D1576553

More Praise for

Rockonomics

"If you like music (we learn here it would take six lifetimes just to listen to every song once) and going backstage to see how things work (touring, streaming, scalping) and the stories behind the stories (how Reginald Dwight met Bernie Taupin and became Elton John), then rock on! Or, in this case, RockOnOmics!"

—Andrew Tobias, author of *The Only Investment Guide You'll Ever Need*

"*Rockonomics* is entertaining, educational, and enlightening. Alan Krueger gives us a backstage tour of the music industry—and in doing so, he creates a brilliant metaphor for our entire economy. Highly recommended."

—Harlan Coben, #1 *New York Times* bestselling author of *Don't Let Go*

"Read this book—whether you are a rock fan or, like me, think the Beatles and Stones were the last good groups. Read it because Alan Krueger makes the subject fun and demonstrates how the workings of this 0.1 percent of the US economy beautifully illustrate upcoming changes in the US and global economies."

—Daniel S. Hamermesh, Distinguished Scholar at Barnard College and author of *Spending Time* and *Beauty Pays*

"I actually majored in economics in college. A few years later, I bumped into a former classmate who asked me what I was doing. I told him I was handling rock radio promotion for Mercury Records. He said, 'What a waste of your education.' I hope he reads *Rockonomics* so he'll find out I didn't end up as a total loser."

—Cliff Burnstein, cofounder of Q Prime with Peter Mensch, management firm for Metallica and the Red Hot Chili Peppers

What the Music Industry
Can Teach Us About Economics
(and Our Future)

ROCKONOMICS

ALAN B. KRUEGER

JOHN MURRAY

First published in Great Britain in 2019 by John Murray (Publishers)
An Hachette UK company

1

Copyright © The Estate of Alan B. Krueger 2019

A CIP catalogue record for this title is available from the British Library

Hardback ISBN 9781473667884
Trade Paperback ISBN 9781473667891
eBook ISBN 9781473667907

Printed and bound in Great Britain by Clays Ltd, Elcograf S.p.A.

John Murray policy is to use papers that are natural, renewable and
recyclable products and made from wood grown in sustainable forests.
The logging and manufacturing processes are expected to conform to the environmental
regulations of the country of origin.

John Murray (Publishers)
Carmelite House
50 Victoria Embankment
London EC4Y 0DZ

www.johnmurray.co.uk

FOR LISA, JUST THE WAY YOU ARE

CONTENTS

ROCKONOMICS

CHAPTER 1

Prelude

Somebody said to me, "But the Beatles were anti-materialistic."
That's a huge myth. John and I literally used to sit down and
say, "Now, let's write a swimming pool."

—Paul McCartney

What walk-on music would you like?" It was a question I had never been asked before or since. I was about to give a speech at the Rock and Roll Hall of Fame, and my hosts wanted to know which songs to play before I took the stage.

No, I wasn't about to be inducted into the Hall of Fame. I'm not a musician and I can't even carry a tune. I'm an economics professor at Princeton. I was then the chairman of the President's Council of Economic Advisers. I had been invited to speak because I had the idea of using the music industry as a metaphor to draw parallels with the U.S. economy—in particular, the financial struggles of middle-class families and the growing gap between the wealthy and everyone else. The key theme was that the U.S. job market had become a superstar, winner-take-all affair, much like the music industry, where a small number of top performers did fabulously well, while almost everyone else struggled to make ends meet.

The speech used the term *rockonomics*—meaning the economic study of the music business—to explain why this was happening, what it means for everyday Americans, and what should be done to bring about a fairer economy that works for everyone. I had a list of bold ideas to restore our national hopes and dreams.

What better venue to give this speech than the Rock and Roll Hall of Fame in Cleveland?

My boss at the time, President Obama, liked the idea. Even better, he liked the speech. I sent him a copy when he was flying on Air Force One, and he subsequently announced at a meeting that "everyone should read Alan's speech." Soon I was getting requests for a copy from the labor secretary and commerce secretary.

This book expands on that original rockonomics metaphor to tell the story of how the whole U.S. economy has changed in recent years—and how each of us can prepare for the changes in store in the twenty-first century. In my career I've found, and psychological research supports, that we learn best not from abstract principles or equations but from stories. And music is all about telling stories.

Economics is also about telling stories, although the field has acquired the unfortunate and misleading reputation as "the dismal science." Economic models, statistics, and regression analyses are all tools used for the purpose of telling stories with rigor and precision. We economists just don't tell the story very well or clearly. This is one of the reasons there was such strong rejection of expertise and basic economic concepts, including gains from trade and the value of impartial, objective economic statistics, during the 2016 U.S. presidential election. We need to find more convincing ways to share the lessons of economics. A broader audience might be willing—even eager—to listen if the story of the economic forces disrupting our world is told through the prism of the music industry. After all, music is one of the few endeavors that unites us, whatever our backgrounds or interests. Almost everyone has a connection to the music industry in one way or another. I call this a theory of "one degree of separation," since we are intimately connected to music and the music industry in one way or another through friends, family, and associates.

To investigate the economic forces shaping the music industry, I conducted dozens of interviews with musicians and music industry executives, from up-and-coming performers and struggling singers to legendary members of the Rock and Roll Hall of Fame, from executives at Spotify and Amazon to those at Universal Music Group, the largest music company in the world—as well as the owner of my local record shop. (Yes, the Princeton Record Exchange still exists and is thriving, despite a challenging environment for retail stores.)

I've interviewed iconic figures who have helped shape the music industry, including Gloria Estefan, the most successful crossover artist of all time, and Quincy Jones, the famed music impresario and performer who produced records for virtually every star from Frank Sinatra to Donna Summer and Michael Jackson. And I met often with Cliff Burnstein and Peter Mensch, the co-founders of Q Prime, which manages Metallica, Red Hot Chili Peppers, Cage the Elephant, Eric Church, and other successful bands. Marc Geiger, the swashbuckling head of music at William Morris Endeavor, shared his optimism for the future of the music biz with me, and top music industry lawyers Don Passman and John Eastman tutored me on music rights and record company contracts. To gain a bird's-eye view of the work and effort involved in putting on a show, I tagged along with musicians and their crews to a number of gigs, and interviewed ushers, vendors, and executives at Live Nation and Ticketmaster.

Answering questions about money and contractual arrangements is always difficult, especially for artists. A disagreement over money helped break up the Beatles.[1] Money can be a treacherous topic. I am thus especially grateful that so many artists, executives, and industry participants were willing to share their experiences, financial data, and perspectives with me. In the pages that follow I have tried to faithfully reflect their stories to explain the economics of the music business. Most important, I try to convey their passion for creating and sharing music. Perhaps the most powerful lesson that I learned is that it is their love for creating music and entertaining audiences that drives most musicians, rather than expectations of earning a fortune (or even a living).

As an empirical economist, I believe that theories, observations, and anecdotes must be evaluated in the cold light of objective, representative data. In researching this book, I analyzed data on hundreds of thousands of concerts collected by *Pollstar* magazine, which gave me unprecedented access to its Pollstar Boxoffice Database. I analyzed data on billions of music streams, millions of record sales and digital downloads, hundreds of thousands of concerts, and thousands of musicians. To fill the gaps, I conducted my own survey of 1,200 professional musicians.* By melding firsthand observations from those on the front lines of the music business with Big Data on the industry as a whole, I developed a richer, more reliable, and more representative picture of how economic forces shape the music industry.

Fortunately, there is also a burgeoning research literature on the music industry by economists, sociologists, psychologists, and computer scientists. Other scholars, too, have found that the music industry provides fertile ground for research, and a scintillating way to inspire and engage students. To provide a forum for researchers to exchange ideas and to support research on the music business across disciplines, in 2016 I helped form a non-profit organization called the Music Industry Research Association (MIRA). This book draws on findings from the innovative social science and related research literature on the music industry.

Although music listeners may not realize it, economics lies at the heart of the music that is created and produced. Economic forces profoundly affect the music that we listen to, the devices on which we hear it, the genres that are produced, and the amount we pay to attend a live performance, stream music, or

---

* Interested readers can access the data from this survey and several other data sources used in this book from www.Rockonomics.com.

buy a recording. When Dick Clark asked Sam Cooke on *American Bandstand* why he switched from gospel to pop music in the late 1950s, the singer smiled and replied earnestly, "My economic situation." And Paul McCartney recently explained to Howard Stern that the Beatles were not trying to create a revolution. "We were just kids from a poor area in Liverpool who wanted to make some money." Even if musicians do not personally feel that they are motivated by economic incentives, economic forces quietly orchestrate success and failure. In his book *In Praise of Commercial Culture* (Harvard University Press), Tyler Cowen has likewise argued that "economic effects have had stronger effects on culture than is commonly believed. The printing press paved the way for classical music, while electricity made rock and roll possible. For better or worse, artists are subject to economic constraints."

To truly understand and appreciate music, you need to understand economics. To take one example, you may have noticed that many more songs today involve collaborations between artists, often where a mega-star is featured with other artists trying to break in or cross over to reach a new audience. "Despacito," the most-streamed song in 2017, is a good example: it is by Luis Fonsi and Daddy Yankee and features Justin Bieber. If you listen carefully to songs that feature other singers, you will notice that the star normally appears early in the song, within the first thirty seconds. This is logical because streaming services only pay royalties for music that is streamed for at least thirty seconds. In other words, economic incentives of streaming are directly affecting the way songs are written, composed, and performed.

Careful economic study of the music industry can shed light on where music is headed, and why. Music and the music business will change over time, but a small number of timeless economic insights can be applied to understand the industry, as new genres and apps are created. More important, understanding the economics of the music industry can yield insights into how economic forces affect our daily lives, work, and society in a myriad of ways.

Seven Keys to Rockonomics

In many ways, the music industry is an ideal laboratory for witnessing economics. From the gramophone and phonograph to on-demand streaming, disruption caused by technological change typically occurs first in music. The music business serves as the canary in the coal mine for innovations. Creative destruction in music occurs in real time. Digitization has changed the way that music is produced, promoted, distributed, discovered, and consumed. Musicians, record labels, radio stations, device manufacturers, and fans all respond to the evolving economic incentives embedded in the music business. Businesses in many industries can learn essential lessons for survival and success from the music industry. Music fans, by reflecting on the economics of music, can learn how economic factors impact their own lives.

In my behind-the-scenes tour of the music industry, seven key economic lessons constantly resonated, like notes in a scale. These seven lessons form the backbone of this book:

♪ **Supply, demand, and all that jazz.** The forces of supply and demand loom large in the music industry, as they do in the rest of the economy. The limited supply of tickets for a Rolling Stones concert, for example, combined with the tremendous demand by fans to see the Stones perform, drives their ticket prices to commanding heights. But other factors—what I refer to as "all that jazz"—matter deeply as well. For example, many musicians are fearful of being perceived as unfair to their fans. That can lead them to underprice their concert tickets relative to the price that supply and demand alone would dictate. This concern for fairness, which suppresses prices and creates a shortage, is the main reason there is a large and enduring secondary market for scalped tickets. You can't understand markets or the economy without recognizing when and how the jazz of emotions, psychology, and social relations interfere with the invisible hands of supply and demand.

♪ **Scale and non-substitutability: the two ingredients that create superstars.** Music is the quintessential example of a superstar market, with a small number of players who attract most of the fanfare and earn most of the money. Economists have long understood what enables superstars to dominate certain markets. These markets have two critical characteristics. First, the top performers, professionals, or firms are able to reach a large audience or customer base; this is what we call *scale*. Second, the sound, service, or product sold in superstar markets must be unique, with distinct features. There is no substitute for it as far as consumers are concerned, and combining the second- and third-best performers in the market does not create a sound, service, or product that is as good as the best. The Internet, digitization, and social media are turning more and more markets into superstar markets, which in turn is causing the middle class to wither, with grave consequences for workers, consumers, politics, society, and the future.

♪ **The power of luck.** Talent and hard work are required ingredients for success, but they are not sufficient. Luck, the unpredictable, random spins of fortune that affect our lives in countless ways, is particularly important in the music industry, where tastes are fickle, quality is subjective, and many talented would-be stars toil away but never get their shot. The right artist might arrive at the wrong time, or at the right time with the wrong song, or at the right time and with the right song but with the wrong manager or label. The impact of luck, for good or ill, is magnified in a superstar market.

♪ **Bowie theory.** The late David Bowie once remarked, "Music itself is going to become like running water or electricity. . . . You'd better be prepared for doing a lot of touring because that's really the only unique situation that's going to be left."[2] His observation highlights the importance of having something unique to sell in addition to recorded music—what economists call *complementarities.* The list of complementarities in music is long: live performances, merchandise, books, music videos, Dylan and Metallica whiskey, Bon Jovi rosé, Questlove popcorn seasoning, Kiss Kaskets, and so on. Successful companies have figured out the importance of Bowie theory. For example, Apple makes money from selling iPhones, iPads, and computers, and runs Apple Music at a loss as a way to drive device sales.[3]

♪ **Price discrimination is profitable.** When a band or business has a unique product to sell, and if it can restrict the resale of that product, it can greatly increase its revenue and profit by charging a higher price to customers who are willing to pay more and a lower price to those who are willing to pay less. Economists use the term *price discrimination* to refer to any practice used to segment customers and charge a higher price to some than to others. Airlines figured this out long ago. Price discrimination is not immoral or illegal. It helps explain why Taylor Swift delays the release of her new records on streaming services until after she sells albums to her most devoted fans. Charging different prices for different seats at a concert is a way for musicians to price-discriminate and charge fans according to their willingness to pay. And *bundling* different products—such as twelve songs on an album, as opposed to selling them individually—can facilitate price discrimination.

♪ **Costs can kill.** Making money, even a lot of money, is not a guarantee of success. Successful bands and businesses have to monitor and minimize their costs to maximize their profits. They invest wisely but not excessively, and negotiate to cut costs when they can. The days of Emerson, Lake & Palmer touring with a fifty-eight-piece orchestra are long gone. As Keith Emerson said, "We had our manager with a shotgun behind us saying, 'Look, if you don't play as a three piece, forget it, you'll be bankrupt.'"[4] At a macroeconomic level, a sector with stagnant productivity will face rising costs and see intense pressure to economize, an ailment known as *Baumol's cost disease*, after the late Princeton economist William Baumol. To illustrate this idea, Baumol used the example of a Schubert string quartet, which takes the same amount of time and labor to perform today as it did two hundred years ago.

♪ **Money isn't everything.** Too many people confuse the underlying motivation of economic life with greed and the blind pursuit of money. At its best, economics recognizes that people are motivated by much more than money. The great joys of life come from pursuing one's passions, spending time with friends and family, and enjoying experiences. As John Eastman, lawyer to Paul McCartney and Billy Joel, told me, "Music is wonder."[5] Music, more than money, is the tonic of happiness. Music helps to create moments and social occasions, memories and emotions. This is the secret of music, and it is the reason that, as Neil Young famously sang, "rock and roll will never die."[6]

Don't fret if these lessons are not entirely clear yet. They are the chorus that repeats throughout the book. The force of these economic ideas can be seen in the pricing of concert tickets, the supply of musical talent to the industry, the way bands and record labels are organized, the nature of collaborations among artists, the structure of streaming contracts, and nearly every other aspect of the industry. The music business also reveals the pervasive role of emotions in decision-making and economic outcomes, a field that economists call *behavioral economics*. Music is inherently the art of eliciting emotions in listeners, the ultimate consumers. Performers pour their emotions into their work. As Lady Gaga has said, "You have to go to that broken place of your heart to write songs."[7]

Economists have a great deal to learn from observing how musicians strive to develop an emotional bond with their audiences, often at the expense of short-term profits, and how emotions guide their work and shape their economic decisions.

Because emotions play such an outsized and explicit role in the music business, the industry reveals behaviors that are often hidden, but just as prevalent and consequential, in other industries and walks of life.

In addition, economists have slowly become aware that individuals' tastes and preferences are not immutable features of their personalities, as is commonly assumed in introductory economics courses. Instead, they are partly determined by social pressures, and subject to change based on experience. This is nowhere more evident than in music. Research shows that the more you listen to a song, the more you tend to like it, and the more likely you are to buy the singer's records.[8] This path-dependent process can explain why payola—the now illegal practice of paying radio DJs to play particular songs on the radio—was so popular and effective, and why new forms of payola are emerging in streaming.

In other words, economics and music are a two-way street. The music industry can help to explain how the economy works and how economic forces are changing our lives. And economists can learn new insights about the economy and human behavior from studying the music industry. That's rockonomics to me.

The Disconnect in the Music Market

There is a fundamental disconnect at the heart of the music business today: the way artists earn most of their money differs dramatically from the way most fans enjoy the music artists create. You can't walk down a city street, ride in a subway car, fly on a plane, or travel by train without noticing people with earbuds or headsets listening to music. The most common content aired on the radio? Music.[9] It is ubiquitous in elevators, doctors' waiting rooms, gyms, bars, and restaurants. The next time you watch television or go to the movies, notice how often music is playing in the background of your favorite TV show or movie. And we spend a great deal of our time listening to recorded music, which, thanks to our smartphones, is accessible anywhere and anytime.

Yet most musicians earn most of their income from live performances, not from sales of recorded music. Even Sir Paul McCartney, who has written and recorded more number-one hits than anyone in music history, earns most of his income from playing live concerts.[10] File sharing and music piracy have widened the gap between the amount of income musicians earn from recorded music and live performances. But even in the pre-Napster days, live performances were a critical source of musicians' incomes. In Chapter 2, I follow the money in music and explain how music manages to punch well above its economic weight.

The advent of paid streaming—the latest in a long line of disruptive technologies—is beginning to cause artists' revenue from recorded music to rebound. Nevertheless, the fundamental divide between how consumers consume music and how artists earn a living will almost surely persist.

Steely Dan's Donald Fagen, at age sixty-nine, gave a simple explanation for why he went back on tour in 2017: "For me, touring is the only way to make a living."[11] Established artists such as James Taylor, the Eagles, and Billy Joel, who used to tour to promote record albums, now tour without having new music to hawk. Popular music concerts today devote far more resources to costly pyrotechnics, video displays, dancing, and other stage theatrics to entertain and engage fans. No longer is the focus just on the music. Concerts and festivals sell experiences.

A Star Is Born; a Superstar Is Super Lucky and Talented

There would be no music without the songwriters, composers, and musicians who create and perform it—at least until machine-learning algorithms and artificial intelligence (AI) advance to the point that computers can compose popular music and write lyrics. You may laugh, but AI is already being used in a growing number of applications to compose melodies for commercial purposes and to train musicians. In the future, musicians may be replaced by computer programmers.

In the meantime, it is important to ask, "What draws musicians to the risky business of music? How have the backgrounds of musicians changed over time? How, and how much, are musicians compensated?" These are among the questions I raise in Chapter 3, as I examine musicians from garage bands to mega-stars.

Most working musicians are unknown performers who labor away at their craft in relative obscurity, barely earning subsistence pay. Only a select few become superstars. Why do some performers ascend to superstardom while other, equally talented musicians remain anonymous and impoverished? Economists start by asking a more basic question: why are some industries prone to superstars in the first place? There are no superstar retail clerks, insurance salesmen, or nurses. What makes music and a small but growing number of other fields susceptible to the superstar phenomenon?

With the music industry as a guide, economists have developed a time-tested model of superstars that has repercussions for the wider economy. As I explain in Chapter 4, two essential features of a market are necessary for a sector to be dominated by a small number of stars. First, there must be *scale economies*, meaning that someone can apply his or her talents to a large audience with little additional cost per audience member. Second, the players need to be *imperfect substitutes*, meaning that their work is differentiated and unique. Both elements are present in music. Every successful singer, band, and orchestra has a unique sound. And recorded music can reach billions of listeners at little additional cost once a recording is made. By contrast, in medicine, for example, some surgeons are much better than others, but they are limited by the number of, say, hip replacements they can perform in a day. The top surgeons do well, but they do not do nearly as well compared to lesser surgeons as top musicians do compared to every other recording artist.

The importance of scalability in producing superstars in a given field was first highlighted by the great economist Alfred Marshall some 125 years ago. Marshall's work highlighted the career of Elizabeth Billington, a leading opera singer of her day. Ironically, he used a musician as an example of a profession that was limited by the scale of the market. Long before the creation of digital recordings, microphones, and music videos, Marshall pointed out that Mrs. Billington was highly constrained in reaching a large audience because the "number of persons who could be reached by a human voice is strictly limited."[12] Today, digital technology enables artists to reach an unlimited audience at virtually zero incremental cost, which in turn has led to the enormous success of a select few superstars.

This ability to create superstars in music is amplified by another feature, one that increasingly applies to other industries: the popularity of a song or artist grows geometrically rather than linearly. This is often called a *power law*. The popularity of the top performer is a multiple of the second-most-popular performer, which in turn is a multiple of the third-most-popular performer, and so on. Scientists have documented power laws in all kinds of outcomes, from the frequency of use of various words to the size of cities and the number of hurricanes in a year.

Networks help to create power laws. Popularity ricochets through networks of friends and acquaintances, creating power law relationships where a small number of performers garner almost all the attention. In the music industry, this can be seen in the extremely skewed distributions of concert income, music downloads, Shazam requests, Facebook and Twitter followers, and artists' merchandise sales. In his bestselling book *The Long Tail*, Chris Anderson, then a *Wired* editor, predicted that the Internet will lead to greater opportunity for those in what he called the long tail of sales, because smaller producers will be able to find niche markets.[13] This has yet to materialize in the music business. Instead, the middle has dropped out of music, as more consumers gravitate to a smaller number of superstars.

Over the past thirty years, the share of concert revenue taken home by the top 1 percent of performers has more than doubled, from 26 percent in 1982 to 60 percent today.[14] The top 5 percent take home 85 percent of all concert revenues. The same pattern holds for recorded music. The long tail remains long and lonely; all of the action is in the head of the tail.

This is an extreme version of what has happened to the U.S. income distribution as a whole. The top 1 percent of families doubled their share of income from 1979 to 2017.[15] In 1979, the top 1 percent took home 10 percent of national income; in 2017 they took home 22 percent. By this measure, incomes in the U.S. economy today are almost as skewed as they were in the rock and roll industry when Bruce Springsteen cut "Born in the U.S.A."

One reason the entire economy has veered toward a superstar, winner-take-all affair is the rise of digital technology. Successful entrepreneurs can turn apps and digital technology into fortunes worth billions of dollars. Five of the six wealthiest Americans (Bill Gates, Mark Zuckerberg, Larry Ellison, Michael Bloomberg, and Jeff Bezos)—whose combined wealth equals nearly that of half of the world's population—made their fortunes because of digital technology.[16] Digital technology is scalable. One day soon the top surgeons may be able to operate on a great many more patients due to improvements in digital technology.

This technological revolution has brought many other profound economic and social changes, all of which are readily apparent in the music industry. Small, often imperceptible differences in quality separate the best from the rest. As a result, luck matters for success more than ever. Releasing the right record at the right moment matters critically for success or failure. The same is true in the economy writ large. Bill Gates might have been Bill What's-his-name if Gary Kildall and Digital Research had agreed to the terms IBM first offered them for developing the operating system for the new personal computer in 1980, before turning to Bill Gates's fledgling company.[17]

Success is hard to judge ahead of time, and in no way guaranteed, even for the best performers. Consumer tastes are fickle, and herd behavior often takes over when an artist begins to become popular. One-hit wonders are common in the music industry because a great deal of luck goes into achieving a hit song, and, like lightning, luck rarely strikes more than once. Even the industry experts, with much at stake, have difficulty picking winners. In Chapter 5, I chronicle how good luck and bad luck play outsized roles in the rock and roll industry, much as in life in general.

Steve Ferrone: Heartbreaker and Session Musician

Steve Ferrone grew up in Brighton, England, and has played drums with almost every major star, from George Harrison, David Bowie, and Eric Clapton to Chakah Kahn, Stevie Nicks, and, of course, Tom Petty for twenty-five years. Ferrone backed Prince during his epic performance of "While My Guitar Gently Weeps" at the Rock and Roll Hall of Fame. Steve Ferrone is both a session musician and a touring musician. I interviewed him in his modest home in Van Nuys, California, on March 15, 2018.

What were the highs and lows of playing at the Super Bowl halftime show with Tom Petty?

We traveled to Phoenix on a private jet. We stayed at a hotel on Camelback Mountain, and it was just gorgeous. The plan was that we were going to blow up the show, go to the airport, sit on the plane—because they weren't letting anyone fly private until the game was over—and then fly back to Los Angeles. I got a phone call the day of the show, and they said, "We're not leaving tonight." The plans had changed. Tom's wife wanted to go to the after parties.

I had a 9 AM flight to Japan the next day. The Heartbreakers never travel before noon, and I had to get back. It turned out that the wife of one of the guys in the band had flown commercial and had a return flight. Through the power of the NFL, they get in touch and change her ticket to my name. We finished the halftime show, waved goodbye, and I went back into my world.

I went from super first class to . . . at the airport and they tell me, "You can't take that cigar cutter on the plane." They throw it away at security. I was drenched after the show because it's hot up on stage. I took a shirt out of my bag and put it on. I arrive at the gate, and there's a little guy from Oklahoma watching the game on TV. He didn't like the teams. He didn't like the referees. He didn't like the ads. He didn't like anything and he was really loud. Then there was a lull, and I could see him looking around with the crosshairs for someone to have a go with. I hadn't realized it, but I had grabbed a T-shirt out of my bag that said "Super Bowl Halftime Show." He saw me and said, "Is that shirt real, or is it bull?" I asked if he saw the halftime show. He said, "Yeah, I didn't think it was much." And, I said, yeah, it wasn't that good.

In just hours I came crashing back to earth, to my musician area.

How did you become a musician?

My parents had started me tap dancing when I was three. Because I used to sit in my highchair with my spoon and listen to the radio, and tap the spoon in time. So, they sent me to tap-dancing lessons. I was always sort of being geared for show business, and they used to take me to see people perform. When I was twelve, I joined a band with older kids because . . . they had a drummer who had appendicitis and had to have surgery, and they were looking for someone to fill in for that weekend.

When I was fourteen, the school started to ask my career plans. Fifteen was the school leaving age. I came from a working-class family. I had no intention of staying in school. They asked, "What do you want to do when you leave school?" I said, I want to be a drummer. And, they said, "You can't do that. It's not a real job." I said, Ringo Starr does it. I can hang with Ringo Starr. And, they said, "What do you know?" So they started to mock me by calling me Ringo.

What was work as a studio musician like in LA twenty years ago? How does it compare to today?

In those times, there was so much work. The studios were working around the clock. Now, they're closing in droves.

Double-scale work is not as prevalent as it used to be and a lot of people today don't want to do it through the union, which is actually what paid for my retirement.

In those days record companies used to invest in artists. They would spot somebody with talent, and they would recognize the talent. But, talent doesn t always hit the first time. Now, they want guaranteed product done, finished.

They used to finance an artist to do demos. I played on Luther Vandross's first demos, and they were turned down. Luther was known back then as a studio musician. He was a session singer. He sang "Be All You Can Be" in the ad for the army. It was kind of difficult to get him to move from being thought of as a great background singer, or jingle guy, to being Luther Vandross the superstar.

Have you come across any musicians who you considered phenomenally talented but were never able to really break through?

Yes, a lot of them, and for varying reasons. For some of them it is about attitude. Probably has to do with drugs and alcohol. And, some of them, I can't figure it out. It's just bad luck.

What was the best-paying gig you ever had?

George Harrison once paid me for what could be the world's most expensive session ever. He called me and said, "Steve I really need you to come over because we're missing some drums on one of the tracks that we recorded. I need you to replace them." He booked me a flight on the Concord. A big limousine was waiting for me when I landed. I get to George's mansion in Henley and say, "What's the problem?" We go into the studio and we're listening to his song and all of a sudden there's no downbeat to the drum. Everything is there, except the bass drum is missing. He said, "Did you hear that?" I said, "It's just one bass drum beat that's missing. You could take one of the other ones and copy it in there." He said, "No no no, I need you to play it." So I hit the bass drum once and that was it. Then we went to eat.

Are you making money from royalties from records you recorded?

I get some royalties from when I was in the Average White Band. And some from work with Eric Clapton and Tom Petty. But royalties were much greater when I first started with Tom.

Were you paid a fee to play with the Heartbreakers or did you get a split of the income?

I was a hired drummer. The founding members were partners. I don't know their splits. Ron Blair was actually a founding member who left the band for twenty years and then came back. He actually came back as a hired hand like me. Tom paid us all very well. He loved his band. And, he kept his band close, took really, really good care of us. I have no complaints about where I stood.

I'll tell you, it was an amazing band that will never be the same. It wasn't just Tom Petty and the Heartbreakers. He was part of the Heartbreakers. He was in the band. This never will be the same again. Even though there are a lot of bands that continue, Tom was really something special, had a special presence.

Cash and Concerts

Digital technology has also led to major changes in the business model of music, with important implications outside the music industry as well. Advances over time, from amplification, radio, vinyl records, eight-track tapes, and cassettes to music videos, CDs, MP3 players, and streaming, have made it possible for performers to reach an ever wider audience. And the increasing globalization and interconnectedness of the world have vastly increased the reach and fame of the most popular performers. Musicians no longer need to rely on physical record stores to stock their albums in a particular city; their music can be streamed almost anywhere in the world, at any time.

But advances in technology have also had an unexpected effect. Recorded music has become cheap to replicate and distribute, and it is difficult to police unauthorized reproductions. This has cut into the royalties of the most successful performers and caused them to raise their prices for live performances. My research suggests that this is the primary reason concert prices have risen so much since the late 1990s, about as fast as inflation in health care costs.

An understanding of concert ticket pricing conveys lessons for understanding and optimally setting pricing for other events, services, and goods. Successful bands have learned how to navigate the trade-off between maximizing short-term revenue as opposed to long-term popularity and profitability. The social constraints on pricing of concert tickets, the ultimate "party good," are quite apparent, and help to explain pricing in other industries and markets, where economists and businesses have come to rely too heavily on the overly simplistic supply-and-demand framework, the workhorse of economics.

Many artists used to treat concerts and touring as a loss leader, a way to gain popularity and hone their skills while promoting record sales. Their goal had been to sell enough records to score another, more lucrative record contract. Concert ticket prices were kept artificially low, below what fans were willing to pay, to gain a loyal fan base and promote album sales. As I document in Chapter 6, this has now flipped. The price of the average concert ticket has increased by more than 400 percent from 1981 to 2018, much faster than the 160 percent rise in overall consumer price inflation.[18] And prices for the best seats for the best performers have increased even more.

The reason for this is that file sharing has greatly cut into the royalties that musicians earn from album sales. Consolidation in the recording industry, after several lean years, further threatens artists' recording income. Concerts are now viewed as a primary profit center, and digital recordings are a means of promoting concerts. Again, rockstar and economic pioneer David Bowie foresaw this development years ago when he said, "Music itself is going to become like running water or electricity. . . . You'd better be prepared for doing a lot of touring because that's really the only unique situation that's going to be left. It's terribly exciting." Sounding like an economist looking at the powerful forces governing the world, Bowie added, "But on the other hand it doesn't matter if you think it's exciting or not; it's what's going to happen."

What I call Bowie theory applies increasingly outside of music as well, to newspapers, books, magazines, and other industries. The *Wall Street Journal*, the *New York Times*, *Bloomberg*, and the

Economist all increasingly rely on live events for revenue. News is available from countless online sources, often for free. Soon newspapers and magazines could be loss leaders for live conferences and lectures.

Navigating these new economic shoals is difficult, not least because norms of behavior constrain economic activity. Artists cannot be seen as gouging their fans or being too greedy. They risk weakening their bond with their audience, not to mention threatening their record sales and royalties, concert revenue, and merchandise sales. Fans and artists are still people, motivated by passions and emotions, even in an era of artificial intelligence and the digital economy.

Rockonomics

Marie Connolly of the University of Quebec and I first used the term *rockonomics* in the title of an article we wrote in 2005. *USA Today* later mistakenly credited me with coining the term.[19] Although we did think of the neologism independently—around the same time as my friends Steve Levitt and Stephen Dubner wrote *Freakonomics*—I subsequently discovered earlier uses.

In October 1984 Bill Steigerwald wrote an article in the *Los Angeles Times* arguing that Bruce Springsteen was economically naive for charging the same price for all his concert tickets, selling out in forty-five minutes, and then complaining about ticket scalping.* The headline of Steigerwald's article was "Supply-Side Rockonomics." As far as I can tell, that is the earliest use of the term (although Chapter 6 explains that Bruce is not really economically naive).

Marc Eliot's 1989 book *Rockonomics: The Money Behind the Music*

---

* Mr. Steigerwald wrote me after the *USA Today* piece came out to claim credit. He presciently wrote, "When you write your book on rockonomics, which I'm sure you will someday (you should; it'd make a great teaching tool for economic principles), please give me credit."

chronicled the sordid details of music contracts. There are many examples of artists being treated unfairly and fraudulently by their labels and managers, but in most cases musicians face disappointing financial results because of the unfavorable economics of the music industry, not malevolence. In Chapter 7, I place music contracts, which can seem unfair to most artists—and recording contracts are unfair to superstars—in an economic context. For example, because only one or two of every ten albums actually pays off for a record label, contracts for records that become successful subsidize recording costs for all those that don't make money, and provide a return on investment for the record companies.[20] Still, there are some simple rules artists can follow to protect themselves financially and to save for the future. For example, I discuss a practice that has evolved in the industry where the artists collect and audit the money and then pay their manager, to prevent malfeasance and misunderstanding.

After the publication of the *USA Today* story, Ron Christopher, a music producer in Los Angeles, informed me that he mixed an album by the band Flash Kahan for Capitol Records in 1985 that included the song "Rockanomics." The song included these long-forgotten lines:

> *Goin' to take a Chevy for a U.S. guitar*
> *Rockanomics, rockanomics*

Needless to say, "Rockanomics" did not become a household word or a hit.

For the purposes of this book, any music that is popular and amenable to economic analysis fits in the rockonomics tent. That's practically every genre of music and aspect of the business, from after-school music lessons and bar bands to Carnegie Hall, Ticketmaster, Live Nation, and Spotify, from ABBA to ZZ Top. To paraphrase Billy Joel: hot funk, cool punk, even if it's old junk, it's still rockonomics to me.

It's a Small World After All

Two things are certain about music: First, musical styles continually change, and each generation looks down upon the next generation's tastes in music. And second, the way in which we listen to music—from vinyl records and digital downloads to YouTube and iPhones—will continually change. Streaming services such as Spotify, Pandora, Tidal, Deezer, and QQ are the latest innovation in how people the world over listen to music. Streaming is bringing profound changes to the music world. On one hand, streaming is boosting revenue for recorded music for the first time in more than a decade. After years of decline—global recorded music revenue fell from $25 billion in 2002 to $15 billion in 2015—industry veterans have a reason to feel some optimism, as revenue rose in 2016 and 2017 thanks to streaming.[21] As I discuss in Chapter 8, with billions of streams and millions of customers, streaming provides a remarkable laboratory to see economics in action.

Pandora, for example, conducted a one-of-a-kind experiment on twenty million subscribers to its ad-supported free service to learn how sensitive their listening habits are to the number of commercials that they are exposed to each hour they listen to music.[22] The results provide about the strongest evidence of a demand curve that one could find in economics. The more listeners were exposed to increased nuisance costs in the form of additional ads, the less likely they were to continue utilizing the free ad-based service, and the more likely they were to switch to the paid service. This is a textbook example of the type of evidence companies can use to maximize profits and improve their customers' experiences.

Streaming has another, broader effect as well. Listeners are not limited to the relatively small number of records that record stores used to stock on their shelves, or to the music playing on the radio. Historically, record stores filled their limited shelf space primarily with local music and popular hits. Today, just about all the music ever produced is available at your fingertips (or with a verbal command to Amazon's Alexa) anywhere in the world. As we'll see in Chapter 10, this change is beginning to affect the music that people are listening to around the world, with less focus on musicians from one's home country. It is a smaller world after all when it comes to music.

Although no one knows for sure how streaming will evolve in the future, it is certain to change. The blending of movie streaming services and movie producers (Netflix, Amazon, Disney) suggests that music may move in the same direction. It is not unreasonable to speculate that in the future music will be bundled with other entertainment programming, such as movies, sports, and television shows, as it is with Amazon Prime. Look for Spotify, Amazon, Apple Music, and other distributors to try to create original content, following the Netflix and Amazon movie model. If so, the economics of the music industry will likely be upended again.

Streaming offers the opportunity for new musicians to break in and reach a broader audience without the need for a record label. And new companies are emerging to take advantage of this opportunity. In Chapter 8 you will meet Rehegoo, a four-year-old company started by Italian and American entrepreneurs that works with undiscovered musicians to improve, market, and stream their music. So far, their music has been streamed more than ten billion times. If the long tail is to offer musicians more opportunity, it will be because of innovations like Rehegoo.

All economies operate under rules. Chief among these rules is the definition, allocation, and defense of property rights—who has the right to own or use certain goods and resources, and how are the rights traded and protected? In the music business, a key set of rules concerns how music is licensed under copyright law. Musicians and labels produce music. The music is copyrighted. Different licenses are required for different uses of music. For example, a synchronization license, or sync license, is required to use music in a movie or video. The laws governing the licensing of music were obsolete before streaming, and they are even more obsolete today, despite major legislation known as the Music Modernization Act, enacted in 2018. In Chapter 9 I discuss why music licenses matter, what trade-offs are involved, and how the licensing process can be improved in the age of streaming.

The Sounds of Happiness

My research with the psychologist Danny Kahneman revealed that the time people spend listening to music is ranked among our most enjoyable activities of daily life.[23] Music is thought of in the same class of activities as participating in sports, religious worship, or attending a party, in terms of the positive emotions that it generates, and the negative feelings like stress and anger that it helps to counteract or chase away. What's more, listening to music improves the experience of other activities, such as commuting to work or cleaning house. Every student who ignored his or her parents' requests to turn off the music while studying knows that music can improve any number of unpleasant activities. In fact, there's a reasonable chance you're listening to music while you read these words.

In Chapter 11, I argue that music is one of the best bargains human society has ever conceived of—and it is getting better by the day. On average, we spend three to four hours a day listening to and enjoying recorded music. Yet the average consumer spends less than 10 cents a day for that music. That is down 80 percent since 1999, after adjusting for inflation.[24] Americans spend more on potato chips than on recorded music.[25]

Now that listening to virtually any song or genre of music anywhere and anytime has become essentially free, human welfare has been greatly increased.

In fact, music is a quintessential part of the "experience economy," the segment of the economy that relies on selling experiences rather than physical goods or services. An increasing share of our GDP is derived from producing and selling experiences.

The rest of the economy can learn a great deal from the music industry about how to sell and create experiences.

What, precisely, is it about music that produces such profound emotions? What leads people to want to experience music when they're feeling blue or happy, when they are feeling lonely or longing to be part of a crowd? What is it about music that led Madison Avenue to discover that playing it helps to sell products, from coffee to cars? Music sets the mood for political campaigns, bars, senior proms, weddings, and countless other events and rites of passage. Music teaches us our ABC's and reinforces our memories. In fact, musical therapy has proved to be helpful in treating some psychological and neurological disorders.[26] Although the magic of music remains in part a mystery, archaeologists have found that musical instruments have been part of civilization for millennia, predating other known human tools and instruments. Music, it seems, is embedded in our DNA. As the lyrics to the ABBA song "Thank You for the Music" put it, "Without a song or a dance what are we?"

Where the Streets Have No Name

In a highly polarized age, music is one of the few endeavors in modern life that unites people from different political, religious, cultural, regional, ethnic, and racial backgrounds. Economic problems are also universal. The challenges of finding dignified and rewarding work, saving for the future, and pursuing happiness are vital for all people. And I would argue that essential insights into understanding and overcoming these challenges can be found in rockonomics.

So what songs were on my walk-on list at the Rock and Roll Hall of Fame in Cleveland? My first selection was perhaps obvious to many: Bruce Springsteen, a fellow New Jerseyan whose heartfelt anthems and three-hour concerts highlight the struggles of the working class in a changing economy. His "Land of Hope and Dreams" was the top song on my playlist.

The second warm-up song I selected was John Mellencamp's "Hand to Hold On To." I wanted the audience to reflect on the simple and universal wisdom of his moving lyrics: "Don't need to be no strong hand / Don't need to be no rich hand / Everyone just needs a hand to hold on to."

And my last two songs? Sixto Rodriguez's "Sugar Man" and Parker Theory's "She Said." To understand why I selected them, you need to read Chapter 5, which documents the outsized role of luck in success and failure.

CHAPTER 2

Follow the Money: The Music Economy

The fact of the matter is that popular music is one of the industries of the country. It's all completely tied up with capitalism. It's stupid to separate it.

—Paul Simon

*P*aul Simon grew up in the music industry. His father, Louis, was a professional bass player, session musician, and dance bandleader who performed under the name Lee Sims. Both Paul and his father understood the music business, from playing bar mitzvahs, weddings, and debutante balls to entertaining half a million fans at Simon and Garfunkel's landmark concert in Central Park.

Although Paul Simon is undeniably correct in saying that popular music is one of the "industries of the country," it is a surprisingly *small* industry, one that would go nearly unnoticed if music were not special in other respects.[1] Total expenditure on music—including concert tickets, streaming fees, record sales, and royalties—were $18.3 billion in the United States in 2017. Although that may sound like a lot of money, and it is enough to support some of the best and most sophisticated entertainment ever produced, it represents a little less than 0.1 percent of GDP, the value of all goods and services produced in the country that year. In other words, less than $1 of every $1,000 in the U.S. economy is spent on music. The music industry employs less than 0.2 percent of the workforce. And the United States is the world's largest music market, accounting for more than a third of all music spending worldwide.[2]

Paul Simon is also correct in saying that music is completely tied up with capitalism and it would be a mistake to separate it from the economic forces that drive our capitalist system. The industry needs a sustainable business model to keep the music playing and permit new artists to enter and succeed in the industry. But at its finest, music has the ability to transcend capitalism— and socialism, communism, and all the other isms. Yes, music is often used by Madison Avenue to hawk products, but it is also used to inspire social activism and political movements. It is not naive to think that music and musicians have played a significant role raising awareness, lifting spirits, and stirring souls in the feminist revolution ("I am woman, hear me roar"), the U.S. civil rights movement ("We Shall Overcome"), the collapse of apartheid in South Africa ("Biko"), and the fall of communism in Eastern Europe (the Velvet Revolution drew inspiration from the Plastic People of the Universe and the Velvet Underground).

More than any other industry, music has the ability to rejuvenate lives, reinvent cities, break down barriers, rally resistance, and give rise to revolutions. As Bruce Springsteen once put it, "In some fashion, I help people hold on to their own humanity, if I'm doing my job right."[3] In economic jargon, music provides substantial *positive externalities*, meaning benefits for society beyond what music costs to create.

Scaling Music

No matter how you cut it, economically speaking, music is a relatively small industry. Global music spending in 2017 was only $50 billion, or 0.06 percent of world GDP.[4] The music industry is small even compared to the rest of the entertainment industry. Worldwide, $2.2 trillion was spent on entertainment and media in 2017. Music represented just 2 percent of that market.

I once commented to Russ Crupnick, a veteran music industry

consultant, that I was surprised there were not more economists advising music companies. He gave a terse explanation: "There isn't much money in music."[5] That's hard to dispute.

To put the music industry in perspective, more than three times as much money is spent on professional sports as on the entire music industry in North America.[6] More revenue is booked by college and pro football alone.[7]

Americans spend over five times more on cigarettes than they do on music. Incredibly, tobacco companies spend more money *advertising* their products than Americans spend on recorded music.[8] Music is also small compared to much of our virtuous spending: Americans spend 50 percent more on health clubs, for example, than on music.[9] Even the fees for *unused* health club memberships in the United States exceed the total revenue collected for recorded music.

The Shape of Music Money

Where do our music dollars go? Figure 2.1 provides one look at how total U.S. music spending was divided among major categories in 2017. You should be warned, however, that comprehensive, unassailable financial data for the music industry do not exist. Contracts are private, and the division of concert ticket and recording revenue is rarely disclosed. As Cliff Burnstein, the manager of Metallica, Red Hot Chili Peppers, and other acts, once cautioned me, "There is a limited amount of transparency in our business."[10] I had to rely on fragmentary data and the informed judgment and advice of industry professionals to apportion the various slices of the music money pie.

This caveat aside, today about half of every dollar spent in the music industry goes to recorded music, and about half goes to purchases related to live performances. Fans experience and enjoy music most of the time through recorded music. Most musicians, however, earn most of their money today performing live events.[11]

Figure 2.1: Estimated Division of Total U.S. Music Revenue, 2017

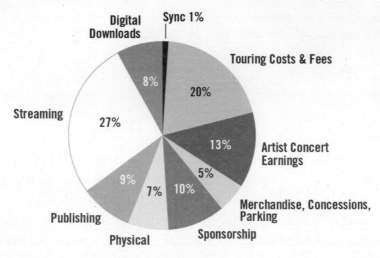

Source: Author's estimates based on Pollstar data, RIAA, Statista, and interviews with managers.

The format on which music is distributed and heard has evolved throughout the twentieth century, with the invention of the phonograph, tape recorder, and radio. But it has changed even more radically and rapidly in the twenty-first century once music was digitized. Figure 2.2 displays record industry revenue collected from three broad formats over time: physical products such as CDs, cassettes, and vinyl records; digital downloads; and streaming. The digitization wave in the early 2000s had two significant effects that rippled through music sales. First, digital downloads eclipsed physical record and cassette sales. Second, file sharing and piracy cannibalized recorded music revenue. Napster, unauthorized ripped CDs, and other ways of illegally copying and sharing music caused the demand for legitimate records to steadily dwindle. For more than a decade, the record business was in secular decline, following the same track as the steel and coal industries. Avery Lipman, the president and cofounder of Republic Records, told me that the record business in this period was like being on a "slowly descending airplane for fifteen years."[12]

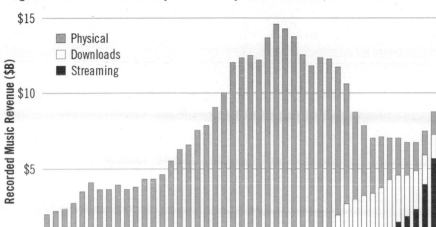

Figure 2.2: Record Industry Revenue by Music Format, 1973–2017

Source: Author's calculations based on data from RIAA U.S. Sales Database. Revenue from synchronized licenses is included in digital downloads.

Then another tidal wave disrupted the industry. Rapid growth of streaming services such as Spotify, Pandora, and Apple Music all but displaced digital downloads. Digital downloads for iPods and other MP3 devices through online services such as iTunes, which seemed revolutionary a decade ago, are now a relic of the past, akin to eight-track tapes and 45s. Economists rarely get to see such creative destruction in real time. It's as if Darwin was able to observe species evolving before his eyes while he visited the Galápagos Islands.

Meanwhile, physical record sales have finally stabilized, albeit at a low level. There is a revival in vinyl record sales to music enthusiasts, and the CD market is propped up for now by customers with older cars purchasing new CDs for their dashboard CD players.[13]

Streaming is having a revolutionary effect on music sales. After fifteen years of decline or stagnation, revenue from recorded music finally began to increase in 2016. And the signs are that this upward trend will continue for some time. The growth in music revenue is entirely due to streaming services, particularly the rapid growth in paid subscriptions for Spotify, Pandora, Apple Music, Amazon Music, and Deezer. These services are the music equivalent of an all-you-can-eat buffet, where fans get access to nearly all music ever recorded for a monthly subscription fee, or for putting up with the inconvenience of occasional ads. One important lesson from this revolution is that fans are willing to pay for music if it is provided in a convenient fashion. Streaming is upending the music business, favoring certain genres such as hip-hop, electronic dance music (EDM), and Latin music, as well as giving a second wind for royalties on deep catalog recordings by older artists such as Tony Bennett and classic rock bands including the Beatles and Rolling Stones.[14]

The amount that artists and other copyright holders are paid when their music is streamed varies, depending on whether their music is played on ad-supported or subscriber-supported services. It also varies across services. But a song typically earns royalties of around $2,000 to $3,000 per million plays.[15] Spotify, the largest streaming service, pays out approximately 60 percent of its revenue in music royalties.[16] We are still in the early days of the streaming era; it has a great deal of room to grow. Given its potential to change the music business, I return to the role of streaming in Chapter 8. For now, it is clear that streaming is providing a much-needed shot of adrenaline for the recorded music business.

Streaming is also giving a boost to publishing revenue, which currently makes up 9 percent of music revenue. Publishing is the complicated and somewhat antiquated business of securing payments for the right to use music. Songwriters can publish their own music; more commonly, they work with a publisher to ensure that adequate payments are made for the various rights to use music. Although concrete figures do not exist, artists who compose music typically receive about 45 percent of publishing revenue.[17] Increasingly, this revenue is being split among a larger number of songwriters and collaborators, as music has become more sophisticated, with more hands and minds involved in the composition.

Another revenue stream that bears mentioning, although it accounts for only 1 percent of all music revenue, is sync licenses. Sync licenses are required to synchronize music in videos, TV shows, movies, and commercials. For example, a sync license is required for music videos played on YouTube, the video-sharing service acquired by Google in 2006. YouTube's role in music today cannot be overstated: fully half of all Americans listened to music at least once a week on YouTube in 2017, exceeding the combined share of Americans in any given week who turn to Spotify and Pandora.[18] Almost organically, YouTube became a major and controversial player in the music business. YouTube accounts for a third of all online music streaming time—and yet only 6 percent of music revenue.[19] This imbalance is likely to change, although industry professionals are pessimistic that it will change quickly. In 2017, YouTube paid out over $1 billion to record labels and other rights holders for music, roughly the same as in 2016.[20]

Is YouTube a positive or negative development for musicians and record companies? There is no straightforward answer. On one hand, the share of YouTube revenue that is paid out for musical copyright is small compared with streaming services, which is a source of anger for many musicians and labels. On the other hand, record labels and artists used to have to bear the cost of distributing and marketing music videos. So to the extent that YouTube has replaced MTV, and has much wider reach, it is a profitable development for record companies and musicians. Because artists generally earn a small share of their income from recordings, on net it is likely that YouTube has been a positive development for artists trying to break in and develop an audience; established stars, however, have a legitimate beef with YouTube's relatively meager royalty payments.

New Business Models

Digitization and the Internet are providing new opportunities for musicians to record and sell their music directly to their fans. An early experiment in this vein was carried out by the English rock band Radiohead. In 2007 Radiohead released its album *In Rainbows* directly on its website and asked fans to pay whatever they wanted to digitally download it. The experiment was a test of music fans' responses to economic incentives. Any payment made was entirely voluntary. Fans could elect to pay nothing for the album. And roughly 60 percent of the million fans who downloaded the recording from the band's site in the first month did pay nothing. Millions more downloaded it for free from unauthorized websites. But 40 percent of those who downloaded the recording from Radiohead's official website did opt to pay, contributing an average of $6 per album that they downloaded. Radiohead, which owned the master license to *In Rainbows*, netted nearly $3 million from their pay-what-you-want experiment. Tom Yorke, Radiohead's frontman, claimed, "In terms of digital income, we've made more money out of this record than out of all the other Radiohead albums put together."[21]

Radiohead's experiment was a harbinger of new music distribution methods to follow. The hottest singers, such as Taylor Swift, Adele, and Beyoncé, now tier the way they release their music. Swift, for example, waited three weeks before she made her latest album, *Reputation*, available on Spotify, Amazon, Apple Music, and other streaming services. Why? The services pay less in royalties than she would have received from full album sales. Her most ardent fans purchased her album. The strategy resulted in over 1.2 million record sales in its first week, edging out Ed Sheeran's for the strongest sales of any album in 2017.[22]

Technology is rapidly facilitating "disintermediation," enabling musicians to produce, record, publish, and distribute their own music without the need of a record label. Companies such as Kobalt are emerging to help independent artists publish music and collect royalties. And services such as DistroKid enable artists to upload their music to streaming services and online stores. With a profusion of new music, the Herculean challenge for new and lesser-known artists is garnering an audience.

One new model that lesser-known musicians are turning to involves subscription services where fans pay the artist directly. At Patreon.com, for example, artists set a monthly subscription fee (or per-download fee) for the music they make available through the site. The artist keeps 90 percent of the revenue, a division that is essentially the flip side of a recording contract. The singer and songwriter Amanda Palmer released her song "Machete" and a David Bowie tribute entitled *Strung Out in Heaven: A Bowie String Quartet Tribute* exclusively on Patreon. With more than 11,000 patrons, she has grossed over $1 million in two years. As Palmer says, "I've been struggling since I got off my label in 2008 to find the right platform for ongoing support, through which I can release constant material (and get paid)." She has also used Kickstarter to crowdfund the cost of producing music and videos.[23]

The Radiohead experiment demonstrated something else, which had already been discovered in countless pie-splitting economic experiments: not everyone is motivated purely by self-interest. In two-person pie-splitting experiments (often called the Ultimatum Game), the first player makes a proposal about how to divide a fixed pie, say $100, between herself and a second player. The second player can accept or reject the proposal. If the proposal is rejected, both players get nothing; if the proposal is accepted, the players divide the pie along the lines the first player proposed. If you were the first player, how much would you offer the second player in this situation? The optimal strategy is for the first player to offer the second player a pittance, say a penny; the second player should accept that proposal because getting something is better than getting nothing, and player one receives the most from this strategy. Of course, many people do not consider it fair to offer such a small amount, and in practice the first player typically offers close to a fifty-fifty split, because she considers it a fair division. When people do attempt to keep most of the money for themselves, they often find that their proposal is rejected. The second player is willing to forfeit the money he would have received, because he feels the offer is unfair.

Radiohead's pay-what-you-want experiment provided real-world evidence that considerations of fairness can motivate human behavior. You can count on some people to be generous—and others to be greedy. Increasingly musicians are figuring out ways to charge more to consumers who are willing to pay more, a practice called *price discrimination*. Indeed, Taylor Swift's strategy for the release of *Reputation* can be seen as a clever form of price discrimination. Her hard-core fans, who were willing to pay the most, opted to purchase her album as soon as it was released, at a higher price. Others who were more price sensitive waited until it was available through streaming services.

Sources of Musician Incomes

Most of the money collected from recorded music does not go to the musicians who created the music. Record contracts typically give the musicians an advance upon signing against a 10 to 12 percent share of future royalties, net of costs. There is a simple reason for this uneven division: most records don't pay off.[24] Only one or two of every ten records that a record label releases actually covers its costs. Music labels take large risks. They are similar to venture capitalists betting on a lot of new artists and music in the hopes that a few will break out in a big way. To cover their costs, record companies must subsidize a lot of music that is in the red—that loses money—with a small number of records that strike it rich, at least until the successful stars can renegotiate their contracts.

Today, even superstar recording artists, whose records account for the vast majority of industry-wide music revenue, make most of their income from live performances, rather than royalties. In 2017, for example, Billy Joel, the original Piano Man, earned $27.4 million from live performances, only $1.3 million from record sales and streaming, and $0.6 million from publishing royalties. In other words, more than 90 percent of his income was derived from live concerts.[25] And that was true for Joel in the early 2000s as well, long before he landed his monthly gig at Madison Square Garden (which insiders sometimes refer to as the Garden's fourth franchise, after the Knicks, Liberty, and Rangers). Or consider Paul McCartney, who has written and recorded more number-one songs than anyone in music history. He netted 82 percent of his income from performing live shows in 2017.

U2, who led all musicians with $54 million in income in 2017, earned 96 percent of their income from touring. And Beyoncé, who topped the list with $62 million in 2016, earned 88 percent of her income from touring that year.

Of the top forty-eight musicians who toured in 2017, on average they earned 80 percent of their income from touring, 15 percent from recorded music, and 5 percent from publishing fees. Touring accounts for the lion's share of income.

There are some exceptions to this pattern, of course, even if they are typically short-lived. Canadian rapper Drake—who is in the rare position of producing his own music and owning his own imprint, OVO Sound—earned $23.3 million from recordings and "only" $13.6 million from live concerts in 2016, according to Billboard. Drake didn't tour in 2017, and earned $10.3 million from recordings that year. "Revenue is lumpy from year to year," Cliff Burnstein pointed out. His client, the heavy metal band Metallica, made a reported $13.2 million from record sales and $3.8 million from touring in 2016, but in 2017 earned $10.9 million from record sales and $30.7 million from touring. Over a five-year period, Burnstein said, the band typically earns more from touring than from record sales. In general, the days when Metallica made more money from records than from touring are long gone, according to Burnstein. And if this is true for Metallica, which ranks behind only Garth Brooks and the Beatles in record sales since 1991, according to Nielsen Sound-Scan, it is presumably true for just about everyone else.[26]

Overall, forty-seven of the top forty-eight artists who toured in 2017 netted more income from live performances than from record sales and streaming.

For most musicians, live concerts pay the bills. Streaming is unlikely to change this balance. While Fleetwood Mac may be right that players love you only when they're playing, it is not too much of a stretch to also say that they make money only when they're playing. And, as if to prove the point, although its members are in their seventies, Fleetwood Mac embarked on a tour of more than fifty cities in 2018 and 2019. [27]

The Disconnect

Musicians, like many other businesses, sell multiple products, the most important of which are live performances and recorded music. In economics terms, musicians are multi-product businesses. Apple, the largest company by market capitalization at the time of this writing, is another example of a multi-product business. Apple sells devices, such as iPhones, computers, and iPads; it sells music through Apple Music; and it sells books through Apple Books.

Musicians are distinguished, however, by the fact that they earn relatively little of their income from their most popular product, recordings. This disconnect distinguishes musicians from other entertainers as well. Movie actors make most of their income from acting in movies, which is how their fans enjoy and consume their art. Some professional athletes make money from endorsing products or starring in films, but they typically earn most of their livelihood in the form of salary for playing their sport, which is how their fans engage with their work. Perhaps the comparison that comes closest to musicians is book writers. They earn most of their money from book advances and from royalties for selling books, but occasionally they leverage their popularity or expertise to earn significant income from the lecture circuit.

As file sharing and piracy cut into musicians' record sales in the late 1990s and early 2000s, the disconnect between how fans consumed music and how musicians made a living grew to possibly unsustainable proportions. The gap is likely to narrow in the future, however, as streaming and social media enable musicians to interact directly with their fans and create stronger links between live performances and recorded music.

Taylor Swift is a pioneer in this regard. Fans can increase their chances of being able to buy a ticket to one of her concerts by watching the pop singer's music videos, joining her email list, or purchasing her albums or merchandise. Such tie-in sales are a natural way for musicians to leverage their connection to fans through recorded music to increase their income.

Technological developments could also narrow the lines between recorded music and live performances, assuming that licensing agreements permit it. A comparison to sports is instructive. In professional sports, most of the revenue that teams earn is generated from selling television and cable rights to broadcast live games.[28] Revenue from the gate for live sporting events is the equivalent of a live concert—but there is rarely an opportunity for musicians to earn additional money from recording or broadcasting their live shows. In the future, it would make economic sense for fans to purchase recordings and videos of live events, and for more artists to experiment with live-streaming their concerts to increase revenues.

Personalization may also be coming to recorded music, just as personalized medicine is the frontier in health care. The multi-talented singer and musician Jacob Collier has offered to personalize music for his patrons on Patreon. Fans submit a recording of their lyrics, and Collier puts it to music and harmonizes it.

Not surprisingly, the music ends up sounding much better once the Grammy Award–winning musician is done. Other musicians offer to sing "Happy Birthday" or other songs for a customer, for a price.

To narrow the disconnect between the money earned for live events and that earned from recorded music, record companies will have to change their business model, which typically prohibits the resale of live recordings. Alternatively, artists could become more independent of their labels. Radiohead's Thom Yorke advises young musicians, "First and foremost, you don't sign a huge record contract that strips you of all your digital rights. . . . If you're an emerging artist, it must be frightening at the moment. Then again, I don't see a downside at all to big record companies not having access to new artists, because they have no idea what to do with them now anyway."

Most music superstars still sign on with one of the three major record companies (Universal, Warner, or Sony) or one of the large indie labels. The most notable recent exception is Chancelor Jonathan Bennett, better known as Chance the Rapper. The Chicago-born twenty-five-year-old is charting his own course by remaining an independent artist. He releases his albums (which he calls mixtapes) for free, and makes money touring and selling merchandise. He has the distinction of being the first artist to win a Grammy without selling physical copies of his music. Chances are that more artists will follow this route, even if most continue to take the safer route of signing with a major label.

The Time of Your Life

Although music represents a small percentage of economic activity, it looms large in our daily lives. The poet Carl Sandburg once wrote, "Time is the coin of your life." In the currency of how we spend our time, music is unquestionably an economic heavyweight.

Time use is difficult to measure. Still, surveys find that more than 80 percent of Americans report that on a typical day they listen to music. And those who listen to music spend two to four hours a day listening to it, on average.[29] Streaming services provide a more precise estimate of the amount of time that subscribers spend listening to music on their platforms. Pandora, for example, finds that active listeners spend about twenty hours a month streaming music. Since streaming represents about a third of all time spent listening to music, that equates to at least two hours a day of music listening in total.

Music is most often a secondary activity, however, playing in the background while people commute, work, do homework or chores, exercise, or socialize at a bar. Even so, music occupies more of people's time than any other leisure activity except television—and music is often playing in the background on the movies and television shows we watch.

At no time in human history have there been so many different ways to listen to music. We can choose from YouTube, Pandora, Spotify, Facebook, iTunes, Amazon Echo Dot, iHeart, and satellite radio, not to mention vinyl records, FM radio, and CDs. The average person listens to music on about four different formats today. Traditional radio still occupies the largest share of music listeners' time, although it is declining fast.[30] Smartphones and computers are now the most widely used listening devices.

The growth of streaming is enabling people to spend even more time listening to music. From 2015 to 2017, Americans increased the amount of time they spent listening to music by 37 percent, according to Nielsen.[31] And not surprisingly, streaming services report an increase in the amount of time subscribers spend listening to music.

As music is made more easily accessible, some economists and pundits have argued that the enjoyment of additional listening time is likely to diminish, due to what economists call the law of diminishing marginal utility. The law of diminishing utility is not a physical law, like gravity, but a tendency for the value derived from additional consumption of most goods and services to decline after a certain point. If you can put only a few songs on your playlist, as opposed to having all the songs ever recorded at your disposal, you will probably choose the songs you put on it more carefully.

Weighing against diminishing returns is the tendency for musical tastes to change as people listen to more music. The more a listener is exposed to a given song, for example, the more he or she tends to like that song (up to a point).[32]

Music Spillovers

Music has many spillover effects for individuals and communities, some monetary and even more non-monetary. A music festival is an example of monetary spillovers. Business and workers who are not directly connected to the music industry benefit when a town such as Manchester, Tennessee, or Indio, California, hosts a music festival. Restaurants, bars, and hotels experience additional demand, and the local workers who set up the stage and equipment and staff the local restaurants, bars, and hotels benefit as well. A major festival such as Bonnaroo or Coachella can put a little-known town on the map. As a result, towns often compete to host music festivals, because of the increased economic activity and publicity that they generate. Indeed, El Dorado, Arkansas, is investing $100 million of public and private funds to build the Murphy Arts District, with a 7,500-person amphitheater and 2,000-seat music hall, in an effort to rejuvenate the city and retain population.

There is an entire ecosystem that benefits from the music industry that is not counted directly in the music economy. Radio stations, device manufacturers such as Sonos, Bose, Beats, and Apple, and rock videographers all benefit from the music economy. Music drove the success of the iPod and later, to a large extent, the iPad and iPhone. These types of monetary spillovers are not unique to the music industry. Sports teams, auto manufacturers, and movie studios, among others, create monetary spill-overs. Even allowing for these spillovers in the music ecosystem, however, the music industry remains relatively small economically compared with other industries.

Of greater importance are spillovers that affect us on a personal, cultural, and societal level, beyond dollars and cents. Renditions of "Amazing Grace" comfort us in times of trouble; "The Star-Spangled Banner" binds our nation together; and "We Will Rock You" rallies arena or stadium sports fans. Erik Kirschbaum makes a credible case that Bruce Springsteen and the E Street Band's concert before 300,000 people in East Berlin in 1988 helped topple the Berlin Wall.[33] Although not all external benefits of music are positive—I still resent the student in the dorm room next to mine blasting music all hours of the day and night—and music can be (and has been) enlisted for evil causes as well as good ones, the positive effect of music on our psyches and in support of social causes is what extends its impact far beyond its monetary contribution to the economy.

Holding On to Humanity

The Sirius XM radio host Eric Alper recently took to Twitter to ask, "What album or song or musician has changed your life?" Some three hundred people quickly responded.[34] A wide range of emotions and a diversity of music poured out, including David Bowie, Linkin Park, Nirvana, Metallica, Big Bang, Joni Mitchell, Kiss, Mozart, Queen, Elvis, Dylan, Beck, Björk, Billy Joel, Ani DiFranco, Pearl Jam, Pink Floyd, Tori Amos, Marvin Gaye, Neil Young, Miles Davis, Prince, Michael Jackson, and Janet Jackson. Here are some of my favorite replies:

"Impossible to answer but I can't imagine where or who I'd be without The Beatles."

CHRISTY COLLINS OF CALIFORNIA

"Bruce Springsteen. And to say he changed my life is an understatement."

FLYNN MCLEAN OF QUEENS, NEW YORK

"Beyoncé's 'Flawless' and 'Formation' basically get me through #chemo and therefore have probably literally helped save my life."

ANYA SILVER OF MACON, GEORGIA

"Tom Petty 'Won't Back Down.' Saved my life."

MEL MARIE

"In 2017, definitely @lorde's 'Melodrama'—got me out of a deep, black hole this year."

KRISHNA N. PATEL

" 'Fools Rush In': danced to it at a wedding with my husband on first date: fell in love: still being fools."

CINDY JOYCE

This hardly qualifies as a scientific study, but clearly many people believe music has changed their lives in a variety of profound ways, from chasing away the blues to reinforcing memories of good times. This conclusion is supported by neuroscience research and clinical studies, which have found that music influences neurobiological processes in the brain. A lot of us rely on music as a source of emotional strength, happiness, courage, and a sense of identity that we might not otherwise have been able to summon or tap into. As Harry Chapin put it in his song "Let Time Go Lightly": "Music has been my oldest friend, my fiercest foe / 'Cause it can take me so high, yes it can make me so low."

Social Causes

The eighteenth-century Scottish writer and revolutionary Andrew Fletcher is often credited with the saying, "Let me make the songs of a nation, and I care not who makes its laws."* The line encapsulates the special power of music to shape the mood and spirit of a nation.

Musicians have, through their music and their personal efforts, promoted a variety of social causes. Here are a few notable examples:

Bangladesh George Harrison and his sitar mentor, Ravi Shankar, led two landmark benefit concerts in 1971, and produced a live album and a documentary film for Bangladesh that eventually raised $12 million in humanitarian aid for the new nation, which was overwhelmed by war, natural devastation, and millions of refugees.[35]

"We Are the World" A charity song written by Michael Jackson and Lionel Richie and produced by Quincy Jones in 1985 that raised over $60 million for humanitarian aid in Africa and the United States. A star-studded cast of more than forty singers appeared on the recording.[36]

Live Aid Benefit Concerts A pair of concerts organized by the Irish and Scottish musicians Bob Geldof and Midge Ure to raise funds for humanitarian relief for Ethiopia, which was suffering a famine at the time. Over $200 million in donations was raised.[37]

---

* Fletcher's actual quote was less poetic, but the sentiment was the same. Centuries later, the great economist Paul Samuelson would have his own riff on this line: "I don't care who writes a nation's laws—or crafts its advanced treatises—if I can write its economics textbooks."

Countless artists have supported social causes. Nina Simone, Harry Belafonte, Pete Seeger, Mahalia Jackson, Aretha Franklin, and many others are identified with the U.S. civil rights movement. Through her music and political activism, Cyndi Lauper has been an advocate for LGBTQ rights and awareness. Bruce Springsteen has passionately supported numerous charities, including the 1736 Family Crisis Center in Los Angeles and the Community Food Bank of New Jersey. U2 frontman Bono was a co-founder of the ONE Campaign, an organization with more than seven million members committed to taking action to end extreme poverty. John Mellencamp, Neil Young, and Willie Nelson have been advocates for family farmers. Chance the Rapper has supported the organization My Brother's Keeper.

Natural and human-made disasters often bring out musicians' support. Marc Anthony, Jennifer Lopez, Ricky Martin, Selena Gomez, and others teamed up to raise millions of dollars for disaster relief for Puerto Rico after Hurricane Maria devastated the island. And Boyz II Men, Imagine Dragons, The Killers, Wayne Newton, Céline Dion, and other stars participated in the Vegas Strong benefit concert to raise money for the victims of the mass shooting at the Las Vegas Route 91 Harvest music festival.

Doing Well and Doing Good

The prevailing view in economics, as articulated by Milton Friedman, is that the business of companies should be to make money, not pursue social objectives. In Friedman's words, "There is one and only one social responsibility of business—to use its resources and engage in activities designed to increase its profits so long as it stays within the rules of the game, which is to say, engages in open and free competition without deception or fraud."[38] But in music the objectives of maximizing profit and pursuing social objectives may not conflict; in fact, they often coincide.

One reason so many musicians support social causes is that activism is often good for business. It helps the musicians create a following and builds stronger connections with fans. This is not to doubt the sincerity of singer-activists' motives, but only to highlight the obvious: being perceived as doing good can also be good for business.

In fact, many corporations have ignored Friedman's advice and used their resources to actively support social causes. It is common for companies to make charitable contributions using funds that would otherwise go to shareholders, or to sometimes forgo lines of business that have negative societal consequences. In what may be a watershed moment, Laurence Fink, the head of BlackRock, the world's largest asset manager, wrote a letter to CEOs of top companies in 2017 arguing that "society is demanding that companies, both public and private, serve a social purpose." He further warned, "To prosper over time, every company must not only deliver financial performance, but also show how it makes a positive contribution to society."[39]

Troubled Water: A Price for Social Activism?

Do musicians pay a steep price for social activism that is out of sync with their fans? There is no sign that Beyoncé or Kanye West paid an economic price for criticizing President Bush's decision to go to war in Iraq; to the contrary, their stars rose after they criticized the president.[40] But their political statements were largely aligned with the views of their fans. After Irish singer Sinead O'Connor tore up a photo of the Pope on *Saturday Night Live* in 1992, her career crumbled, and it never recovered.[41]

A good test of this question occurred on March 10, 2003, just before the start of the Iraq War, when Natalie Maines, lead singer of the country music band the Dixie Chicks, announced at a concert in London, "Just so you know, we're on the good side with y'all. We do not want this war, this violence, and we're ashamed that the President of the United States [George W. Bush] is from Texas."[42] The reaction to Maines's comment was swift and severe. Some radio stations pulled the group's music off the air, and protestors collected and then destroyed the band's CDs. Several country artists, including Reba McEntire and Toby Keith, harshly criticized the trio. Members of the band received death threats.

The conventional wisdom is that the Dixie Chicks paid a sizable economic penalty for Ms. Maines's outspokenness. One article reported that the incident led "to the virtual demise of the band."[43] Looking back at the controversy, Maines herself said, "I feel like we are tainted. I don't know if we put a tour up, if people would come."[44]

The reality, however, is more nuanced. A consideration of hard data suggests that the economic consequences were relatively minor, on net. On one hand, the group's record sales may have lagged after the controversy, and they lost a promotional opportunity with the American Red Cross. Their single "Landslide" fell off the *Billboard* chart after reaching number ten. On the other hand, their touring revenue in 2003 remained healthy, and there is no sign that ticket sales waivered. The Dixie Chicks played forty-two sold-out shows in the summer of 2003 as part of their Top of the World Tour and grossed just over $40 million in that period, according to my tabulation from data in the Pollstar Boxoffice Database. The band's next major tour was the Accidents and Accusations World Tour in 2006, which grossed $34 million from fifty shows. A handful of shows were cancelled because of low demand, but others were added, notably in Canada and Australia. Their 2006 album *Taking the Long Way* debuted at number one on the *Billboard* 200 chart, sold more than 2.5 million copies in the United States, and won five Grammys. The album's top single, "Not Ready to Make Nice" (written by the three band members and Dan Wilson), commemorated the controversy and became the band's only song to be certified platinum and reach the top five of the *Billboard* Hot 100. In 2016, the band grossed $52 million from sixty-eight shows. Given that musicians derive most of their income from live concerts, it is plausible that the Bush controversy caused a drop in their income. But most other bands would be delighted to make the touring money the Dixie Chicks were able to garner after the controversy.

Why didn't they pay a larger economic price? A few factors probably offset the firestorm of criticism directed at the band. First, the controversy generated attention and publicity, supporting the old adage "All publicity is good publicity as long as your name is spelled right." Second, although some fans may have been turned off by Natalie Maines's comment, the band gained new followers, especially outside the United States. Third, even for superstars, concerts are a niche market. The Dixie Chicks' 2003 Top of the World Tour sold around 900,000 tickets in the United States in 2003.[45] With a population of close to 300 million people in the United States at the time, that amounts to less than one customer per 300 people. This is quite a different market than that for products such as Dove soap, Coca-Cola, or Bayer aspirin, which are purchased by a much higher percentage of households. The Dixie Chicks could afford to offend a segment of their fan base and still sell out because they continued to have a strong niche following. And one can argue that many of their fans became more devoted because of Maines's political stance.

Gold Isn't All That Glitters

Music makes a relatively small contribution to the economy in terms of the amount of money consumers and businesses spend on music and the incomes and jobs afforded by the music industry. The effect of music on our lives, however—as suggested by the considerable amount of time we spend listening to music, and the intense feelings that music evokes in us—is greatly out of proportion to its economic impact. For consumers, music is probably the best bargain ever.

Music transcends its economic value precisely because of the powerful emotional connection it creates with listeners. The emotional bond between musicians and their audiences is what sells records and concert tickets, and enables musicians to have an outsized influence on social causes. The "soft power" of music can topple autocrats and soothe souls. As Bono has said, "Music can change the world because it can change people."[46]

CHAPTER 3

The Supply of Musicians

There's a reason they call it playing, not working.

—Max Weinberg

Max Weinberg, the longtime drummer for Bruce Springsteen and the E Street Band, has told me on more than one occasion that performing music is great fun; there's a reason musicians call it playing and not working, he says. When he once let me climb onstage and bang the tambourine to "Glory Days," I got a small glimpse of what he meant. Even the illusion of entertaining a live audience is pure joy.

Weinberg has had a storybook career. In 1974, while attending college and playing drums in Broadway pit bands to help make ends meet, he came across an ad in the *Village Voice* that said the E Street Band was auditioning drummers. He was the fifty-sixth of some sixty-plus drummers to audition. He didn't know much about Springsteen or the band at the time, but he'd never seen a band so focused on its leader. After the audition he told Bruce, "I don't know who you are going to choose, but I'll tell you what, I'll play with you for nothing."[1] His father didn't object when he left school a handful of credits shy of graduating and postponed plans for law school to join the band. A year later, Bruce Springsteen and the E Street Band had their first hit, "Born to Run." More than forty years later, the drummer whom the Boss calls "Mighty Max" says, "I'd still do it for nothing."

A passion for creating and sharing music is what draws most

musicians into the profession and keeps them there despite the long odds of achieving commercial success or fame. Many describe the appeal of music as if it were a religious calling; they simply can't imagine spending their lives doing something else. From an economic standpoint, this inner drive creates a ready supply of musicians who are willing to sacrifice higher income and steadier work in order to practice their art. The lucky few are paid, as the Bruce Springsteen lyric says, "a king's ransom for doin' what comes naturally."[2] The rest just do what comes naturally and struggle to make ends meet.

Musicians by the Numbers

There were 213,738 workers in the United States who identified their main occupation as "singer, musician or related worker" in 2016, according to Census Bureau data.[3] These musicians represented only 0.13 percent of all employees that year; musicians' share of the workforce has hovered around that same level since 1970.

What do we know about working musicians? First, their salaries as a group are low. The median musician earned $20,000 in 2016, some $15,000 less than the median of all other workers. Lee Sims, who hustled to make ends meet, is more representative of musicians than his son Paul Simon.

Second, about two-thirds of musicians are men; the gender balance in the overall workforce is much closer to parity. And while women have increased their share of the U.S. workforce since World War II, there has been essentially no change in the two-to-one ratio of male to female musicians since the 1970s.

Third, 13 percent of professional musicians are African Americans, which is close to the share of African Americans in the workforce overall. Hispanics, by contrast, represent a much smaller share of musicians than their share of the workforce overall: 10 percent of musicians are Hispanic, versus 17 percent of the workforce. Following trends in the rest of the workforce, however, musicians have become more racially diverse over time. In 1970, 89 percent of musicians were white non-Hispanics. In 2016, their share was down to 71 percent.

Fourth, professional musicians are a little overrepresented in the South, but by and large they match the geographic distribution of people across the United States.

Despite the image of musicians as young school dropouts with wild hairdos, as a group musicians are actually older and better educated than the workforce overall.[4] The average working musician was forty-five years old in the latest data available—four years older than the average worker overall. Only 4 percent of musicians left school before completing high school, which is less than half the dropout rate of other workers. Fully half of musicians are four-year college graduates, compared with one-third of the workforce overall.

The gig economy started with music. Not surprisingly, musicians are almost five times more likely to report that they are self-employed than non-musicians. In 2016, 44 percent of musicians were self-employed, while just 9 percent of other workers were their own boss. Like other freelancers, self-employed musicians have the freedom to perform their work however they please and to work for a variety of employers. But they also face greater risk than traditional employees when it comes to finding steady work, and they are responsible for managing their own careers, securing benefits, and saving for the future without the aid of a human resources office.

About 30 percent of musicians currently work for a religious organization as their main gig. There are a lot of church choirs and organists. A great many singers got their start performing in church, including Aretha Franklin, Whitney Houston, John Legend, Katy Perry, Faith Hill, Justin Timberlake, Janelle Monáe, Usher, and many others.

The average musician earns income from engaging in three distinct music-related activities a year, according to a survey of

1,227 musicians that Princeton's Ed Freeland and I conducted in 2018.[5] Live performances are the most common source of income. Eighty-one percent of professional musicians earned income from performing live events over the course of a year. The second- and third-most-common sources of income are giving music lessons (42 percent) and performing in a church choir or other religious services (38 percent). These three activities accounted for more than two-thirds of the average musician's music-related income. They also take up a lot of time. The average musician spends 14.1 hours a week performing or rehearsing for a performance, 5.7 hours traveling to or from performances, and 3.6 hours giving music lessons.

These statistics tell us who works as a musician, what they do to make a living, and how much they earn, but not how and why they became musicians—neither the joy they derive from music nor the hurdles they face in pursuing their passion. In other words, they tell us everything about the backgrounds of musicians except what makes a musical career magical and maddening.

Gigging for a Living

The term *gig* was coined by jazz musicians in the 1920s to refer to a short engagement to perform music. Life as a jazz musician then, and now, often involved traveling from one town to the next to play a set or a show. The term stuck and eventually spread outside of music. Any temporary paid work today is often referred to as a gig.

In the age of Uber and Airbnb, *gig* has taken on additional meaning, often referring to a short-term work assignment through an Internet app that matches customers and workers. Both online and offline, gig work has grown in the United States in recent years, although the amount of money is relatively small.[6]

Freelance musicians account for most of the growth in musician jobs since 1970.[7] There are two main drivers of this trend. First, record companies have been under intense competitive pressure to reduce costs because piracy and file sharing have cut into revenues. Second, technology has made it easier for parts of music jobs to be outsourced and carried out remotely. And the proliferation of Uber-like online platforms that match musicians with gigs—such as GigTown.com, Gigmor.com, and ShowSlinger.com—is likely to propel freelance musical work in the twenty-first century.

Musicians have long been at the vanguard of the gig economy, facing many of the same problems that gig workers face today: obtaining health insurance, saving for the future, paying down debt, planning for taxes, and recordkeeping. In 2013, before Obamacare established health insurance exchanges and provided income-based subsidies for individuals to purchase insurance, 53 percent of musicians lacked health insurance, which was triple the uninsured rate for the population as a whole.[8] Self-employed workers as a whole saw a greater rise in health insurance coverage after Obamacare passed than other employees. The health insurance coverage rate of musicians jumped to 86 percent by 2018.[9] Not surprisingly, musicians and other freelancers have generally been more supportive of the controversial law than the public as a whole.[10] Given the mental stresses and physical wear and tear that a musical career entails, the low rate of health insurance coverage historically has been a serious problem for musicians.

Musicians, like other gig workers, struggle to find enough work. New Jersey musicians I've interviewed often say that gigs used to be easier to come by, and that their pay—around $100 for each musician per performance—has hardly increased over recent decades.[11]

Another challenge musicians and other gig workers face is getting paid. Musicians tell countless stories of being stiffed by club owners and promoters. Their experience is not unique. A quarter of self-employed workers overall say that they were paid less than they were owed at some point in the past year.[12] Aretha Franklin and many others used to insist on being paid in cash before performing.

Today, bands hire their own accountants to collect the money from the shows they perform, and they then pay their manager's commission. In the early days of music, it was the manager who would pay the performers. As one manager told me, there are lots of ways that a manager can lose artists; this practice eliminates one of them.

In light of the very real challenges that musicians face earning a living, Billy Joel's advice to young musicians is worth repeating: "Deciding to become a musician for life is a big decision, and it's scary because there's no safety net. A lot of your friends will say you're crazy; you're never gonna make it. Your parents worry about how you're gonna make a living. Most musicians that play in clubs or restaurants have to have another job."[13]

Human Capital

As noted, musicians as a whole are well educated. This is not so surprising, perhaps, given that music mastery requires years of devotion and practice, the same attributes that are necessary for academic achievement. Even those who drop out of high school to pursue a musical career often possess the focus that could lead to educational excellence.

Despite Pink Floyd's claim that "we don't need no education," training and devotion to one's craft are key ingredients to success in music. Education and training build what economists call "human capital." Decades of research has found that human capital is an important contributor to economic success for both individuals and countries. My statistical analysis shows that professional musicians who graduated from college earn considerably more income than those who left school after high school.

Grammy Award–winning songwriter Dan Wilson has said, "Even to be a moderately successful musician takes a huge amount of repetitive effort and a lot of luck. The repetition is necessary for practice but also as fertile ground for the luck."[14]

The economic and professional benefits that accrue from practice, persistence, and training can be seen in the music industry's most successful bands, such as the Beatles and Rolling Stones. Even a presumed slacker such as Kurt Cobain recognized the fundamental role of human capital in musical success. In a letter dismissing his drummer, Dave Foster, from Nirvana, Cobain admonished, "A band needs to practice, in our opinion, at least 5 times a week if the band ever expects to accomplish anything."[15] Even immensely successful bands, such as Bruce Springsteen and the E Street Band, still rehearse on the day of every show, even after decades of performing together. Practice may not make perfect in music, but a lack of practice is a sure way to turn a symphony into a cacophony.

The Magic of Music

What draws people to pursue a career in music? After interviewing music stars and newcomers and reading several musicians' own accounts, I am convinced that the main reason—and the best reason—for pursuing a musical career is a deep, abiding love of music, one that creates a nearly mystical appeal, rather than dreams of fame or fortune.

Nile Rodgers, the legendary singer, guitar player, record producer, songwriter, composer, and arranger, gives a simple and yet often told explanation for what draws him to music: "to be heard."[16]

Patti Smith describes the creative process in mystical terms: "The artist seeks contact with his intuitive sense of the gods, but in order to create his work, he cannot stay in this seductive and incorporeal realm. He must return to the material world in order to do his work. It's the artist's responsibility to balance mystical communication and the labor of creation."[17] Who, after all, could resist an opportunity to talk to the gods?

Bob Dylan, too, alludes to the transcendent appeal of music:

"Songs, to me, were more important than just light entertainment. They were my preceptor and guide into some altered consciousness of reality."[18]

Jason Pierce of the alternative rock bands Spiritualized and Spacemen 3 explained the allure of music this way: "All I know is I feel so alive when I'm out there playing and that makes me want to keep going more than anything else."[19] Sheila Stratton-Hamza, a sixty-year-old blues singer who attended one of my focus groups, said, "I'm in pain before taking the stage, but euphoric once performing. I feel my essence comes out. I'm transformed as a person." Jacob Collier, a humble, multi-talented twenty-four-year-old musician who won two Grammys for music he created in his bedroom, told me that he feels "invincible" when he is on tour.[20] Remembering that he has a serious peanut allergy is the only thing that brings him back down to earth, he said.

Musicians that I surveyed highlighted the opportunity for artistic expression, performing, and collaboration with others as their favorite aspects of being a musician. They overwhelmingly selected "financial insecurity" as their least liked aspect of being a musician.[21]

From an economic standpoint, the fact that there is an endless supply of people who are willing to create and perform music virtually for free because of its intrinsic appeal puts downward pressure on incomes in the industry for all but the superstars. As J. P. Mei, an economist and founder of the Shanghai Peking Opera Company, put it, "The idea of a starving artist may be an equilibrium."

Even music superstars are relatively low-paid compared to superstars in other arenas. *Billboard* magazine compiles a list of the top fifty moneymakers in music each year. Some are solo performers and others are multi-person bands, which split their income among their members. If we focus on the twenty-nine solo performers in the top fifty, the average of these music superstars earned $19.5 million in 2017. That's a lot, to be sure, but only about half of what the average of the top fifty CEOs at publicly traded companies earned that year ($37 million), and less than half of the average pay of the top fifty athletes that year ($51.1 million).[22] And all of this is small change compared to the incomes of top hedge fund and private equity managers.

I advise students to go into fields that they are passionate about. My argument is that they will spend a huge amount of time and energy working, so they should find something that excites them and makes them proud; the rest will take care of itself. But if possible, I advise students, they should find a field that they enjoy and that others find *less* enjoyable, because that limits the supply of people going into their field, thereby increasing pay for those who do go into it.

Music falls squarely in the first of these categories. I used to think that musicians entered the field because of overconfidence, with oversized expectations that they will attain fame and fortune despite the long odds. After all, Adam Smith, the eighteenth-century founder of economics, long ago argued that "the contempt of risk, and the presumptuous hope of success, are in no period of life more active than at the age at which young people choose their professions."[23] But even presumptuous young musicians seem to me to be under little illusion that they will achieve fame and fortune. They simply can't imagine another career path that would provide them with more joy or a better outlet for their creative passions. And musicians typically do not work alone—they work with other musicians, who are united in their comradery and common purpose, helping to strengthen that commitment and drive. As the Grateful Dead sang, "But I can't stop for nothing, I'm just playing in the band."[24]

Steve Liesman: Reporter by Day, Musician by Night

Steve Liesman has two great gigs. You probably recognize him as the economics reporter on CNBC's business show *Squawk Box*. But he also plays guitar in the Stella Blue's Band, one of the best Grateful Dead cover bands. Liesman exemplifies the thousands of musicians who have managed to earn a living doing something else, but who work passionately as musicians on the side. I interviewed him about the role of music in his work and life on September 21, 2018, at CNBC's studio in Times Square, New York.

How do you manage to work as both a TV reporter and a musician?

I live this double life. I go to work every day around 5:30 in the morning, then I play a gig at night that sometimes starts at 9:00 pm. I go to every gig with a little five-hour energy drink in my car thinking I'll need it for the ride home or somewhere in the middle of the show—but I never need it.

When did you start playing music?

I was sixteen years old. I was sitting there drinking beer and smoking cigarettes on the curb of the local elementary school in Edgemont, New York, and I decided there had to be more to life than this.

What's funny is that everyone played. But, somewhere around twenty-one or twenty-two years old, everyone else got a memo that said you can stop playing now, and I never got the memo.

How many guitars do you own? Is gear a big part of your budget?

I'm not a big expensive guitar or gear guy. I use two or three guitars playing and each one has a backup. I think a lot of guys spend an awful lot of time worrying and fretting about gear, and I spend more time worrying and fretting about how I'm playing.

You go to a gig with $3,000 or $4,000 of gear in the car. And, sometimes you're doing it for $50 or $100, so that difference is quite remarkable.

When did you decide to earn a living as a reporter instead of a musician?

I was in my early twenties. I was playing in Manhattan every week. I walked into Kenny's Castaways at midnight and there was an amazing guitar player playing in the vestibule. I looked at how good he was, and I decided that if he's that good and playing in the vestibule, the world doesn't need me playing as a professional guitar player.

I was the international diamond reporter for the *National Jeweler Magazine* at the time. So I always pursued these two professions, journalism and music. I'm not sure why and how they come together. I wrote my essay for Columbia Journalism School on that.

Do you feel that music and reporting complement each other?

To me, there's a connection that I cannot describe between crunching data on the spreadsheet and figuring out the right notes on a Jorma Kaukonen song, or what Bob Weir plays. There's an analytical part of music that really works in my brain with the economics and the math that I use in my life.

Does being a live performer in front of an audience help you perform before a television audience?

No. Sitting in front of a camera, you just don't get the feedback from the audience.

What I do know about performing live is that I've got to know something one hundred times better on guitar in my living room to play it live. There's this disconnect between how well I know something in my living room versus what I need to know playing live.

You only have so many hours in the day. What do you sacrifice to practice music?

Sleep.

How many bands have you been with over the years?

I've played with eight to ten bands. I just always had a band, wherever I was. People don't get how much it takes to play live. Having a gig and a band makes you work to perfect stuff.

How often do you perform with the Stella Blues Band?

I do a paid gig with the Stella Blues Band two to four times a month. On a good night, the band makes $1,500 or $2,000, and we divide that by seven. We take a part of that and put it into advertising and other things the band might need. So, on a good night, we walk away with $200 or $150 each.

We did a free show in Central Park and there were probably a thousand people there. Most nights we play before one hundred and two hundred people. And, they pay between $10 and $20.

As an economics reporter, I know that playing music is economically ridiculous. Yet, I would even play more if I could. I have separate buckets in my head for what I should be paid in music and what I should be paid in my day job. If we make $150 a night playing, that's usually a good night. If we make $300 a night, that's an amazingly good night. But that's a fraction of what I get paid with my day job. So, they're ridiculously incongruent. Perhaps behavioral economist Richard Thaler could explain it.

Have you ever played with any members of the Grateful Dead?

I've played with Bob Weir a couple of times. Stella Blue's played the Capitol Theater in Westchester, and Phil Lesh came on and played a set with us.

What was it like playing with Bob Weir and Phil Lesh?

It's such a sort of awestruck moment, and you're trying so hard not to screw up, that you don't even know the moment's there. Bob was a little weird to play with because I play his parts with the Dead band, so it was a little hard to play with him.

The tough part of playing with them is that they're true creative geniuses that, in my opinion, were involved in creating some of the most classic American music ever. They love to jam but have little interest, as true artists, in repeating what they've already done. No artist does. So, the idea that I'm doing stuff that they did before means that they're less interested in what I'm doing now.

I know Bob Weir pretty well, and he thinks it's funny that people try to imitate his sound. Bob rarely goes back and listens to his live performances. I constantly do. We're sort of on a different plane than them.

What do you think is the source of creativity in music?

I have a very easy answer for that: walking my dog. All of the songs I've written have basically come from walking my dog.

For the Grateful Dead, I think drugs were part of their secret. But I don't think it was all of it. They really knew music very well. Jerry Garcia was a world-class banjo player and then he became a world-class jazz musician.

Bob Weir has essentially innovated his own style of rhythm guitar. It's the ability to take unrelated things and put them together and kind of make them work together or layer together. They knew jazz and blues and country, and they kind of melded it all into one thing and that's doing their own thing, and I think that's creativity.

It's like trying to find previous analogs for the Beatles. You can do it, but they represented, in my opinion, such a revolutionary step that it's hard to go back and say, "Oh this was the precursor to the Beatles, or that was."

On my day job, the most creative thing that I do is I think about metaphors to explain economics and business.

Do you have a good metaphor for the difference between musicians like yourself and Bob Weir?

I divide the world into two different kinds of musicians: there's mutants and there's everybody else. The mutants are the great players; they're the guys who hit the hundred-mile-per-hour fastballs, or throw them. In music, they hear a song once and know it forever. Even if they haven't heard a song before, they know where the next chord is. They invented music that we know and love. And, there's everybody else. I consider myself somewhere toward the top of everybody else. But, fairly early on, I realized I wasn't a mutant, and that I was not going to be a mutant.

I'm good enough to keep pace with the mutants on a song that I know, but when they go off into LaLa Land, they leave me behind. A friend in the music business says they have a name for someone like me, but he told me I've proven myself not to be one of those people. They're called "dentists with Alembics." That's a rich professional person who can afford expensive gear but doesn't play well. They're a big group. Some of them pay musicians $500 to $600 a night to play with them. That's a business.

This is why the money modestly matters to me. It distinguishes me from the dentists. I'm not paying to play; I'm trying to make it work.

The Organization of Bands

"I couldn't possibly think of any adjectives to introduce this next group," Frank Sinatra declared on his live album recorded at the Sands on his fiftieth birthday, "so I merely say the magnificent Count Basie and his great organization."[25] Sinatra's description of a band as an *organization* struck a chord with me as an economist. A band *is* an organization, like any other small business or association. Musical groups, from garage bands to symphony orchestras, can be analyzed with the tools of the economic field of industrial organization.

Every organization must confront several essential questions: How many members should the group contain? How should decisions be made? How should income be divided among members of the organization?

The number of members in a musical group has fallen over time. The bands listed in the *Billboard* Top 100 in 1976, for example, had an average of 4.5 members. In 2016 there were far more solo artists in the Top 100; even excluding solo performers, the average size of a group fell to 3.2 members.[26]

Why have bands been shrinking? The likely explanation is that technology has made it easier for fewer musicians to create more music. All else being equal, there is a significant economic benefit to having a smaller number of members in a band, given that the money the band generates is divided among its members. A smaller band means more money per person. It is what I call the *1/N problem*, as revenue must be divided among *N* members of the band.

While the size of bands has been getting smaller, an increasing number of songs recorded by superstars today feature other artists. Some examples are "Stand Up" by Andra Day (feat. Common); "Perfect" by Ed Sheeran (feat. Beyoncé); and "Despacito" by Luis Fonsi and Daddy Yankee (feat. Justin Bieber). Figure 3.1 shows the sharp rise in the number of songs in the *Billboard* Top 100 that involve collaborations among artists.

Figure 3.1: Number of Songs on *Billboard* Top 100 That Are Collaborations

Source: Author's calculations using data from *Billboard* Year-End Top 100.

Another trend is that songwriting has become much more of a collaborative endeavor since the 1980s, as the number of writers per song in the *Billboard* Top 100 almost doubled.

There are many potential explanations for the trend toward greater collaboration. In some cases it reflects the fact that music is becoming more complicated, and artists are reaching out to others to contribute when their expertise is needed. In this regard, music reflects the trend toward outsourcing that has affected the rest of the economy.

Singer-songwriter Dan Wilson mentioned that, in his experience, more composers are contributing to songs because the process of recording music has become compartmentalized, with various contributions transferred around the world and inserted into the finished product. He cited as an example a song by Halsey (featuring Big Sean and Stefflon Don) called "Alone," which credits seven songwriters. Wilson explained how so many musicians came to be credited with the song:

"Alone" started with a groove that Josh Carter from Phantogram created, and he brought it to a Phantogram session that I was working on. . . . I sang a verse right there. And then, it got rejected for their album, but [Eric Frederic's] next record that he was working on was with Halsey, and he and she wrote a song that magically needed that verse that we had done. And then they sent the files to a couple of other producers and I'm wondering, "It's a lot of people on the record." So they got a rap on it from Big Sean and Stefflon Don. . . . [Tony Hester is credited] because Josh's original version of the song had a sample from a Marilyn McCoo and Billy Davis Jr. song from long ago that he wrote. Then Halsey and Ricky wrote the song and they included that verse that I wrote. So part of the reason there are so many people writing on a song is because you can do it now.[27]

Interestingly, Wilson thought that the compartmentalization of music means that music has become simpler, with complex melodies often dropped from the finished recording because they don't fit in, or because a contributor down the line doesn't appreciate the value of the variation.

In some cases, collaborations are also a means for artists to cross over to reach a new audience—for example, for a pop artist to reach hip-hop fans, or vice versa. And certain genres, such as hip-hop, rely more on collaborative efforts because of the nature of their sound and work practices.

Today, it has also become much more acceptable for musicians to acknowledge the collaborative input of other artists on their songs. In the early days of recorded music, collaborative contributions were rarely acknowledged, even when they occurred. We have come a long way since the time when Tommy Dorsey was credited with the number one song on the very first *Billboard* Top 10 Chart in 1940, for "I'll Never Smile Again," which in fact was a collaboration with an unnamed Frank Sinatra.[28]

It took the rise of hip-hop as a mainstream genre in the 1990s for collaborations to become popular. We have since reached the point that Dr. Dre's attorney, Peter Paterno, could quip, "The biggest artist in the world right now is *Featuring*. That guy is on every record."[29]

1/N

Most bands start out by dividing their income evenly. This is a transparent and fair method. When he was the lead singer and songwriter for Semisonic, which produced the hit "Closing Time," Dan Wilson agreed that his three-man band would divide their earnings equally, in exchange for Wilson receiving creative control over all musical decisions.[30]

"At the beginning," manager Cliff Burnstein told me, "a band has to be a democracy, because it is all about survival. Everyone has to get the same amount."[31] He stressed that "at the early stage a band is only as strong as its weakest link." It must earn enough money to keep everyone committed to the group. "Think about the minimum amount of income that the guy with three kids and a wife needs to make to stay in the group," he said. Suppose there are four members in the band. "The microeconomics of the band," he explained, "requires that you multiply this minimum amount by four, and the band must earn at least that much to survive." One challenge, of course, is that constantly touring to generate the income they need can kill the band's creativity and chemistry. Burnstein tries to find a balance between touring and writing and studio time to generate enough revenue to keep the band going, while maintaining their creativity and chemistry.

When should a band stop splitting its income evenly and reward the more creative contributors more generously? Burnstein's answer surprised me: "Not until their third arena headliner tour." When I commented that it could be a long time before a band had a third arena tour, he responded, "Yes, but after their first arena tour they might not have another one. They need to demonstrate that they're more than ephemeral."

If a band achieves superstardom, there is a risk that the biggest star will leave unless he or she is paid a bigger share. This is when a band usually makes a transition from a democratic model, where all revenues are split equally, to more of an authoritarian one, in which the rewards are more heavily skewed to the stars. As Cliff gently put it, "Only once you have the confidence that this is going to be a long-term proposition, you can evaluate the ways to incentivize the creative guys a little more. This is the economics of fairness." This is also when good management becomes essential to maintain the band's chemistry, and to minimize resentment and friction among the members who are receiving less than their $1/N$ share.

In Burnstein's experience, managing a band is more art than science. He tries to make dealings with band members transparent, to explain the rationale for decisions, and to convince the band members that they are all making more money together than they ever thought they would.

Career Longevity

"The trick is to become an institution, like me," Count Basie once said. "I can work until I die, even if I don't have another record."[32]

Of course, becoming an institution is not so easy. Very few performers stay at the top for very long.

There are some notable exceptions, including Paul McCartney, the Rolling Stones, Barbra Streisand, Bruce Springsteen, U2, Billy Joel, Madonna, and James Taylor, but they are few and far between.

In hard rock, no band has come close to the worldwide popularity of Metallica since they released their *Black Album* in 1991.[33] What is the secret of Metallica's longevity? Cliff Burnstein admitted that he often asks that question himself. "You would think there should be some competition to come by and knock them off their perch at some point, but it hasn't happened," he said.

Burnstein posited that Metallica's long run came about because they have a large canon of hits, because lead singer James Hetfield "is an unbelievable talent" who has stayed with the band, and because drummer Lars Ulrich is an outstanding arranger and organizer. They are professionals with "a drive to succeed at the highest level."

Burnstein did some research on Metallica's fan base and discovered that their fans are evenly distributed in age from teenagers to fans in their forties. That wide demographic should ensure that Metallica has an audience for years to come. Burnstein highlighted another important aspect of the way Q Prime manages the band that contributes to their longevity: they don't tour the way they did before. They take more time off because of age, family obligations, and physical demands. When they do tour, demand is high. And they put on an amazing show. On winning the 2017 Swedish Polar Prize, sometimes called music's Nobel Prize, Metallica's Lars Ulrich remarked, "It's a great validation of everything Metallica has done over the last 35 years. At the same time, we feel like we're in our prime with a lot of good years ahead of us."[34]

Many performers transition to other roles in the industry, such as songwriting, composing, or producing, all of which creates a steadier stream of income and requires less travel. This progression could also account for why many popular bands and musicians are making a leap from the concert stage to the Broadway stage. The success of ABBA's 1999 Broadway hit, *Mamma Mia*, has been followed by many others, including Green Day's 2010 Tony Award–winning *American Idiot*, Duncan Sheik's 2006 Tony Award–winning *Spring Awakening*, Bono and The Edge's 2011 musical *Spider-Man*, Boy George's 2003 musical *Taboo*, Sting's 2014 *The Last Ship*, and Cyndi Lauper and Harvey Fierstein's Tony Award–winning 2013 musical *Kinky Boots*. Elton John has also had great success writing the score to the Disney hit *The Lion King* in 1998, *Aida* in 2000, and *Billy Elliot the Musical* in 2009.

Perhaps no one has had as long and varied a career in music

as producer Quincy Jones. At age sixteen Jones so impressed Lionel Hampton that he was scheduled to tour with his band, until Hampton's wife insisted that Jones finish high school first. At nineteen he toured with Hampton, playing trumpet. Later, he played trumpet and served as musical director for Dizzy Gillespie's band. He went on to produce records for nearly everyone in the business, from Frank Sinatra and Ray Charles to Michael Jackson and Donna Summer; composed countless film scores; and, after discovering Will Smith, produced the hit TV series *The Fresh Prince of Bel-Air*. He produced the hit song "You Don't Own Me" *twice*—first with Lesley Gore, and then with Grace and G-Eazy—and both versions made it to the *Billboard* Hot 100, fifty years apart. Jones has won twenty-eight Grammys, and at age eighty-four, the music icon told me he has given up alcohol and is excited about writing a new street opera.

Sitting down with Jones in the living room of his 25,000-square-foot Bel Air mansion, I asked him how he managed to enjoy such a long and successful career. Quincy's answer: "Work hard, play hard." [35] Later, he gave a more revealing insight: "Curiosity." That curiosity has pushed him to work in new genres with new artists and with new technology. He did not go into music to become rich or famous, he said, but because of his passion for creating music. The head of his music production company, Adam Fell, mentioned another secret to Quincy's success: he surrounds himself with young people, embraces new ideas, and is comfortable being challenged. [36] That strategy has made him a financial as well as a musical success. For example, Jones was an early investor in the music streaming company Spotify.

Drugs, Mental Health, and Life Expectancy

The Heartbreakers' drummer Steve Ferrone told me that by 2017, Tom Petty's broken hip had become so painful that "he couldn't walk up the steps. He'd hang on to my shoulder to get up onstage." Why didn't he cancel the fifty-three-show tour they had scheduled? Ferrone said musicians feel "bulletproof" while on-stage. "With 50,000 or 60,000 people in the audience that love you, what problems do you feel?" Thanks to adrenaline and pain medication, "sometimes Tom could walk back up there on his own without any problems for the encore," Ferrone said. In addition to fentanyl, an autopsy conducted after Tom Petty accidentally over-dosed on October 2, 2017, found sedatives and an antidepressant in his system. "He must have been in agony," Ferrone whispered over and over.[37]

The sad fact is that fatal drug overdose, substance abuse, alcoholism, anxiety, depression, and suicide are major risks for musicians. Life on the road, the pressure of performance, and the availability of drugs and alcohol take a toll on many. Some musicians may also take drugs in the belief that they enhance creativity. My survey found that musicians are three times more likely than the general population to suffer from substance abuse problems.[38] Among the superstars who have died from drug over-doses are Jimi Hendrix (died at twenty-seven in 1970), Janis Joplin (died at twenty-seven in 1970), Elvis Presley (died at forty-two in 1977), Kurt Cobain (died at twenty-seven in 1994), Michael Jackson (died at fifty in 2009), Amy Winehouse (died at twenty-seven in 2011), Whitney Houston (died at forty-eight in 2012), Prince (died at fifty-seven in 2016), and Lil Peep (died at twenty-one in 2017). Musicians have a two to three times greater risk of dying in their twenties or thirties than the rest of the population, according to careful research.[39]

Several prominent musicians have also struggled with depres-sion, anxiety, and other mental health problems. Mariah Carey, Sia, and Demi Lovato have opened up about having bipolar dis-order. Bruce Springsteen, Logic, Khalid, Selena Gomez, Janet Jackson, the Beach Boys' Brian Wilson, and Heart's Ann Wilson have discussed their struggles with anxiety and depression.

Half of the musicians in my survey reported feeling down, depressed, or hopeless at least several days in the last two weeks, compared with less than a quarter of the adult population as a whole. An alarming 11.8 percent of musicians reported entertaining "thoughts that you would be better off dead or hurting yourself in some way" in at least several days in the last two weeks, compared with 3.4 percent for the general population.*

In 2017, 72,306 Americans died of drug overdoses according to the Centers for Disease Control, up 14 percent from the preceding year. The opioid epidemic, in the form of heroin, struck musicians long before it spread to the general public. As in many cases, problems in American society began earlier and are amplified in the music industry.

Rise Up: Family Backgrounds of Top Musicians

Historically, music has provided an avenue for upward mobility for individuals from disadvantaged backgrounds, and a means to effect cultural influence. It provided a prominent voice for African Americans during the struggles of the Jim Crow era. Among the brilliant musicians who were able to rise from poverty and racial discrimination to enrich American culture and society are Mahalia Jackson, Harry Belafonte, Nina Simone, Chuck Berry, Ray Charles, and Stevie Wonder.

Does music still provide that avenue for upward mobility today for children from disadvantaged backgrounds, the chance to reach the top echelons of American cultural and economic life? With the help of a team of Princeton students, I tracked down the family backgrounds of the musicians who participated in songs listed in the *Billboard* Top 100 in 1976 and in 2016. The 1976 cohort included such stars as Paul McCartney, Freddie Mercury, Peter Frampton, Mick Fleetwood, Elton John, Diana Ross, Steven Tyler, David Bowie, and Steve Miller. The 2016 class included Drake, Adele, Justin Bieber, Rihanna, Shawn Mendes,

---

* After the survey was completed, one musician wrote back, "The very process of completing the survey led me to realize how long I had been feeling depressed and I *am* taking steps to deal with it. . . . I hope it helps to know that you made a difference in ways you may not have anticipated."

Selena Gomez, Ariana Grande, Beyoncé, Jay-Z, and Meghan Trainor. The average age of musicians on the Top 100 charts was about the same in both periods (close to thirty). Discovering the family backgrounds for many musicians proved a challenge, as we attempted to classify them based on their families' economic circumstances.[40]

The results showed a clear and encouraging pattern: music continues to provide a means of upward mobility. In 1976, 15 percent of the musicians in the *Billboard* Top 100 had come from family backgrounds that placed them in the bottom 10 percent of all families economically. In 2016, the corresponding figure was 26.5 percent. The increase in upward mobility was a result of the rise of the hip-hop/rap genre. More than half of hip-hop/rap musicians came from families classified in the bottom half of the income distribution. Excluding hip-hop and rap artists, about 14 percent of musicians with top songs in 2016 came from the bottom 10 percent of families in terms of income. As a point of reference, only 2 percent of all individuals in the top 1 percent of the U.S. income distribution today came from families ranked in the bottom 10 percent when they were growing up.[41] Musicians with a top 100 song are likely to reach the top 1 percent of income earners in that year, so a career in music is associated with much greater bottom-to-top mobility than in the economy overall.

Superstar musicians also come from a more diverse set of geographic regions in the digital era. In 1976, nearly 20 percent of musicians in the *Billboard* Top 100 came from only four cities: Los Angeles, Chicago, New York, or Nashville. In 2016, the number of musicians who came from those cities was down to 15 percent. The share of superstar musicians who grew up in a small city or rural town (population of 50,000 or less) rose from 18 percent to 29 percent over the forty-year span.

Regarding race, there was a slight increase in the percentage of African Americans among top musicians over the intervening years, from 34 percent in 1976 to 38 percent in 2016. African Americans were overrepresented in the top performers when compared to the music workforce overall. The percentage of musicians who grew up in two-parent households fell from 80 percent in 1976 to 66 percent in 2016.

Reflecting the increased polarization of American society, top musicians were more likely to come from families in the top 10 percent of the income distribution in 2016 than in 1976. Seventeen percent of top musicians in 2016 grew up in families with incomes in the top 10 percent; only 6 percent came from such privileged families in 1976. Nonetheless, music remains more democratic than the economy as a whole: in the overall economy, 45 percent of the individuals whose earnings place them in the top 1 percent in the United States grew up in families that were in the top 10 percent of the income distribution.

Music appears more meritocratic than the top ranks of American society in another respect: only a handful of top musicians had parents who were superstar musicians. Although many musicians who have achieved stardom have talented children who follow in their footsteps and achieved some prominence (think Frank Sinatra and his children Frank junior and Nancy, Johnny Cash and Rosanne Cash, Nat King Cole and Natalie Cole, John Lennon and Julian and Sean Lennon), it is hard to name a parent-child combination in which *both* became superstars. Top athletes and corporate executives are more likely than top musicians to have parents who excelled in their profession. The rarity of dynasties in music probably reflects the outsized role of luck in achieving stardom.

A Man's World?

Looking at music as a whole, there have been roughly twice as many men as women working as professional musicians since 1970, according to Census Bureau data. The gender gap is even larger among elite musicians who make it to the *Billboard* Top 100 chart. But at least the trend is improving. In 1976, only 10 percent of the musicians with top hits were women; by 2016 that had increased to 27 percent, still a bit below women's percentage of all musicians, but much higher than forty years ago.

There are many signs that women are underrepresented in music. Only two women (Madonna and Céline Dion) are in the top twenty of all-time performers in terms of concert revenue, according to the Pollstar Boxoffice Database. In the words of former Spice Girl Melanie Chisholm, "As soon as we were heading into the music industry, we started to be faced with some sexism. We were told girls don't sell."[42] Chisholm is not alone. A survey I conducted in 2018 found that 72 percent of female musicians felt that they had been discriminated against because of their sex, and 67 percent said they had been a victim of sexual harassment.[43] After female artists were selected for fewer than 20 percent of the Grammy Awards given out in 2018, the Recording Academy appointed a task force to examine "barriers and biases affecting women and other underrepresented voices in the music industry.*

The gender imbalance is greater in some music genres than in others. Country music, for example, is particularly male oriented. Only three female artists made it to country radio's Top 40 in 2017.[44] Classical music is also a challenge. Zubin Mehta, the celebrated conductor of the Los Angeles Symphony Orchestra (1964–78) and New York Philharmonic (1978–90), once baldly stated, "I just don't think women should be in an orchestra."[45] And there is a dearth of female producers and record company executives.[46]

It may be that women are underrepresented in music because they prefer to go into other fields, or because they face discrimination, as illustrated by the attitude expressed by Zubin Mehta.

---

* A report by Stacy L. Smith, Marc Choueiti, and Kate Pieper of the USC Annenberg Inclusion Initiative drew attention to the low percentage of women who won Grammy Awards in 2018, and launched a national conversation on the issue. The Recording Academy established its sixteen-member task force, chaired by Tina Tchen, in the aftermath of the report. I served as a statistical consultant to the task force.

To determine the role of sex-based discrimination, economists Claudia Goldin of Harvard and Cecilia Rouse of Princeton studied a remarkable, real-life experiment involving auditions for symphony orchestras.[47] In the 1970s and 1980s, most major symphony orchestras started conducting blind auditions, where the candidates performed assigned pieces behind a screen that concealed their identity. In some cases, they even rolled out a carpet so the judges couldn't hear whether the candidates were wearing heels. The share of women selected for orchestras rose considerably in this period, from 10 percent before 1970 to 35 percent in the 1990s. By 2016, women made up just over 47 percent of musicians in American ensembles, according to the League of American Orchestras.

To determine the role that blind auditions played, Professors Goldin and Rouse collected year-by-year data on eleven major symphony orchestras, each with 90 to 105 musicians. With their data, they could look at the male and female hiring rates and the sex composition of orchestras before and after each orchestra introduced the practice of blind auditions. Not surprisingly, female candidates fared far better when they auditioned behind a screen. The two economists concluded that the switch to blind auditions can explain a quarter of the increase in the percentage of women in orchestras from 1970 to 1996.

Blind auditions cannot be applied in every industry or at every step of the hiring process. And members of minority groups continue to be underrepresented in orchestras. But several companies outside of the music industry have implemented strategies to shroud the gender of job applicants to increase the representation of women at work and counteract discrimination, and these strategies have had some success.[48] More progress is needed, however, to nurture women's careers, eradicate explicit and implicit forms of sexual harassment, and change attitudes. These challenges are especially difficult in industries that are characterized by large imbalances of power and industries in which independent contractor relationships are common, conditions now common in music and in a growing number of other industries.

A Musical Life

The life of most musicians is often economically challenging but personally rewarding. Only a lucky few achieve fame and fortune. The rest struggle to make ends meet. Most of their rewards come from the intrinsic joy they derive from pursuing a profession that they are passionate about, from collaborating with similarly passionate musicians to entertain others, and from honing their craft. A growing number of workers in the rest of the economy are facing the same types of challenges as musicians. The advice that Billy Joel gives to young musicians seems to me to be particularly appropriate: "Forget about being a star or a recording artist: If you can pay your rent and make enough money to buy food and necessities of life as a musician, that's already a success."[49]

CHAPTER 4

The Economics of Superstars

The winner takes it all
The loser's standing small.

—Benny Andersson and Björn Ulvaeus

*T*he hit song "The Winner Takes It All" was released by the Swedish pop group ABBA in 1980. That year also happened to be a turning point for economic inequality. Since 1980, more than 100 percent of the total growth in income in the United States has gone to the top 10 percent of families. A whopping two-thirds of all income gains have gone to the top 1 percent. The bottom 90 percent saw their combined income actually *shrink*.[1] Europe and Asia have also experienced a rise in the share of income accruing to top income earners in recent years.[2] Why has the economy become more of a winner-take-all affair?

The income distribution has become more skewed in the direction of top earners for a variety of reasons. Studying the music industry helps shed light on one key factor: the role of superstar markets. Labor markets have been transformed into superstar markets in many professions, where a small number of top performers earn an outsized share of income. Music has long—though not always—been a textbook example of a superstar market, and holds many lessons about the economy as a whole.

Serious study of the economics of superstars began with the great English economist Alfred Marshall in the late nineteenth century. Marshall was interested in understanding why a small number of successful businessmen were earning greater and greater salaries. As you'll see later in this chapter, his answer related to improvements in technology that enabled businesspeople to command far-flung empires and reap the rewards of operating on such enormous scale. Ironically, he used music as a counter-example to this phenomenon, as a case study of a profession where superstar effects were limited, because only people within earshot of a singer's unamplified voice could enjoy his or her performance.

Times have changed. Marshall didn't envision speakers, microphones, amplifiers, digital recordings, streaming media, or Jumbotrons. It is a powerful reminder of the central role that technology plays in determining economic winners and losers. But technology exists within a legal and social framework that also influences economic success or failure, the size of the economic pie, and the distribution of rewards in an economy. For example, the rather meager royalties paid for song publishing rights restrains incomes for songwriters. For musicians, and those in many other fields in our increasingly celebrity-driven culture, the process by which popularity grows or decays is a critical gatekeeper for entry into superstar status, and for all that superstardom entails. Finally, norms of fairness, which constrain salaries, concert prices, and other economic variables, also play a role in determining the rewards to achieving superstardom.

Making a Superstar Market

Alfred Marshall (1842–1924) was the most influential economist of his generation. He marveled at the shifting income distribution taking place during his lifetime. Commenting on the 1870s, Marshall wrote, "A business man of average ability and average good fortune gets now a lower rate of profits . . . than at any previous time, while the operations, in which a man exceptionally favoured by genius and good luck can take part, are so extensive as to enable him to amass a large fortune with a rapidity hitherto unknown."[3] Sound familiar? The same might be said of Jeff Bezos, Bill Gates, and Mark Zuckerberg today.

Marshall's explanation for the growing income gap between superstar businessmen and everyone else rested on new developments in communications technology—namely, the telegraph. The telegraph connected Great Britain with America, India, and even places as far away as Australia. As a result, Marshall recognized, top entrepreneurs were able "to apply their constructive or speculative genius to undertakings vaster, and extending over a wider area, than ever before." In other words, technology increased the scale of the market, an essential ingredient for a superstar to be able to earn a supersized income.

Marshall, as I mention in Chapter 1, pointed to the example of Elizabeth Billington (1765–1818) to make his argument. Mrs. Billington was widely regarded as the greatest soprano of her era. But, Marshall observed, "so long as the number of persons who can be reached by a human voice is strictly limited, it is not very likely that any singer will make an advance on the £10,000 said to have been earned in a season by Mrs. Billington at the beginning of the last century, nearly as great [an increase] as that which the business leaders of the present generation have made on those of the last." Because Mrs. Billington and other outstanding singers could not reach a large audience, they lacked the scale required to become superstars.

Thanks to the work of Sherwin Rosen (1938–2001), a hard-nosed University of Chicago economist who possessed a dry wit and sharp mind, we have subsequently learned that scale is necessary but not sufficient in and of itself to create superstars. Rosen developed a formal economic model of superstars that showed that a second essential ingredient is needed for a market to be dominated by a small number of superstars. The contenders for the top of the market have to be imperfect substitutes, meaning that each superstar has his or her own unique style and skills that raise or lower profitability.

If all managers were identically talented—that is, if they were perfect substitutes—it would not matter whom a company appointed as its CEO or top executives. The top businesspeople would be unable to command a premium because they would face stiff competition from equally qualified rivals. Likewise, if every musician sounded the same, it wouldn't matter which ones we listened to on our smartphones and radios, and all musicians would be paid the same. It is only when the top contenders can distinguish themselves from everyone else in some relevant dimension that there is a chance for a market to be dominated by a superstar. And it must be the case that combining the efforts of workers of lesser talents does not overtake the output of the most talented. As Rosen put it, "Hearing a succession of mediocre singers does not add up to a single outstanding performance."[4]

In other words, both scale and uniqueness have to be present to create a superstar market. Mrs. Billington's voice was unique, but she lacked scale. Scale magnifies the effect of small, often imperceptible differences in talent. With the ability to scale, the rewards at the top can be much greater for someone who is slightly more talented than his or her next-best competitor, because the most talented person's genius can reach a much greater audience or market, in turn generating much greater revenue and profit.

Because small differences in talent can generate large differences in economic rewards, and talent is often hard to judge and predict, luck also plays a significant role in determining winners in superstar markets. Luck refers to the myriad random factors and chance occurrences that can lead one person to rise to the top and another, equally talented person to fall behind. This is particularly the case in the arts, where talent is difficult to assess and requires subjective judgment, and where tastes are fickle. People in the music business often call this "the X factor." In fact, Alfred Marshall specifically noted the importance of good luck as well as talent for achieving superstar status. In my view, the power of luck is so important that I have devoted Chapter 5 to the role of good or bad luck in determining success or failure in the music business, and in life in general.

From Billington to Beyoncé

Nineteenth-century contemporary accounts described Elizabeth Billington as a singer with a singular voice of great sweetness, compass, and power.[5] She performed in all the great opera houses in London, Dublin, Milan, Venice, Trieste, and Paris. Rumors of turbulence in her marriage were the subject of tabloid publications and widespread gossip. In other words, Billington was the Beyoncé of her day. Citing figures from the *Encyclopaedia Britannica* and *Grove's Dictionary of Music and Musicians*, Sherwin Rosen reports that Elizabeth Billington earned between £10,000 and £15,000 in the 1801 season singing Italian opera at Covent Garden and Drury Lane. (With characteristic wit, Rosen adds, "No information is given on endorsements.")

In current dollars, Mrs. Billington earned between $1 million and $1.5 million a year—a significant sum, especially in her day, but less than 2 percent of the $105 million that Beyoncé earned in 2017, according to *Forbes*.[6]

What changed from Billington to Beyoncé? Apart from general economic growth that has raised living standards across the board, the obvious development that propelled superstar musicians' incomes was the invention of sound recordings and amplification. First physical records, and subsequently digital recordings, have vastly increased the scale that musicians can achieve. Beyoncé is able to reach a practically infinitely large audience through streaming platforms. And once a song is produced, the cost of distributing it to a mass audience is nearly zero.

Technology has also increased the scale that musicians can achieve in live performances. On a crystal clear night in July 2016, I joined 56,368 other fans to hear Bruce Springsteen perform at Circus Maximus in Rome.[7] No one left the four-hour show disappointed; most were singing "Thunder Road" on their way out.

And while the venue was available back in Billington's day, it is likely that fewer than five hundred fans would have been able to hear her had she performed at Circus Maximus in her day. Today, the number of people who can be reached by a human voice has become virtually unlimited. Just imagine how many people could have heard Elizabeth Billington sing if she had had access to a microphone and amplifier, let alone to MTV, CDs, Apple Music, Spotify, YouTube, and Tencent; her own station on Sirius XM Radio; and a private jet to transport her around the globe.

The ability to record and replay musical performances has enabled today's top artists, those most in demand, to dominate the music business. Before recordings, many restaurants and bars would hire live performers to play the hits from sheet music. Now live performances are less common, and restaurants and bars instead play music recorded by the stars. After all, why would you pay for a cover band to play "Born to Run" when you can hear Bruce Springsteen and the E Street Band perform it themselves on a recording? The technology that made it possible to achieve scale in the music industry has made it a challenge for musicians below the very top echelon to earn a middle-class living. While demand for superstars has risen, demand for lesser performers has declined.

Album sales and digital streaming clearly reflect the superstar phenomenon. The top 0.1 percent of artists accounted for more than half of all album sales in 2017. Song streams and downloads are similarly lopsided.[8]

But a funny thing happened to musicians' incomes as recorded music became more accessible. Because digital recording technology and the rise of the Internet made it easy to copy and share recordings, artists' and record labels' revenue from selling recorded music has plummeted since the 1990s. Touring, always an important source of musicians' incomes, has become even more important with the demise of record sales.

Today, recorded music is primarily a means for musicians to become popular, so that they can earn superstar incomes from touring and related merchandise sales. As David Bowie predicted in 2002, "Music is as available as running water."[9]

Touring has become more of a superstar market over the last forty years, with a rising share of revenue tilted to the top performers. Figure 4.1 shows the share of worldwide concert box office revenue accruing to the top 1 percent and top 5 percent of performers, based on my tabulations from the Pollstar Boxoffice Database. The underlying data are reported to *Pollstar* magazine by venues, promoters, and managers. Information is reported for box office revenue; tickets resold in the secondary market are not counted, but that money (overwhelmingly) does not filter back to the artists anyway. The Appendix provides a statistical evaluation of the strengths and weaknesses of the Pollstar Boxoffice Database, and efforts I made to adjust the data for underreporting. Although there are some lapses in the Pollstar data, and coverage was particularly incomplete in early years, the Pollstar Boxoffice Database remains our best and most comprehensive source for historical data on concert revenue.*

The Pollstar data indicate that the top 1 percent of artists increased their percentage of total concert revenue from 26 percent in 1982 to 60 percent in 2017. The top 1 percent now take in more revenue than *the bottom 99 percent combined*. And the top 5 percent of performers increased their percentage of total concert revenue from 62 percent to 85 percent over the same period. The top 5 percent of performers earn almost six times as much revenue as the bottom 95 percent combined—a superstar market if ever there was one.

Some have argued that the music industry has become more egalitarian because of streaming, computer music production technology, and lower entry costs. But as far as artists' incomes are concerned, it is becoming more unequal. The driver of this rise in inequality is the rapid increase in ticket prices for the

---

* I am grateful to *Pollstar* for providing me unprecedented access to its data.

Figure 4.1: Percentage of Total Ticket Revenue Accruing to Top Performers, 1982–2017

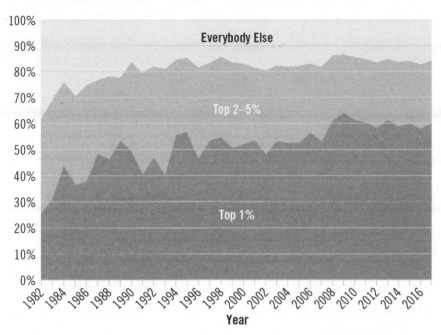

Source: Author's calculations based on Pollstar Boxoffice Database.

superstar performers. The top performers' share of tickets sold and of shows has remained more or less constant since the early 1980s. What has changed is that superstars are commanding higher prices for their live performances.

And the Pollstar Boxoffice Database probably *understates* the degree of inequality in artists' net incomes, because costs vary. Although data on revenue net of costs are not available, it is likely that costs are a lower share of revenue for superstars than for less popular artists, because the superstars have greater bargaining power and can strategically organize touring locations to minimize costs. As Q Prime's Cliff Burnstein told me, "When you're coming to town with a hot show, the venue pretty much has to do what you want."[10]

Merchandise sales, sponsorship income, endorsements, and

other potential sources of income would likely skew the industry further in the direction of a superstar market, as the superstars receive a greater share of such income.

Before turning to the question of *how* superstars become so popular, it is worth emphasizing how the rules of an economy constrain or amplify superstars' incomes. In the United States, most top musicians are independent contractors, who, together with their managers, are free to negotiate their own compensation and touring schedule.[11] In South Korea, however, K-pop groups sign long-term contracts with their management companies, which essentially prevent them from receiving a large share of the profits that they generate.[12] Similarly, in Japan, musicians typically work on a work-for-hire basis, which restricts their upside earning potential. And in China it is common for record labels to take a large slice of performers' touring revenue. Economic forces affect the types of contracts that musicians are able to negotiate, but history and local customs matter as well.

The Power of Power Laws

A total of 33.2 million different songs were streamed in 2017, according to BuzzAngle Music, which gathers data from the various online streaming services.[13] Spotify itself offers 35 million tracks. It would take six lifetimes for any single individual to listen to all those songs just one time.[14] Obviously, with such an enormous volume of music available, we cannot possibly sample every song to decide which ones we like or dislike. Instead, in forming our musical preferences, we rely heavily on the advice of our friends, family, and associates; on what we hear on the radio or other media; and on expert opinion (such as the *Billboard* Hot 100 and curated playlists). Musical tastes do not develop independently across individuals.

This process creates *bandwagon effects*, or a tendency for what is popular to become even more popular. Bandwagon effects can come about because we gain information about the existence of particular songs or musicians from our friends, or because our friends encourage us to like certain types of music. Bandwagon effects are likely to be particularly strong in this instance because music is often a social activity. Listening to music is a common experience that people like to share with others. We want to be familiar with the music that our friends are familiar with because it strengthens bonds of friendship and enhances the experience of listening to (or dancing to) music. Thus, there is a tendency for music that is popular in our networks to become more appealing to us. And bandwagon effects are further reinforced by the well-established psychological tendency for people to grow to like a particular song the more they hear it.[15]

There are two key economic implications when the popularity of a good is determined, in large part, by transmission through social networks. First, the distribution of what is popular will be highly skewed, with the most popular items absorbing most of the oxygen. Second, the determination of what is most popular is highly susceptible to random perturbations in the ways in which new products are introduced to a market and ripple through networks of potential customers.

In statistical jargon, the cascade of information and musical preferences through networks of fans generates a *power law distribution* of popularity—the popularity of the most popular item is a multiple of the next-most-popular item, and so on down the line. As a result, a small number of players—superstars—come to dominate a market. The so-called 80/20 rule (Pareto's law), where 20 percent of a firm's customers are responsible for 80 percent of sales, is an example of a power law that is common in business.

To conceptualize the way in which social influence operates, suppose each person who is considering making a purchase of a song sometimes follows her own judgment and at other times follows the behavior of a friend. Specifically, in p percent of cases she buys the recording if, in her own, independent judgment, she believes the recording is worth purchasing. In the remaining cases, she simply follows the decision of her friend. So in $(100 - p)$ percent of cases, she either buys the recording if her friend bought the record or she doesn't buy the recording if her friend didn't buy it. Her friend acts the same way, relying on her own judgment part of the time and on another friend's judgment part of the time.[16] This decision-making process would generate a power law distribution of song purchases. Even if all the people in this example like every song equally, the reliance on the behavior of others in forming one's own decision creates a bandwagon effect and a highly skewed distribution of song purchases. Some unlucky songs that were not purchased initially will wither away with hardly anyone purchasing them, because no one recommends them, and others will grow in popularity because the fact that they were already purchased by many early consumers leads additional consumers to purchase them. Mathematically, this copycat procedure will result in a multiplicative relationship in popularity, with a small number of songs responsible for most of sales. Such is the way that popularity snowballs up- or downhill.

The idea of a power law, in my view, is fundamental to understanding the music market as well as the superstar phenomenon. For one thing, the distributions of streamed songs, album sales, and concert revenue are all closely approximated by a power law. And so are the numbers of Twitter followers, YouTube subscribers, and Facebook likes that musicians attract.

Figure 4.2 shows, for example, the number of times each of the top 2,500 artists were streamed in 2016, ranked from the most popular to the least popular, based on my tabulation of BuzzAngle data. The most popular artist, Drake, was streamed 6.1 billion times. He was followed by Rihanna (3.3 billion streams), Twenty One Pilots (2.7 billion streams), and The Weeknd (2.6 billion streams). Moving down a hundred places from Drake, the 101st-ranked group was the California band Los Tigres del Norte, which was streamed 0.5 billion times, or less than 10 percent as much as Drake. The sharp drop-off near the top is characteristic of a power law.

Figure 4.2: Number of Music Streams of Top 2,500 Artists in 2016, by Rank

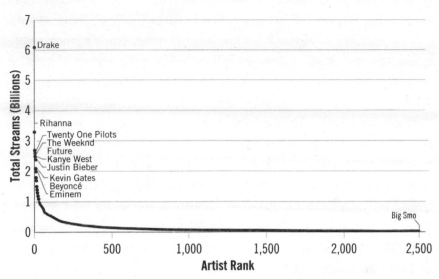

Source: Author's calculations from BuzzAngle Music data.

At the other end of the distribution, the country rapper Big Smo was streamed 25 million times, and most of the lowest-ranked artists were bunched around that level. A complete list of the 2,500 artists depicted in Figure 4.2 is available on my web page (www.Rockonomics.com), where curious readers and the statistically inclined can download a spreadsheet and analyze the data. (Oh, and don't feel too bad for Big Smo and the other bottom-dwellers in the figure. Approximately three million artists are included on streaming platforms, so in the grand scheme of things, Big Smo does fairly well. With 25 million streams, he would net around $35,000 in royalties in 2016.) What this figure tells us is that the distribution of music streaming across artists follows a power law, which is what one would expect if popularity is determined in large part through social transmission.

A landmark experiment conducted by the sociologists Matthew Salganik, Peter Sheridan Dodds, and Duncan Watts demonstrated the importance of social influence on our music choices, as well as the tendency for social influence to increase the gap between the most and least popular songs.[17] The researchers created parallel universes in which a total of 14,341 participants had an opportunity to download forty-eight songs from hitherto unknown bands. Participants were randomly assigned to a website in which they were either informed of the previous participants' download rates for the songs or not informed of previous participants' behavior. In the first website, participants' preferences could be shaped by social influence effects, and in the second one preferences were determined independently. If participants were aware of how often others had downloaded various songs (social influence), there was a much greater tendency for superstar songs to emerge, and the frequency of downloads more closely resembled a power law relationship than when preferences were determined independently.

Further experimentation yielded another fascinating result: if participants were randomly divided into groups, allowing social influence to affect song selections resulted in different rankings of the forty-eight songs across the groups. That is, if a song happened to start off popular with early participants in one set of subjects, its popularity grew, and if it happened to start off unpopular in another group, its popularity faded by comparison. This is an example of what sociologists call *cumulative advantage*, as a small edge acquired over a rival, for whatever reason, snowballs into a much bigger advantage over time. Now, some songs had no chance of ever making it to the top. But among the set of better songs (as judged by the rankings of the songs in the experiment with independently determined preferences), almost any song could have ended up on top. It appears that quality gives a song a chance of becoming popular, but quality is not sufficient in and of itself, given the haphazard interactions in social networks.

It is likely that the sociologists' experiment actually understates the true role of social influence on the popularity of music in the real world, for several reasons. The number of songs to choose from in the experiment was relatively small, so participants could listen to all of them if they were so inclined. Also, marketing, radio play, product placement, media attention, and—probably most important—informal interactions between friends all play a large role in the actual music market, but they were not a factor in an experiment with anonymous participants.

The importance of social network transmission and getting off to a good start is not news to music industry professionals. The multi-talented musician Jacob Collier told me: "The first set of comments posted on one of my YouTube videos can affect whether it goes viral or not."[18] And a good or a bad inaugural *Pitchfork* review can make or break a new band. Many recordings have bombed because they did not receive radio airtime when they were released. In other words, chance interactions through social networks create a tendency for a market to be dominated by superstars, and elevate the effect of good or bad luck.

Once you start looking at the world in terms of power laws, or extremely skewed distributions, you can't miss them. Power laws have been used to describe the frequency of words used in the English language (and practically all other languages), the number of people living in cities, the number of electrical grid failures, the distribution of income, stock market returns, the pattern of musical notes in songs, the number of people joining protests, the frequency of web page links, and multiple physical phenomena.[19] More important, the social or physical network mechanism that can generate a power law illuminates the process that leads to spectacular success or dismal failure. In many walks of life, an understanding of how reliance on interconnections generates a power law relationship can help us understand why extreme events—like a neighbor's daughter becoming the next Taylor Swift, or a devastating blackout that lasts for days—sometimes occur.

The type of social dynamic that generates power laws—where people's beliefs, knowledge, and behavior are influenced by the beliefs, knowledge, and behavior of their associates—can help explain the occurrence of critically important macroeconomic phenomena, including bank runs, financial crises, and housing bubbles. In particular, this type of social dynamic, where individuals' views are influenced by others', can create a self-fulfilling prophecy. For example, the widespread belief that home prices will rise causes more and more people to jump into the housing market before prices rise, in turn causing home prices to be bid up even further. That upward movement can last for a period of time before collapsing under its own weight. Indeed, this social dynamic underlies Citigroup CEO Chuck Prince's famous July 2007 description of the forces that would soon lead to the worst financial crisis of our lifetimes: "When the music stops, in terms of liquidity, things will be complicated. But as long as the music is playing, you've got to get up and dance. We're still dancing."[20] Sad to say, his bank was not dancing much longer, and needed to be rescued by the U.S. government. The same type of dynamic that creates fads in music also can inflate and burst financial bubbles.

What About the Long Tail Hypothesis?

Some have predicted that the decline in the cost of producing music and distributing it over the Internet will lead to greater variety in music consumption, and move music away from a superstar market and toward a niche market. In his blockbuster book *The Long Tail*, Chris Anderson argued:

> Our culture and economy is increasingly shifting away from a focus on a relatively small number of "hits" (mainstream products and markets) at the head of the demand curve and toward a huge number of niches in the tail. As the costs of production and distribution fall, especially online, there is now less need to lump products and consumers into one-size-fits-all containers. In an era without the constraints of physical shelf space and other bottlenecks of distribu-

tion, narrowly-targeted goods and services can be as economically attractive as mainstream fare.[21]

Anderson applied this logic to forecast that the market for books, movies, music, and essentially all retail products will become less concentrated and more diversified. The implication is that the shape of the distribution would tilt away from superstars, and a power law would become less powerful in predicting relative performance.

Echoing this theme, the economist Paul Krugman wrote a short *New York Times* blog post in 2013 in response to my Rock Hall speech, raising the question, "Is this (still) the age of the superstar?" His argument: "Basically, the music business has been hugely disrupted by the Internet. I'd be very curious to know whether that hasn't changed the calculus: radio play matters much less, the audience has fractured, performers can build a following on Pandora and YouTube." He ended his post by commenting, "So I wonder if even Alan Krueger is now behind the curve here—and in any case I'd love to see how the trend for the music business looks since 2003."[22]

Although it is possible that music will become more of a niche market someday, this has not happened yet. Figure 4.1 makes clear that the music industry has become even more unequal over recent decades insofar as touring revenue—the main source of musicians' income—is concerned. Since 2003, the share of concert revenue going to the top 1 percent rose from 54 percent to 60 percent.[23] And although it is difficult to compare record sales over time because of rapidly changing formats, Harvard Business School's Anita Elberse finds that song sales became more skewed toward the very top performers from 2007 to 2011.[24]

So to answer Paul Krugman's question, this still appears to be the age of the superstar.

The Internet has, to some extent, changed the process by which superstars become superstars—Justin Bieber and Jacob Collier were discovered through their YouTube channels. But it has not leveled the distribution of income or enabled a large number of musicians to earn a middle-class livelihood.[25] The Internet may well lead to more music being produced by more musicians, but even in the age of the Internet, a handful of artists remain much, much more popular than everyone else.

The multitalented Questlove, leader of The Roots, recently lamented the highly skewed nature of the music business when I saw him in Miami Beach:

> In my world I'd just like to see a balance. A place where Donald Glover and Tyler Perry can exist on opposite ends of the spectrum. The same for Issa Rae and Whitney Cummings, and for Cardi B and Roxanne Shante. I think oftentimes—especially in music, especially in hip-hop—it's like just one person and no one else. And whoever is the most digestible gets that spotlight and that attention. Meanwhile, there are zillions and jillions of artists who are just as worthy of getting these things. My position is more or less, while the spotlight is still warm, to show people options.[26]

To a considerable degree, he is fighting an uphill battle against the power curve.

My guess is that—contrary to the long tail hypothesis—the availability of just about all music on the Internet is unlikely to change the tendency for musical preferences to be largely socially determined and, as a consequence, highly skewed toward a relatively small group of musicians. In fact, the number of musical choices facing individuals greatly expanded—and became even more bewildering—with the advent of streaming services, which is likely to lead us to rely even more on our social networks for clues in selecting songs and artists. And the rapidly growing set of curated recommendation systems that use Big Data to help us discover new music is also likely to reinforce network effects, unless there is a surge in demand for curation systems that recommend songs that are both unpopular and likely to stay that way.

Gloria Estefan: Music of the Heart

Gloria Estefan is the most successful crossover artist of all time. With her husband, Emilio, and the Miami Sound Machine, and as a solo artist, she has sold over one hundred million records worldwide and won seven Grammys. She has performed at the Super Bowl and Olympics, for popes and presidents. I interviewed Gloria Estefan on October 4, 2018.

You came from a musical family and starred in the movie Music of the Heart, *about music education in schools. Did a school music program influence you?*

Very much so, but I also come with the genetics of music. My mom was the diva of her family and school. On my dad's side, there were also a few artists: there was a classical pianist, a salsa band leader, and a classical violinist. I sang since I talked.

In fifth grade I joined the school band at St. Michael the Archangel School. At the time I wanted to play saxophone, but they would only let boys play the saxophone. So I played the clarinet. To this day I have a deep fondness for the clarinet and reed instruments, and the wooden sound. But it was very important because I didn't like being the center of attention. I played from fifth to eighth grade. It was helpful in a myriad of ways. The first time I left Miami was to go to Tampa with the school band for a state competition. You learn cooperation. You learn math, because music is math. People think for some reason that art and music are less important than math and other subjects, but it is quite the contrary. Music is really symbiotic with other courses.

Every time I see a school music program cut it really hurts. That's why I focus on trying to fill in the gap when government takes funds away, and through private donations try to put music back in the schools.

You earned a degree in psychology from the University of Miami. What do you think it is about music that produces an emotional connection in people?

I've thought about that a lot because if we had that secret then it would go far beyond a hit record on the radio. Music, just like colors, can change your mood.

Music is something that unites us. I've had the opportunity to travel the world, and despite whatever linguistic difference the people in the audience had, I saw literally the same emotional reactions in the same parts of the show. It was totally about the music. It wasn't about whatever language was being sung.

Most definitely there is a very strong connection from music to our emotional well-being. And likewise, music can have a negative effect as well. Sometimes very hard core, violent music can drive people to do very tough things. Music is a very powerful force.

How has the economics of the music business changed?

The economics of music has changed a lot. It is like we've gone full circle back to the 1950s, where it's become about singles—and people not getting paid for their work. Artists had difficulty getting paid in a different way in the 1950s because a lot of the pop music was literally pilfering R&B and African American music, then making it pop and not paying the writers or the original artists that created the music.

Now, it is just really tough for artists to get paid, period. Before you could be a recording artist and never tour. Now, recording artists aren't going to get paid. And the Catch-22 is you can tour, but who will go see you if nobody knows your music.

And the fragmentation of the market has hurt a lot because even though the Internet has freed people from having to find a record company—and Garage-Band and the technology that now exists has put that ability to create music in the hands of pretty much anyone, and you can upload your tune to iTunes or Spotify or wherever you want to put it—the challenge is getting ears on it!

Before, for example, when we first did "Conga" on the Johnny Carson show, you were guaranteed a top ten hit the next day. . . . You have so many options today that it causes fragmentation.

Nowadays, artists are not even thinking about albums, they're thinking about EPs, four songs, or just one song. It is very difficult for a young artist to grow the kind of audience that is going to last through the decades that we've been lucky enough to have.

What has led to your business success?

A lot of artists have suffered at the hands of their handlers. It is not usual to have an artist that is very much about the business. But my husband and I both are. We both had careers, so when it came the moment to decide do we go for a music career full-time, it was a risk.

We did it because we loved it, not to become rich or famous. I joined the band as a hobby and for fun. Emilio and I were kind of destined to be together. And we were making a lot of money in the late 1970s and early 1980s here in Miami as a gig band. We made our own record. We got it on the air. We could do the disco music, the Latin music. We were in high demand. But we made a conscious decision that we had to stop being a gig band because we couldn't continue to do weddings and bar mitzvahs and *Quinceañeras* and try to have a career where you went out and did concerts.

That happened simultaneously. We became very well known in Latin America. We would go down there and do a concert in a 50,000-seat stadium and then come back home and do a wedding for 200 people in Miami.

Can musicians control the arc of their careers?

It is not something you can control. You can do your best at trying to do everything the right way—but what you said about luck, a lot of it is *momentum*. You have to be ready to latch onto the momentum that you have and continue working so you can follow it up. I remember that when we were just breaking through, they would say, "You're really not a cemented artist until your third album." A lot of artists' sophomore records would fail, and they never make it past that. If your third record is a hit, you pretty much have a career, and enough music to tour on for a long time—because, if you stay true to your fans and deliver, when you come out live or when they hear you in an interview, it is a relationship like a marriage; if each time you cement it more, your fans are loyal. We were lucky enough to have a worldwide response.

You have had a storybook career and a wonderful life. How have you managed to avoid the problems, such as drugs and alcohol, that have afflicted so many other superstars?

First of all, it is not in my nature. I do not like to be out of control. And Emilio and his father went to Spain before coming here, and they were eating out of soup kitchens in Spain. His personality is very driven, and he wanted to succeed. Work is his drug and alcohol. He is a workaholic.

Together, we made a family first. By the time I had huge success I already had my son. I went through a lot with my father. He was a political prisoner after the Bay of Pigs in Cuba for two years, then he joined the U.S. Army and when he came back from Vietnam he had Agent Orange poisoning, and I had to take care of him. Having to deal with these things early on in my life, and the struggles that Emilio went through, when we had the opportunity to do something that we loved, and be together doing it—and be able to bring our family with us—we were not going to waste that opportunity.

If you're a young kid and you don't know anything and you haven't gone through any struggles, and all of a sudden you have all this money flowing in, you don't have a basis for knowing where you're coming from as to what is of true value. . . . We went through a *lot* of struggles early on in life that show you the value of things.

That's why we wanted to help out other artists and give a hand up. Emilio has produced and was instrumental in the careers of Shakira and J. Lo. He did J. Lo's first record, with the song "Let's Get Loud," which I wrote. Jennifer fell in love with the song. It was supposed to be for my record. I preferred her to do it, rather than me, because she was a freshman artist. . . . Emilio was happy every time he was able to help in the success of another artist, such as Ricky Martin and Mark Anthony.

Superstar Careers

The cumulative advantage that accrues to superstars can compound over the career. Figures 4.3a and 4.3b display the cumulative amount of concert revenue generated by top male and female headliners over the span of their careers. A few observations in connection with the figures are worth noting. First, superstars seem to be launching into orbit at younger ages. This is clearly the case of female artists—such as Taylor Swift, Lady Gaga, Rihanna, and Beyoncé, who are on a trajectory to eclipse Madonna and Céline Dion before long—but it is also the case for Justin Bieber. It took Billy Joel until his fifties to earn as much touring revenue (in inflation-adjusted dollars) as Justin Bieber earned by age twenty-three.[27] Second, the female superstars tend to be solo

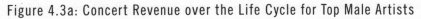

Figure 4.3a: Concert Revenue over the Life Cycle for Top Male Artists

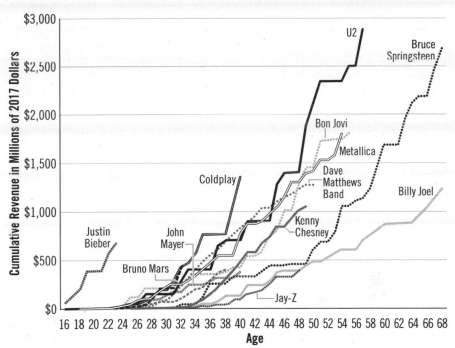

Source: Author's calculations based on Pollstar Boxoffice Database, and adjusted for underreporting of concerts using data from Setlist.fm; see Appendix. Figures in constant 2017 dollars.

artists, while many of the male superstars are lead singers of their long-established bands. Third, top male bands tend to earn more concert revenue over their careers than top female artists. U2 and Bruce Springsteen, for example, have grossed $1 billion more in revenue than Madonna and Céline Dion over their careers. This is primarily because male musicians spend more time touring. Ticket revenue per show for the top male and female performers are roughly equal.

The younger superstars are benefiting from the general rise in concert ticket prices and revenue, and this rising tide is lifting their lifetime earnings. Thus the life cycle data do not provide any evidence of a pending decline in the winner-take-all nature of the music industry for the rising generation of pop stars.

Figure 4.3b: Concert Revenue over the Life Cycle for Top Female Artists

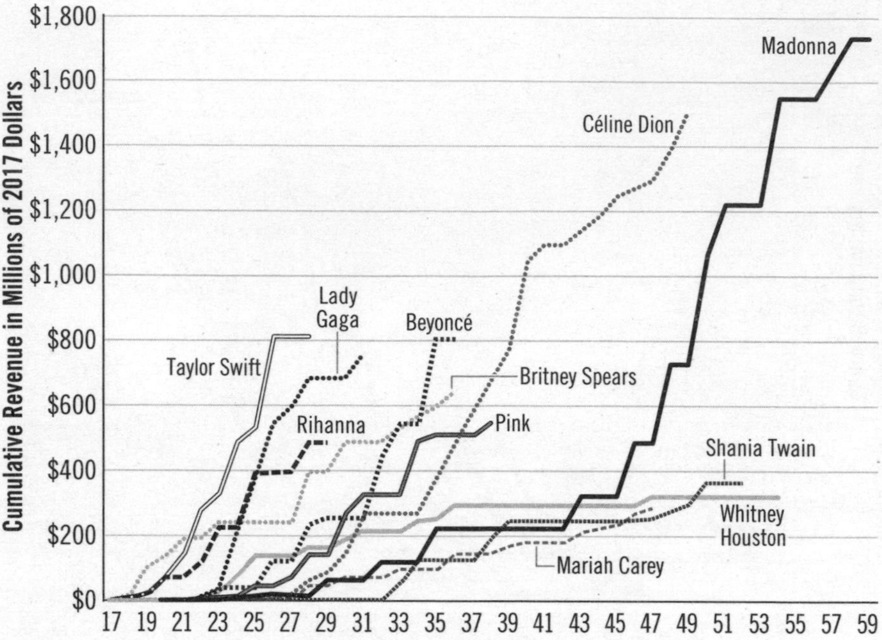

Source: Author's calculations based on Pollstar Boxoffice Database, and adjusted for underreporting using data from Setlist.fm; see Appendix. Figures in constant 2017 dollars.

Superstars in the Rest of the Economy

How does the music industry compare to the rest of the economy? Since 1980, the entire U.S. economy has moved in the direction of a superstar market. Figure 4.4 shows that after falling for decades, the share of national income accruing to the top 1 percent of families more than doubled, from 10 percent in 1980 to 22 percent in 2017. The distribution of income in the United States overall is not as skewed as it is in the music industry, where the top 1 percent of performers take in about 60 percent of all income, but the United States as a whole is now back to the same level of inequality that existed during the Roaring Twenties.

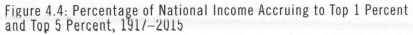

Figure 4.4: Percentage of National Income Accruing to Top 1 Percent and Top 5 Percent, 1917–2015

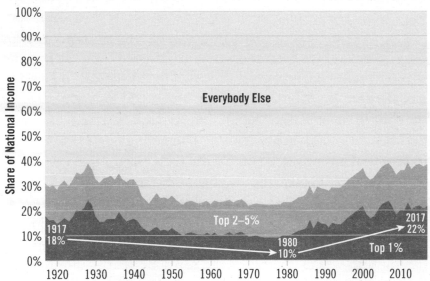

Inequality has also risen among the bottom 99 percent of Americans. In the 1980s the bottom 10 percent of earners saw their inflation-adjusted wages decline, and they have barely recovered since then.[28] And beginning in the mid-1990s the middle class started to hollow out.

Reasons commonly cited for the rise in inequality in the United States are varied. They include the effects of globalization and technological change that have shifted demand away from less skilled workers; an erosion in union membership and decline in the real value of the minimum wage; changes in employer practices, such as non-compete clauses that restrict workers from accepting a job at a competitor, which have weakened worker bargaining power; and a breakdown in norms of fairness and corporate policies that historically compressed pay and constrained the earnings of top executives.

Journalists often ask me to summarize the relative importance of each of these factors. In truth, it is a fool's errand to try to quantify the percentage contribution of each factor, since the various factors overlap and interact, and their quantitative impact varies across the wage structure. A shift in demand against low-wage workers due to automation, for example, will weaken labor unions and hasten the erosion of norms of fairness, especially for blue-collar workers. Nevertheless, when pressed I usually respond that the traditional economic drivers of technological change and globalization probably account for around 35 to 40 percent of the shift in income distribution that we have observed, and non-traditional factors, such as shifting bargaining power and erosion in norms of fairness, account for the remainder.

At the very top of the income scale, technological changes that increased scalability have clearly intensified superstar effects. The University of Chicago economists Steven Kaplan and Joshua Rauh, for example, write, "We believe that the U.S. evidence on income and wealth shares for the top 1 percent is most consistent with a 'superstar'-style explanation rooted in the importance of scale and skill-biased technological change."[29] They highlight that the wealthiest Americans increasingly come from the technology, finance, and mass retail sectors, which, they argue, are the most scalable industries.

One related part of the inequality story that has received a lot of attention lately involves the rise of "superstar" firms.[30] That is, research has found that concentration in output within industries has increased, with a small number of superstar companies increasingly dominating the market. For example, over the last decade the four largest U.S. airlines increased their share of industry revenue from 41 percent to 65 percent.[31] Larger hospitals have gobbled up smaller ones, and Amazon and Walmart have put tremendous pressure on mom-and-pop stores. Even in the beer business, despite the proliferation of craft breweries, the four largest breweries produce 90 percent of the beer consumed.

This phenomenon is clear in the music industry as well. The three major record producers—Universal Music Group, Sony Music Entertainment, and Warner Music Group—hold a two-thirds share of the U.S. record market.[32] The promoters Live Nation and the Anschutz Entertainment Group (AEG) have come to dominate the concert business.

Superstar firms tend to have high profits and high productivity. Workers at superstar firms are paid relatively well, although the top firms tend to use relatively less labor than their competitors for the output they produce. As a result, the rise in superstar firms has contributed to the decline in labor's share of national income.

Superstar firms, including Google, Apple, and Amazon, have probably benefited from successfully deploying the technological innovations that enable them to take advantage of enormous scale economics. But there is also a concern that such firms use their dominant position to stifle competition.

The rise of superstar firms has also contributed to the increase in inequality among the bottom 99 percent of workers. The superstar firms tend to employ higher-paid and more highly educated workers, and they often outsource jobs for lower-paid workers, such as those in janitorial, cafeteria, and security positions.

Another feature of superstar firms is that they can exploit complementarities to grow and generate even more revenue and profit, meaning that they can leverage their scale in one market to have an advantage in another market. Apple, for example, uses Apple Music to help sell iPhones. Facebook purchased the photo-sharing app Instagram to leverage the service in its core social network platform and reach a younger demographic. In a sense, superstar companies can act like superstar musicians who use their YouTube popularity to sell concert tickets and endorse products. These complementarities don't always work out—witness the unsuccessful merger between Citigroup and Travelers, which was eventually unwound. But superstar firms have an opportunity to take advantage of strategic complementarities that do not exist for smaller firms.

Often these complementarities arise because growth begets improvement in service, which begets more growth. Consider the "Amazon flywheel"—the notion that by lowering costs and providing better prices, Amazon would attract more customers, and by attracting more customers it would attract more sellers, which in turn would help to lower prices further and provide more diversity of products, which would attract more customers, which would keep the flywheel spinning. Similarly, if Spotify attracts more users, it gathers more data on users' preferences and can provide better song recommendations, which helps it to retain and attract more users.

It is easy to see the hand of **supply and demand** in the rise of inequality, but reverberations of what I call **"all that jazz"** of political, corporate, and social choices are also evident. For example, the federal minimum wage has remained at $7.25 an hour since 2009, the second-longest stretch in American history in which it has remained constant, and therefore has been eroded by inflation. In real terms, the minimum wage today is below its value in the late 1960s. Cities and states that have raised their local minimum wages have boosted earnings for low-paid workers and reduced inequality.

Collusion among firms to restrain wage growth and refrain from poaching one another's workers, which is easier when there are a few dominant employers in a market, has also constrained wage growth for many workers. Apple's Steve Jobs, for example, once threatened Google co-founder Sergey Brin, saying, "If you hire a single one of these people [software engineers] that means war."[33] And it appears that for years, the railway equipment giants Knorr-Bremse AG and Westinghouse Air Brake Technologies Corporation have had an agreement—which they don't consider to have been illegal—to refrain from soliciting, recruiting, and hiring each other's workers without prior approval from their competitor—something which they have now agreed to stop but only after being sued by the Justice Department.[34]

Adam Smith, the father of economics, predicted this behavior long ago when he warned us that employers "are always and everywhere in a sort of tacit, but constant and uniform combination, not to raise the wages of labour above their actual rate."[35]

The Justice Department and Federal Trade Commission made clear in guidance issued in October 2016 that "agreements among employers not to recruit certain employees or not to compete on terms of compensation are illegal."[36] A government hotline was created for employees to report instances of wage fixing and no-poaching agreements. Shortly after taking office, Maka Delrahim, assistant U.S. attorney general responsible for antitrust enforcement, said in January 2018, "I've been shocked about how many of these [no-poaching agreements] there are, but they're real."[37]

The ways we choose to write and enforce the laws affect inequality. The impact of supply, demand, and all that jazz on inequality is clear from comparisons across countries. While the United States and the United Kingdom have had almost equally sharp rises in inequality, other countries, such as Sweden, Germany, and France, have had much more moderate increases. Local laws, culture, customs, institutions, and business practices matter.

Recall, too, that luck plays an outsized role in success or failure in superstar markets. There are many examples of unlucky companies with superior technology that failed because they were launched at the wrong time or in the wrong place. The rise of superstar employers adds an additional dimension to luck: workers might be lucky or unlucky when it comes to landing a job, and their company may turn out to be a superstar or may fall behind. The implications of good or bad luck in climbing the career ladder are magnified in a superstar job market, as small differences in one's step on the job hierarchy translate to large differences in earnings.

The role of luck is perhaps nowhere more evident than in the music industry, the subject of the next chapter.

CHAPTER 5

The Power of Luck

I been in the wrong place, but it must have been the right time
I been in the right place, but it must have been the wrong song.

—Dr. John

Reginald Dwight was growing frustrated playing piano in Blues-ology, a "mediocre" band, as he describes it, performing for "people eating fish and chips in a cabaret thing." So when the shy twenty-year-old spotted an ad saying "Singers and songwriters wanted," he showed up at Liberty Records in London to audition. Upon arriving, he found an office overflowing with reel-to-reel tapes and piles of envelopes. Many other would-be singers and songwriters had seen the ad, too. Here's how he tells the rest of the story:

> The guy behind the desk said, "What do you do?" I said, "I can sing and I can write songs, but I can't write lyrics. I'm hopeless." So he said, "Well, why don't you just take this envelope.' And he went through a pile of envelopes—it could have been any envelope! Talk about kismet. He gave me an envelope which was sealed. I took it back on the tube train (or the subway), and I opened it and I read it—and it was Bernie. It could have been any envelope; that was just the envelope he gave me.[1]

Fifty years later, the singer now known to the world as Elton John still seems mystified recalling his chance meeting with the seventeen-year-old Bernie Taupin. The duo have since collaborated on more than thirty albums and sold more than three hundred million records, forming one of the most enduring and successful singer-songwriter collaborations in history.

It is hard to imagine that Reginald Dwight would have won five Grammys and been inducted into the Songwriters Hall of Fame and the Rock and Roll Hall of Fame had the guy behind the desk plucked a different envelope from the pile. More likely he would still be playing before the fish-and-chips crowd rather than following the yellow brick road to gold.

Elton John attributes his meeting Bernie Taupin to "kismet." He may be right, but to the less mystically inclined it seems less like destiny than a totally random occurrence that brought them together. Both men were surely lucky that their chance connection led them to make beautiful music together and share it with the world—and so are we.

There are many other well-known examples of chance events that changed music history: Mick Jagger and Keith Richards meeting on a train, Clarence Clemons strolling into an Asbury Park bar on a stormy night, Paul Simon and Art Garfunkel growing up a few blocks away from each other.[2] There are also many cases of bad luck, such as tragic plane crashes that took the lives of Buddy Holly, Ritchie Valens, the Big Bopper, Patsy Cline, Otis Redding, and Jim Croce in their prime. And we never hear of the chance meetings that *didn't* occur. Most important of all, there are numerous musicians who are just as talented and hardworking as the superstars, but for whom good luck never shined. They may have come out with the wrong song at the wrong time or in the wrong place. For any number of reasons, their careers never took off.

In this chapter I consider the effect of luck—the random factors beyond our control that influence success and failure, both in the music business and in life in general. The effect of good or bad luck is magnified in a superstar market, which makes its influence readily apparent in the music business. But given the increasingly important role luck plays in the economy writ large, it is important to understand the impact of chance occurrences on our lives, and how best to tilt the odds in our favor.

Oooh, What a Lucky Man He Was

In a superstar market—where the top performers reap the benefit of enormous scale, while many others struggle to get by—the stakes of moving up or down the hierarchy are greatly amplified. As a result, anything that gives one performer an advantage over another provides an important edge. If good luck pushes someone up the ladder, then the consequences of luck are greater as well.

For middle-level performers, luck is of relatively little consequence, as good and bad luck tend to average out. Yet a streak of good luck—along with prodigious talent and effort—is essential for someone to reach the top of the ladder and achieve superstar status. Think of it this way: you could be a supremely talented poker player, but you also need luck to draw a straight flush. There are, by contrast, any number of ways that you could draw a mediocre hand. It is the combination of luck and skill that leads to greatness.

The role of luck is easy to identify in sports competitions—the ball bouncing the right way at the right time, a referee making a bad call, a key player getting injured at an inopportune time. The economist Robert Frank points out in his book *Success and Luck* that track athletes had a tailwind propelling them in seven of the eight events in which the current world record was set in the men's and women's 100 meter dash, high hurdles, long jump, and triple jump.[3] The wind was certainly beyond their control but in their favor. (There have also been unlucky sprinters who had their world records invalidated because the wind was too strong; sometimes too much good luck can be a bad thing.)

In music, talent and effort surely matter—as in sports—but they are harder to assess. And the challenge of spotting talent is made all the more difficult by the way that tastes change and popularity spreads, as discussed in Chapter 4.[4] The market for books, movies, and television programs presents a similar environment. Luck looms large in the creative arts.

One of my favorite examples of luck in the arts involves J. K. Rowling, author of the Harry Potter series. Her literary agent, Christopher Little, sold the U.K. rights to *Harry Potter and the Philosopher's Stone* to Bloomsbury for just £2,500, and then waited two years for the book to become popular by word of mouth before auctioning the U.S. rights to Scholastic. The book took off after that point.[5] How did the thirty-two-year-old Rowling select Mr. Little as her literary agent in 1995? After being rejected by the first agent she sent her manuscript to, she searched for another in *The Writers' and Artists' Year Book* at her public library in Edinburgh. She latched onto Christopher Little because his name sounded like a character from her children's book. Little (who was dismissed by Rowling in 2011) was surely one of the luckiest men in the world. His commission for the Harry Potter book series has totaled in the tens of millions of dollars.

There are many indications that luck plays a pervasive role in the music industry as well. Even experts in record labels' artists and repertoire (A&R) divisions, with much at stake and years of experience, have difficulty picking winners. Columbia Records turned down Elvis Presley in 1955. Decca famously rejected the Beatles when they auditioned in London on New Year's Day, 1962. And Capitol Records in the United States initially passed on the Beatles in 1963.[6] Legendary talent scout John Hammond described the opposition he faced over signing Bob Dylan in 1961: "I brought in Dylan and signed him, and this was over everybody's dead body. One vice president at Columbia was annoyed at me because I had let Joan Baez go to Vanguard."[7]

After EMI passed on releasing their album in the United States, the Swedish rock band Roxette broke through because an American high school exchange student in Sweden happened to take their record home with him to Minneapolis and pestered local radio stations to play their song "The Look."[8]

Entertainment lawyer John Eastman told me that he once congratulated David Geffen, whom he considers one of the smartest people in the business, for signing Kurt Cobain and Nirvana to his eponymous record label.[9] Geffen replied that he was as surprised as Eastman by Nirvana's success. Eastman recalled Geffen saying, "John, I admit we didn't know we had them. It came over the transom. We put it out, barely, and boom!"

Or consider Sixto Rodriguez, the subject of the Academy Award–winning documentary *Searching for Sugar Man*. Rodriguez recorded two albums between 1970 and 1975 that were commercial flops in the United States, and he was in the middle of recording a third when he was dropped by his record label. But he was a huge success in South Africa, where his music became the anthem of the anti-apartheid movement. Amazingly, for decades he was unaware of his fame and influence. Instead of making music, he spent the rest of his career doing construction and production-line work in Detroit—until the Swedish filmmaker Malik Bendjelloul discovered his story (another instance of luck), which resuscitated his career.

Steve Rowland, who produced Sixto Rodriguez's second album, *Coming from Reality*, in 1971, said, "I've produced a lot of big-name artists with big hits, like Peter Frampton and Jerry Lee Lewis, but I've never worked with anyone as talented as Rodriguez." He added, "I never understood why he didn't become a big star, so to see him rise like a phoenix from the ashes, it's just as inexplicable, but it makes me really, really happy."[10]

Despite their significant investment in A&R and promotion efforts, major record labels do well if one in ten of their records ends up covering its costs.

Have you ever heard of Carly Hennessy? Chances are you haven't. Hennessy, an Irish singer and actress, was signed to a big contract in 2001 by MCA when she was just eighteen years old.

She recognized her good fortune: "Some people just struggle," she said. "I was very, very lucky." Evidently, though, Hennessy wasn't lucky enough. Despite the label investing $2.2 million to produce and promote her debut album, *Ultimate High*, the record turned out to be a commercial flop.[11] *Ultimate High* sold only 328 copies in the first three months following its release, and MCA dropped her the next year. Hennessy's record could have bombed for any number of reasons. Her album came out shortly after 9/11, which cut into the nation's appetite for upbeat songs. Record stations didn't pick up her songs, and retail stores were reluctant to stock her album.

Suppose a band is both good and lucky enough to release a song that does become a hit. Is it likely to do so again? Possibly, but the odds are against it. Of the 2,591 artists who recorded a Top 100 song since 1960, only 40 percent managed to do it more than once.[12] The odds of repeating for a Top 10 song are even longer—only 22 percent of the 490 bands who produced a Top 10 song from 1960 to 2017 managed to do it again.

Figure 5.1 shows the number of times that each of the artists who ever had a song reach the *Billboard* Year-End Top 100 made the list from 1960 to 2017. Selection for the *Billboard* Top 100 is based on a complex weighting of physical and digital sales, airplay, and streaming, so making it to the Top 100, out of the tens of thousands of songs released each year, is a mark of extraordinary success. Since a musician's talent is unlikely to change much from year to year, and since making it onto the *Billboard* charts should give an artist's future songs increased attention, the fact that having a repeat hit is so uncommon underscores the importance of luck.

"There's plenty of room at the bottom; there's only so much room at the top," said bassist Rudy Sarzo, who played with Ozzy Osbourne and Quiet Riot. He succinctly captured the message of Figure 5.1 with his observation: "Getting to the top is hard. Staying at the top is virtually impossible."[13]

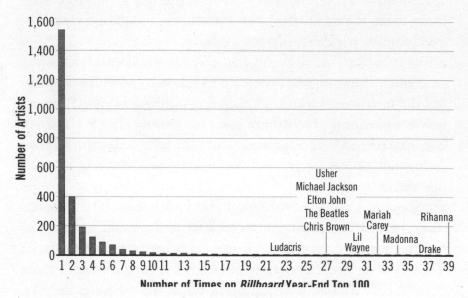

Figure 5.1: Number of Appearances on *Billboard* Year-End Top 100, 1960–2017

Source: Author's calculations using data from *Billboard*'s Year-End Top 100.

The extremely skewed distribution of hit songs, even among the most talented and successful in the music business, is consistent with a power law, with popularity spreading through cascades of networked individuals. A tiny fraction of extremely lucky and talented phenoms—Rihanna, Madonna, Drake, the Beatles, Mariah Carey, Elton John, Michael Jackson—made the list multiple times. But was even their success guaranteed?

The role of luck in determining a song's popularity was demonstrated in another clever experiment conducted by the sociologists Matt Salganik and Duncan Watts.[14] As in their other experiments, the researchers posted forty-eight songs in an online music library, with the musicians' permission. Listeners were invited to log in to the library and sample the songs, with the opportunity to download the songs for free. Participants were shown the list of songs, ranked by the number of times each one had been downloaded up to that point. They could also see the exact download counts, so they were aware of the popularity of each song, based on the collective wisdom of other participants. From there, the subjects could click on a song to play it, and then were given the option to download the song.

For the first 750 participants, the researchers faithfully tallied and displayed the number of downloads for each song. But here's the twist: the subsequent 6,000 participants were randomly—and unknowingly—assigned to one of two alternative scenarios. In one scenario, they continued to see the true download counts. In the other scenario, the researchers surreptitiously flipped the initial download counts, so that the forty-eighth-most-popular song was listed as the most popular song, the forty-seventh song was listed as number two, and so on. After this inversion in the ranking, the researchers let the download tallies grow on their own.

Did the cream rise to the top? Or did the artificial boost in the ranking cause the worst song (based on the original, accurate download count) to become popular?

In the scenario where the download counts were presented accurately, at the end of the experiment the top song was "She Said" by Parker Theory, which had been downloaded more than five hundred times. The least popular song, "Florence," by Post Break Tragedy, had been downloaded just twenty-nine times. So the natural outcome of the experiment was that the most popular song was nearly twenty times more popular than the least popular song.

In the alternative scenario, where the true rankings were reversed, Post Break Tragedy's "Florence," previously the least popular song, did surprisingly well; in fact, it held on to its artificially bestowed top ranking. (In full disclosure, I could barely stand to listen to it.) "She Said," the most popular song in the first scenario, rose in the rankings, so fundamental quality did have some effect. But overall, across all forty-eight songs, the final ranking from the scenario that began with the reversed popularity ordering bore hardly any relationship to the final ranking from the experiment that began with the true ordering. The belief that a song is popular had a profound effect on its popularity, even if it wasn't truly popular to start with.

Duncan Watts summarized the findings from his experiments as follows:

> [W]hen people tend to like what other people like, differences in popularity are subject to what is called "cumulative advantage," or the "rich get richer" effect. This means that if one object happens to be slightly more popular than another at just the right point, it will tend to become more popular still. As a result, even tiny, random fluctuations can blow up, generating potentially enormous long-run differences among even indistinguishable competitors—a phenomenon that is similar in some ways to the famous "butterfly effect" from chaos theory. Thus, if history were to somehow rerun many times, seemingly identical universes with the same set of competitors and the same overall market tastes would quickly generate different winners: Madonna would have been popular in this world, but in some other version of history, she would be a nobody, and someone we have never heard of would be in her place.[15]

Cumulative advantage undoubtedly plays out in the actual market as well.

A musician can come out with the wrong song at the right time, or the right song at the wrong time. He or she can be too early to catch a wave, or too late to stay afloat. Superstars have to hit the right wave at the right time, in exactly the right way. Tony Bennett bombed at rock and roll. Kid Rock would probably fail at swing tunes if he'd been born in another era. Only a handful of performers, such as Paul Simon and the Beatles, have been able to excel in more than one genre, and across multiple decades.

As a top merchandiser once remarked to me, "A one-hit wonder is a miracle." Past success is no guarantee of future success in the music business because chance factors—including timing, the national mood, initial reviews, and airplay—must all align to create a hit. This explains why less than 30 percent of the 706 bands that scored a number-one hit in the weekly *Billboard* charts from 1960 to 2017 managed to achieve the same feat again.

What is true for a song also holds for a musician's career. Bruce Springsteen acknowledged the uncertainty inherent in a musician's career when he wrote:

> You never completely control the arc of your career. Events, historical and cultural, create an opportunity; a special song falls into your lap and a window for impact, communication, success, the expansion of your musical vision, opens. It may close as quickly, never to return. You don't get to completely decide *when* it's your time. You may have worked unwaveringly, honestly, all the while—consciously or unconsciously—positioning yourself, but you never really *know* if your "big" moment will come. Then, for the few, *it's there.*[16]

Had he not auditioned before John Hammond at Columbia Records in New York City, who knows if Springsteen's big moment ever would have arrived.

And that goes for the rest of the E Street Band as well. Max Weinberg, for example, has said he often wonders, "What if I hadn't answered that ad?" As he put it:

> What would have happened to my life had I not met Bruce and the E Street Band? What would have happened to the Beatles had they not gotten Ringo? What would have happened had they stuck with Pete Best? He was a very, very good drummer. But as I think as he himself has said, Ringo was a much better Beatle. Chemistry is everything.[17]

Chemistry adds another dimension in which chance can play a role. The band members' sound may or may not strike a chord.

The group may or may not get along. The band's personality may or may not shine through, or may or may not be appealing. For any number of reasons, the chemistry might not be right.

The outsized role of luck in launching a musician's career helps explain another anomaly that I mentioned in Chapter 3: why, compared to top business executives and athletes, did only a handful of top musicians have parents who were superstars in their profession? If all that mattered was talent, training, and connections, Frank Sinatra Jr. and Nancy Sinatra should have been enduring superstars.

Even the elder Sinatra, who never doubted his own prodigious talent, acknowledged a role for luck. Sinatra said, "People often remark that I'm pretty lucky. Luck is only important in so far as getting the chance to sell yourself at the right moment. After that, you've got to have talent and know how to use it."[18] From the standpoint of the music business as a whole, there are a great many talented people, but talent takes you only so far. In addition to talent, arbitrary factors can lead to success or failure, like whether another band happens to release a more popular song than yours at the same time.

The difference between a Sixto Rodriguez and a Bob Dylan, or even a Post Break Tragedy and Post Malone, depends much more on luck and timing than we commonly acknowledge. In hindsight, it is hard to imagine the world without Madonna or Dylan, but if the chips had fallen a slightly different way at a critical point in their careers, or in a rival's career, we might well feel that it would be hard to imagine the world without some other superstar's music. Just ask Sixto Rodriguez how easy it is for the flame of fame to be ignited or extinguished.

Making the Most of Luck

Becky Weinberg, Max's better half, once asked me how I got my job at Princeton University. I explained that luck played a major role. I just happened to sit next to Ginna Ashenfelter, the wife of one of Princeton's greatest economists, Orley Ashenfelter, on a flight to the American Economic Association Meeting, where I was interviewing for jobs. Perhaps thinking about Max's audition forty years earlier, Becky responded by echoing Seneca: "Luck is what happens when preparation meets opportunity." I consider myself extremely fortunate to have been able to take advantage of the opportunity that presented itself when Princeton called to invite me to interview for a job, which never would have happened if I had had a different seat on that airplane.

Allen Klein, who managed Sam Cooke, the Rolling Stones, and the Beatles, started out as an accountant. His career in the music business advanced because he ran into an old classmate, music publisher Don Kirshner, on the street in New York. Kirshner offered to steer some clients Klein's way to audit their record labels' books. "It was really happenstance that I got into the music business," Klein told his hometown newspaper, the Newark *Star-Ledger*, in 2002. "I never wanted to be a manager. It was going over the books that I loved. And I was good at it."[19] Chutzpah also helped. When Klein met Bobby Darin at Kirshner's wedding, he immediately promised to get the singer $100,000 if he hired Klein to audit his royalty payments.

Luck—factors beyond your control—affect where you are born, who your parents are, where you go to school, your health, and nearly every other aspect of life. As Michael Lewis, the author of *Liar's Poker* and a dozen other bestsellers, told the graduating class of 2012 at Princeton University in his baccalaureate speech:

> You are the lucky few. Lucky in your parents, lucky in your country, lucky that a place like Princeton exists that can take in lucky people, introduce them to other lucky people, and increase their chances of becoming even luckier. Lucky that you live in the richest society the world has ever seen, in a time when no one actually expects you to sacrifice your interests to anything.[20]

In other words, we are all better off if we recognize the role that luck plays in contributing to our successes, and if we are more tolerant and supportive of those who are less lucky.

An unbiased look at our economic successes and failures shows that luck plays a significant role. Consider identical twins. For four summers in a row, my colleague Orley Ashenfelter and I conducted a survey of twins at the world's largest twins festival, in Twinsburg, Ohio.[21] We interviewed identical twins about their education, how long they dressed alike, and their incomes. Our goal was to find twins with differences in educational attainment and determine whether the twin with more education earned a higher income than the other twin. Most twins have the same education, but we did survey some with different schooling levels. On average, we found that a twin who completed four more years of education than his or her sibling earned about 60 percent higher wages.

But luck also matters in terms of economic success. Identical twins with the *same* level of education who were raised by the same family, under the same roof, and typically dressed alike and went to the same school, often have very different economic outcomes as adults. Earnings differed by 50 percent or more in a quarter of the identical twins with identical schooling levels, and by 25 percent or more in half of the sample. These large disparities for two genetically identical individuals with such similar backgrounds suggest that luck is an important factor in the overall labor market, as it is in the music industry. Sometimes one twin was lucky to land a high-paying job, while his sibling was scrambling because the plant where he worked closed. One twin may have had a supportive, agreeable boss and the other a difficult boss. In other cases, one of the twins had a spouse who kept him on a straight and narrow path, while the other was not so fortunate. For many reasons, identical twins were not treated identically by the economy, and chance factors accounted for much of the differences in their outcomes.

As in music, timing matters as well. A worker can be lucky and enter the job market when it is strong, or unlucky and enter the job market in the middle of a recession. Research has shown that the labor market consequences of graduating from college in a year when the economy is weak are large, negative, and persistent.[22] Another study of MBA students found that graduating from business school in a weak year for stocks reduces the chances of getting a high-paying Wall Street job, while graduating in a bull market boosts the chances of landing a high-paying career in investment banking.[23] The study concluded that "investment bankers are largely 'made' by circumstance rather than 'born' to work on Wall Street."

And, as in the music industry, the effect of luck is amplified in a winner-take-all market in the general economy. Consider CEOs. The pay of top executives relative to their workers has soared since the 1980s. In 1978 the average CEO earned about 18 times as much as the average worker; today the average CEO carns more than 250 times as much.[24] As in Alfred Marshall's time, successful executives can now undertake initiatives and new ventures on a much vaster scale, which has undoubtedly played a role in their outsized compensation.

But luck and an erosion of norms of fairness have also boosted CEO pay in many cases. In a landmark study, Marianne Bertrand and Sendhil Mullainathan show that the compensation paid to CEOs of oil companies jumps when the price of oil rises.[25] Since the price of oil is set on the world market, with gyrations caused by geopolitical forces well beyond the control of oil company CEOs, movements in the price of oil have nothing to do with their job performance. Yet they benefit when the price of oil rises. Some of the profit windfall from oil price spikes is also shared with workers further down the wage scale, but not with those at the bottom, according to my latest research.[26]

Cliff Burnstein: Even Managers Get Lucky Sometimes

Superstar managers as well as superstar musicians benefit from luck. Over Chinese food, Cliff Burnstein told me that luck played a critical role in his music career on four occasions.[27]

First, he was lucky to get his start in the music business. While he was finishing up studying demography in graduate school at the University of Pennsylvania in 1973, Burnstein mailed letters seeking a job to several music companies. The only one that invited him for an interview was Mercury Records in Chicago. Why? According to Burnstein, it was pure luck. Mercury's president, Irwin Steinberg, was from his hometown, Highland Park, Illinois, and one of Steinberg's sons was a student at the University of Pennsylvania. As a result of these coincidences, the personnel department probably thought that Burnstein would be an interesting candidate to interview. With his foot in the door, Burnstein was offered and accepted a job in the finance department at Mercury, and soon moved to promotion and A&R.

After a year at Mercury Records, he caught another break. Early one Monday morning, he was given the assignment to listen to an album by an unsigned—and then unknown—Canadian hard rock band called Rush. Mercury needed to decide by the end of the day whether to sign the band. Why was Burnstein asked to make a recommendation about Rush? He was the only one in the office that day. To his surprise, Burnstein thought the music was excellent. He did some homework, called someone at radio station WMMS in Cleveland, who confirmed the record was hot, and convinced Steinberg to sign the band. Rush subsequently garnered seven Grammy nominations and was inducted into the Rock and Roll Hall of Fame in 2013. The band's success increased Burnstein's credibility and self-confidence.

In 1980, Burnstein left Mercury Records for Leber-Krebs in New York City, where he worked with his close friend Peter Mensch. Burnstein and Mensch decided to strike out on their own and form Q Prime Management in 1982. At the time the duo was ready to leave Leber-Krebs, they were managing AC/DC, the Scorpions, Michael Schenker (younger brother of Rudolph Schenker, the Scorpions' guitarist and songwriter), and Def Leppard. They could not take AC/DC with them, and the Scorpions and Schenker preferred to stay with a big, established firm. Burnstein and Mensch were able to take Def Leppard because, as luck would have it, David Krebs thought the band was destined for failure. The only time Krebs saw Def Leppard perform, Cliff Burnstein told me, the band was the opening act in an outdoor show held outside Atlanta on a brutally hot day. A guitar player, who Burnstein estimates weighed only 105 pounds, passed out from the heat and excess alcohol consumption. A stagehand dragged him offstage by the scruff of his neck, and the show wobbled on. Needless to say, Krebs was unimpressed. But the young lads from South Yorkshire were more than happy to join Cliff and Peter at Q Prime when they split from Leber-Krebs. Cliff and Peter managed Def Leppard, their first Q Prime client, for a quarter of a century, and the band sold more than 100 million albums. Who knows what would have happened if the temperature had been cooler during that Atlanta show.

Q Prime immediately recognized that they needed more than one act. Cliff's view has long been, "Don't manage one act, because then they manage you. Then you're just doing their bidding. You have to diversify." The fourth time luck struck in Cliff Burnstein's storybook career was surely a grand slam. On the lookout for another band to manage in 1984, Burnstein and Mensch were in London and visited a record store. They happened to notice a couple of shoppers wearing homemade Metallica T-shirts. Only vaguely familiar with Metallica at the time, Burnstein and Mensch surmised that any band that generated such engaged fans must be special. They have managed Metallica since 1984, and the band has consistently been among the top acts in the music business.

In all of these examples, luck was necessary but not sufficient to launch and advance Burnstein's career. Someone with less persistence, less talent, and less perceptive judgment could not have taken advantage of these opportunities. Cliff Burnstein and his longtime friend and business partner Peter Mensch are routinely included on the *Billboard* list of the most powerful people in the music industry because of their business acumen, and because they treat their artists fairly and with respect. But some lucky opportunities that arose along the way opened the door for them to apply their skills. To use a baseball analogy, skill is required for a baseball player to hit a grand slam, but luck is also necessary to place three of the previous batters on the bases at the time of his at-bat.

Harmonizing Good and Bad Luck in Your Portfolio

The unpredictability of financial assets such as stocks is well known. Although the stock market does not exactly follow a random path, movements in prices may seem random. "A blind-folded monkey throwing darts at a newspaper's financial pages," Burton Malkiel wrote in his 1973 bestseller *A Random Walk Down Wall Street*, "could select a portfolio that would do just as well as one carefully selected by experts."[28] Experience has borne out this prediction. In 2016, for example, two-thirds of actively managed large-capitalization stock funds underperformed the S&P 500 large-cap index.[29] And even when an actively managed fund does beat the overall market index in one year, the odds of it doing so again the next year are not very good. What's more, actively managed funds tend to charge higher fees for the privilege of earning unimpressive returns. Unless you're as savvy an investor as Warren Buffett, the best advice economists can give is to invest your savings in a well-diversified, low-cost passive index fund.

Although we cannot control luck, we can seek a balance between risk and reward. If, for example, you have a job that is tied to the ups and downs of Wall Street, it would behoove you to consider investing in safe assets, such as CDs (certificates of deposit, not compact discs) or Treasury bonds, to reduce your risk. Financial economists have long emphasized that we can minimize the effect of bad luck by deliberately diversifying our portfolios.

An alternative approach is to "invest in what you know." This philosophy is often associated with legendary mutual fund manager Peter Lynch. Lynch's advice has been summarized as follows: "Use your specialized knowledge to home in on stocks you can analyze, study them and then decide if they're worth owning. The best way to invest is to look at companies competing in the field where you work."[30]

In a 1984 interview in *Playboy*, Paul McCartney described his investment philosophy in similar terms:

> The music publishing I own is fabulous. Beautiful. I owe it all to [my wife] Linda's dad Lee Eastman and her brother John. Linda's dad is a great business brain. He said originally, "If you are going to invest, do it in something you know. If you invest in building computers or something, you can lose a fortune. Wouldn't you rather be in music? Stay in music." I said, "Yeah, I'd much rather do that." So he asked me what kind of music I liked. And the first name I said was Buddy Holly. Lee got on to the man who owned Buddy Holly's stuff and bought that for me. So I was into publishing now.[31]

This worked out splendidly for Paul McCartney. The "buy what you know" philosophy has been employed by many others, including Michael Jackson (who once outbid McCartney to purchase the rights to the Beatles' catalog) and Quincy Jones.

Although there can be some benefits from investing in what you know, it can also be quite risky. Enron employees knew Enron very well, for example, and a great many of them invested their retirement savings in Enron. This didn't work out well when Enron failed in 2001. They lost their jobs and their life savings along with it.

As investors, we tend to be overconfident, which means that we may know less than we think we know. Studies find that retail investors (especially men) tend to sell stocks that go on to outperform the market and tend to buy stocks that subsequently underperform the market.[32] We also tend to trade too often. Buying and holding a diversified portfolio is a better strategy for most investors. Evidently we know less than we think we do when we're buying and selling stocks.

In any event, there is some common ground between a diversified portfolio and buying what we know. We can invest in what we know to diversify our portfolio and find a good balance between risk and reward. Gloria Estefan, for example, told me that she knew from the beginning of her career that women singers "have a much shorter shelf life in this industry," and that fans' tastes can be fickle. "You should not put all of your eggs in one basket, especially something that is as volatile as music." She and her husband, Emilio, consciously invested in hotels, real estate, and restaurants to diversify their sources of income outside of music.[33] They invested in Cuban and Lebanese restaurants because they knew the food from their heritage.

This is a simple but profound idea. Portfolio theory—the strategy of assembling a mix of investments to maximize return for a given level of risk—has been around for a long time. But I have been struck by the resistance to this idea in the music business. Musical tastes are subject to fads and large swings. Success in music is difficult to predict and unlikely to last. Record labels, promoters, and managers hold risky portfolios if their client rosters consists of a small number of bands. And even if that list has a large number of bands, the portfolio is risky if they are in the same genre or subject to the same market swings. Why not look for ways to diversify their risk? Yet this doesn't seem to be the nature of the business. Instead, most companies in the music business seem heavily invested in one artist, one genre, or a single risky asset in one way or another, with little effort devoted to diversification.

One exception is Q Prime, which manages a mix of heavy metal, rock, and country bands. I asked co-founder Cliff Burnstein if the eclectic mix of artists—from Metallica to Eric Church and Gillian Welch—was a deliberate strategy to diversify risk. If preferences for heavy metal, for example, were to wane, interest in country music might well rise, keeping a constant demand for his clients. I was expecting to hear a portfolio theory of music. Instead, Cliff gave a simpler answer: he just liked country music because that was what he heard on the radio when he was growing up. It is hard to argue with success, no matter how you get there.

Invictus

My high school English teacher assigned the poem "Invictus" by William Ernest Henley because, she said, at our tender age we would be able to relate to the poem better than we would when we were older. At the time, I had no idea what she meant. But I still haven't forgotten the lines: "I am the master of my fate:/I am the captain of my soul." As time goes by, it becomes increasingly clear that we are not quite the invincible captains of our ships that we once thought we were. Both good luck and bad luck intervene.

Sometimes it takes an incredible shock of bad luck to realize that "Invictus" is the stuff of fairy tales. The *New York Times* columnist Frank Bruni recently wrote about this epiphany after waking up one morning with severe, probably irreversible damage to the vision in his right eye:

> I went to bed believing that I was more or less in control—that the unfinished business, unrealized dreams and other disappointments in my life were essentially failures of industry and imagination, and could probably be redeemed with a fierce enough effort. I woke up to the realization of how ludicrous that was.[34]

Bruni's eventual solution was to focus on what he could still accomplish, and to recognize how lucky he was despite his impairment. "Show me someone with a seemingly unbroken stride and unfettered path," he wrote. "More often than not, he or she is hampered and haunted in ways that you can't imagine."

One person who was not haunted despite his run of bad luck in the music business and his own vision problems (due to glaucoma) is Sixto Rodriguez. The movie *Searching for Sugar Man* revealed a man who seemed perfectly at peace with his life after his music career fizzled in the 1970s. The filmmaker Malik Bendjelloul, who later committed suicide, said that Rodriguez gave most of his money away, despite his impoverishment.[35] After the movie was released, Rodriguez's music career had a second wind, this time a strong tailwind. At age seventy-six, he is touring internationally and enjoying fame and a measure of fortune, all the while maintaining the same Zen-like presence that he possessed during his years of obscurity. When asked about switching from construction back to his musical career, Rodriguez told a reporter, "Well, you never throw away your work clothes. But this thing is like a monsoon."[36]

CHAPTER 6

The Show Must Go On: The Economics of Live Music

*I am a salesman. I come from a long line of traveling sales-
people on my mother's side. And I think I'm a good salesman of
ideas, songs, melodies, if I believe in them.*

—Bono

I'm very sorry," Bono kept saying. "Something went wrong that
night, the energy wasn't right." Bono, whose given name is Paul
David Hewson, was profusely apologizing to me about a concert
he had performed in Madison Square Garden almost a decade
earlier. I'd attended the show in New York that night, November 22, 2005, with a team of grad students to survey the audience about how they bought their tickets, how much they paid,
and why they went to the show. The Irish rock band U2 has sold
more tickets and made more money touring than anyone since the
early 1980s. U2's Vertigo tour grossed well over $350 million from
131 shows held from 2004 to 2006, and was the subject of three
documentary films.[1] Their 2009–11 U2 360° tour grossed a record
$736 million from 110 shows. What better laboratory to study the
economics of live entertainment, the main source of income for
most musicians, than a U2 concert in Madison Square Garden?

So when I bumped into U2's frontman, Bono, outside the
West Wing of the White House almost ten years after that night,
I finally had a chance to share my research findings with him. He
listened intently as I explained that almost a third of the tickets
for the show had been resold on the secondary market for about

twice their list price, and they were disproportionately good seats. But mostly he wanted to apologize for the show not living up to his expectations. Of all the shows he has performed, I was amazed he could recall this one so clearly. Here was a true professional. Weeks later, he told a mutual friend that he was still sorry that that show had not gone as well as he had hoped.

Concerts sell experiences, not only music. "People go to a concert for the experience, with friends, to have a drink and have fun," the billionaire businessman Mark Cuban recently told the annual Pollstar Live! conference.[2] He likened selling concert tickets to the way he sells Dallas Mavericks basketball tickets—sell the experience. "There's not much in entertainment that provides an experience like live music," says Q Prime's Cliff Burnstein.[3] There is some kind of a "magical thinking quality to music," he said, that creates a unique connection between the performers and the audience. In his view, only a great novel comes close. Jeannie Wilkinson, the former head of research for Live Nation, said that fans attend live performances "to lose themselves in the artist's music and performance, and to connect with other fans in this experience. For many, it would be likened to a euphoric, religious experience."

As recorded music is becoming more widely available than water, people are flocking to concerts and music festivals in record numbers. In a typical summer week, about three million people attend a live show in North America.[4] And top performers like Bono know how to give the fans what they're looking for. Emotional experiences are the stock in trade of live entertainment. Supply, demand, and all that jazz are all on vivid display in the concert market. Performers want sellouts, but they don't want to be viewed as *being* sellouts. Fans want to feel good about participating in an exclusive, one-of-a-kind, communal experience. When emotions and markets collide, the result is often an uneasy harmony.

Live Entertainment 101

"The ticket price is not up to us, man," David Crosby told the *Dallas Morning News* when he was asked why Crosby, Stills, Nash and Young tickets were so expensive.[5] He elaborated: "The way all big tours go down now is one company buys the entire tour, and they give you an enormous amount of money, and then they control everything." I love David Crosby's harmonies, but his description of the concert business strums over some important details.

Musicians *do* have a say over ticket prices for their tours. In fact, I have had several bands' managers tell me they wish I could convince their artists to charge more. Ticket prices are a major component of the negotiation that takes place between a band's agent and the concert promoter, and the band has to sign off on box office prices and other terms of the contract for the deal to be completed. The show won't go on if the band objects to the ticket prices specified in the contract.

The band's manager (or management company) plays a central role in the band's development and business decisions. The manager negotiates on behalf of the band and advises the band. Arrangements vary depending on the bargaining power of the respective parties, but a typical agreement pays the manager a commission of 15 percent of the band's net touring revenue and other income for his or her services.[6] Terms may differ. Sometimes the manager may take a 20 percent commission, and sometimes the commission may be based on gross revenue instead of net revenue. In any of these cases, the manager's take can approach or even exceed the average band member's. Suppose, for example, a concert grosses $1 million in revenue. It is not unusual for travel and other expenses to equal 60 percent or more of revenue. So if the band's net revenue is $400,000 and there are five members in the band, and the manager's share is 15 percent of net revenue, the manager's commission from the show is $60,000. That leaves $340,000 for the band to split, or $68,000 for each member if they divide it equally. If the manager's commission is based on gross revenue, or if the commission rate is higher than 15 percent, he or she would make more money than the average band member.

A top band is also assisted by a cadre of other professionals: a lawyer (who reviews contracts and structures deals), an agent (who books appearances), a tour accountant (who counts the money), and a business manager (who invests the money). They are all important, but no one is more important than the band's manager, who handles tasks big and small. The manager negotiates with record labels, merchandisers, and—most important— concert promoters for major tours. On the aesthetic front, Paul McCartney credits the Beatles' first manager, Brian Epstein, with raising the band's level by hiring a tailor to make the Fab Four's matching suits.[7]

In a typical business arrangement for a concert, a band's manager or agent negotiates with a concert promoter on behalf of the band. The promoter could be interested in signing the band to perform one show in a single venue or, increasingly often, signing the band to perform several shows in different venues across the country or on several continents. The concert promoter's role is to organize a show by booking the musicians, securing a venue, and marketing the event. The promoter typically needs to rent the venue and contract with a ticketing company (e.g., Ticketmaster) to sell and distribute the tickets (if the venue doesn't already have an exclusive deal with a ticketing company).

Burnstein's dictum that "everything is negotiable" notwithstanding, a common arrangement between the promoter and band resembles a book contract, with an initial advance against future ticket sales and then royalties if sales exceed a certain level. Consider a typical agreement covering a single concert, which a manager provided to me. According to the agreement, the band receives a "guaranteed advance" equal to the first $100,000 of ticket sales. Then, before additional revenue is distributed, the promoter recovers expenses and sometimes a "minimum profit"—say, $50,000 for expenses and $22,500 for profit. The expenses could include advertising, rent for the venue, costs of unloading equipment, security, and so on. The band also has expenses (e.g., travel, crew, security, extra lights, video, sound engineer, choreographer, pyrotechnics), which it pays for out of its income. The promoter and the band split any ticket revenue above the guarantee plus expenses and minimum profit (above $172,500 in this case), usually with the band receiving 85 percent and the promoter receiving 15 percent of these revenues. The band's guaranteed advance and percentage of revenue after expenses is higher for bands with greater bargaining power. A superstar, for example, could command a seven-figure guaranteed advance and a 90 percent or higher split on revenues beyond a certain point.

Concert promoters used to be local monopolies, operating in their regions with little competition. Bill Graham Presents controlled San Francisco. Jam Productions was dominant in Chicago. And Ron Delsener held sway in New York for fifty years. These promoters played a critical role in boosting the careers of the Grateful Dead, Bob Dylan, Frank Zappa, Rod Stewart, and many other household names. Then in 1996, the media entrepreneur Robert Sillerman formed SFX Entertainment and began acquiring and consolidating local promoters to form a national company. In 2000, Sillerman sold SFX to Clear Channel Communications, a conglomerate of radio and television stations, amphitheaters, and billboard businesses, for $4.4 billion. In 2005, Clear Channel spun off its concert promotion business into a new company called Live Nation. Live Nation continued to grow and merged with Ticketmaster, the giant ticketing company, in 2010, forming Live Nation Entertainment.

Live Nation Entertainment's biggest competitor is AEG. In addition to promotion activities, AEG owns and operates several venues in the United States and around the world, such as the

Staples Center in Los Angeles and the Manchester Arena in England. So the largest promoters have horizontal as well as vertical monopoly power.

At a national level, the concert promotion business has become much more concentrated in recent decades, following the trend in many other U.S. industries. In 1995, for example, the four largest promoters booked 22 percent of concert business nationwide. But in 2017, based on my calculations from the Pollstar data, the four largest concert promoters were responsible for 67 percent of concert revenue in the United States.

At the city level, however, there was not much competition before 2000. The local monopolies that have survived and remained independent now have to compete with Live Nation and AEG. As a result, margins are tight for concert promoters. Profit margins for concerts are so thin that they have been dubbed the "river of nickels."[8]

Consolidation of the concert industry has facilitated national and international tours, and promoters are willing to pay a premium to sign a major act to an exclusive tour. Live Nation CEO Michael Rapino said that bundling tours "is the best way for an artist to get the best deal."[9] He acknowledged that Live Nation pays a premium for the right to promote an exclusive run of concerts for a band. In economic terms, this is a case of bilateral monopoly, where a large buyer (the promoter) is negotiating with a seller of a unique product (the band). In such a situation, each party tries to leverage its strategic assets and reach the best bargain for its side. For example, Live Nation's connection with Ticketmaster provides vertical reach and greater profit opportunities, especially in the United States, where Ticketmaster has a larger share of ticket distribution than in Europe.[10] AEG, on the other hand, has tried to lock artists into performing in its venues around the world, a practice called *block booking*.[11] If a promoter holds a show in a venue that it owns, it receives income from food and beer sales as well as parking. These complementary revenue streams give promoters an incentive to prioritize their own venues. As a result, it is not unusual to see a tour wend its way through O2 in London and the Staples Center in Los Angeles, because AEG owns both venues. Azoff MSG Entertainment likewise reportedly tries to block-book its venues, Madison Square Garden and the Forum in Los Angeles.[12]

In principle, leveraging complementary assets in this way can maximize the joint surplus for the parties to split, although there is also a risk that a promoter could monopolize a segment of the industry and suppress competition, to the detriment of fans and performers. Sharon Osbourne, Ozzy Osbourne's wife and manager, raised exactly this concern when AEG tried to use its muscle to require Ozzy to give a concert at the Staples Center in exchange for performing in London's O2 stadium. "There's enough for everyone without you trying to monopolize the world of entertainment," she wrote.[13] (Osbourne dropped a lawsuit against AEG after the company announced it would drop block booking in September 2018.)

As the concert industry became more consolidated, several managers have told me that it also became more professional. Although tour accountants still find reasons to challenge promoters' receipts and revenues—and there still are notable scams, such as the Fyre Festival fraud in 2017—the fact that Live Nation is a publicly traded company, for example, legally obligates it to accurately report financial information. Michael Lorick, a tour accountant who began his career with Hootie and the Blowfish at the Jones Beach Theater in 1995, said the industry has come a long way since then.[14] Lorick discovered at the time that some tickets never went on general sale. In 1998 a box office employee of the theater pled guilty to grand larceny for skimming tickets from the first ten rows of the theater at Hootie's and others' concerts and reselling them to ticket brokers for a profit.[15] This practice is much less common today because there is an electronic paper trail, he said. But digitization has enabled bots controlled by ticket brokers to swoop up premium tickets to many shows ahead of ordinary fans.

How do these developments affect fans and performers? The fact that promotion is a low-margin business suggests that competition exists among promoters despite the high degree of concentration on a national level. Live Nation's profit margins are only 4 to 5 percent.[16] Promoters are pressed by higher advances for performers and by increased concert costs. In view of these low profit margins, Michael Rapino has pointed out that Live Nation is always looking for ways to monetize concerts outside of the gate. "As important as ticketing is for Live Nation," he said, the "sponsorship arm," which brings in money from Anheuser Busch and other companies, "is just as important." For the long run, he advises promoters to obsess about the art of the show—the quality and artistry of the production—and not just the art of the deal.

Pricing and Distribution

In the hit Estelle song "American Boy," the featured rapper Kanye West grumbles, "Tell the promoter we need more floor seats. We just sold out all the floor seats." This is actually a common problem. To an economist, the lyric should be: "Ask the promoter why we didn't charge more for the floor seats. We just sold out all the floor seats."

Historically, concert tickets were underpriced compared to what supply and demand would bear. Tickets to see the Beatles play at Shea Stadium in 1965 cost between $4.50 and $5.65 (or $32 to $40 in today's dollars). A ticket for Billy Joel at the Forum in Los Angeles in 1978 was just $9.75 (or $34 in today's dollars). "We're still coming out of the age of rock and roll socialism," according to William Morris's top agent Marc Geiger.[17] The data bear him out. Figure 6.1 shows that the average price of concert tickets has soared in recent years. The average list price of a concert ticket purchased in the United States rose from $12 in 1981 to $69 in 2017. If prices had grown with overall inflation, the average concert price would have been just $32 in 2018.

Figure 6.1: Average Price per Ticket and Overall Inflation Rate, 1981–2018

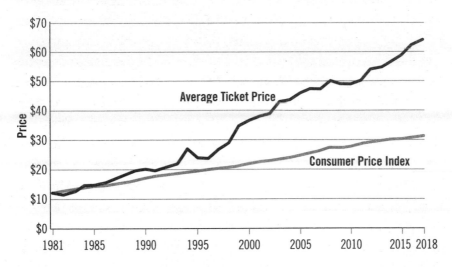

Source: Author's calculations based on the Pollstar Boxoffice Database for concerts held in the U.S. from 1981 to 2018. The figures shown each year are total box office revenue divided by total tickets sold. The price for 2018 is estimated based on a regression of the percentage change in the average price for all tours on the percentage change in the average price of the top 100 North American tours from 1996 to 2017, and the percentage change in the price of the top 100 tours in the first half of 2018. Inflation is measured by the CPI-RS, through the first half of 2018.

Concert prices have increased especially rapidly relative to inflation since the late 1990s. From 1996 to 2018, the average concert ticket price rose 190 percent, while overall consumer prices rose by 59 percent. To put the rapid growth of concert prices in perspective, the average concert price over this period grew faster than medical care inflation (113 percent) and almost as fast as college tuition and fees (204 percent), the two sectors of the economy with runaway price inflation.

Ticket prices have grown even more quickly for the best seats and for the hottest shows. If you rank all concerts by their average ticket price and weight the prices by the number of tickets sold for each show, from 1996 to 2017 the price of the 90th-percentile ticket (near the top) in the Pollstar data increased by 218 percent, that of the median ticket increased by 140 percent, and the price of the 10th-percentile ticket (near the bottom) rose by 108 percent. And for the most expensive seats at the biggest shows, prices have risen even faster: the highest ticket price in the house for concerts increased threefold from 1996 to 2017 (again weighted by tickets sold for each show). The cost of a ticket to one of the hottest shows is growing faster than college tuition.

In my research I have examined several hypotheses for the rapid rise in concert prices. Surprisingly, the consolidation of promoters discussed earlier in this chapter, which started shortly after concert prices began to accelerate, *does not* appear to account for the rise in prices, as ticket prices also rose in Canada, Europe, and regions of the United States that did not experience an increase in consolidation.

In part, the rise in concert prices reflects the general rising cost of attending entertainment events. The prices of tickets for sporting events, movies, and theatrical performances have all grown faster than overall price inflation, according to Bureau of Labor Statistics data. This most likely reflects the fact that consumer demand for leisure activities rises over time when countries become richer. Concert prices grew in lockstep with the price of other entertainment events until the late 1990s. But after 1999 the growth in concert prices was consistently stronger than the growth in other entertainment prices. Notably, 1999 was the year that Napster was founded.

Napster was a disruptive force in the music industry. As the rampant file sharing and piracy ushered in by Napster eroded record sales and artists' royalties from recordings, musicians began to view concerts as more of a profit center. In economics terms, musicians can be viewed as selling complementary products. In the pre-Napster days, it made more sense to keep concert prices low to gain popularity and sell more albums. In the post-Napster days, recorded music can be viewed as a way for artists to gain popularity, to increase demand for live performances.[18] It is this progression that led David Bowie to advise fellow musicians to tour a lot.

The consequence of this development has been to turn the music industry into even more of a winner-take-all affair. And that has imperiled the livelihoods of middle-class musicians and workers in the music industry. As John Eastman, Paul McCartney's lawyer and brother-in-law, explained to me:

> The century-old music world beginning with Edison's breakthrough (analog) technology spawned a business which happily supported numerous musicians and companies economically, much as the nation's then broad industrial base did.
>
> It was digital "disruptive technology" beginning with Napster which destroyed the industry's century-old economic underpinnings, manufacturing and distribution, leaving just a handful of stars depending only on personal appearances who were the winners taking all . . .
>
> My guess is this is broadly analogous to the digital revolution (again disruptive technology) in our post-industrial world which led to the nation's dangerous winner-take-all economics with a cancerous income disparity so threatening to our democracy.[19]

One other aspect of the evolution of concert pricing bears attention. When live entertainment began, in many respects it operated more like a block party than like an impersonal commodity market. In a commodity market, price is just the result of balancing supply and demand. But in a block party, while it is appropriate to charge your guests for attending—perhaps enough to cover the cost of food and utensils—it is inappropriate to be viewed as charging them too much. The fact that everyone pitches in to make a block party work enhances the experience. No one wants to be seen as gouging their friends and neighbors.

Similarly, to fans the price that a band charges for a show is often considered a reflection of the band's ethos and fundamentally a part of the experience. Artists want their fans to feel that they are being treated fairly, and they want their fans to contribute to the experience at a concert by singing along, dancing, holding up cellphones, and posting photos on Instagram. Many sporting events as well, including the Super Bowl, had a block party spirit when they first started (and if you have ever attended a tailgate party before a football game, you can relate to this experience).

But over time, entertainment events evolve to behave more like a market and less like a block party. That is, commercial sporting events, concerts, and perhaps other live entertainment events tend to go through a phase where they are more like a social gathering initially, and then over time—because of excess demand and changing expectations of appropriate norms of behavior—they transform to become more of a market, with prices determined by the forces of supply and demand. If an event turns into an impersonal market too quickly, it risks losing its allure and destroying the goose that has the potential of laying the golden egg. I call this "block party economics," and it is a rational way to build an industry and loyal customer base (although to agents like Marc Geiger, it smacks of rock and roll socialism).

It is not surprising to see tension between the desire to treat customers fairly and the desire to price to whatever the market will bear in a block party economy. This tension often causes the invisible hand of the market to appear to be all thumbs when it comes to setting the price of concert tickets. Some artists hold to the practice of charging fans a reasonable price irrespective of the price that supply and demand would dictate. Musicians can be sensitive. They care about what is said about them on social media. They may also consider it in their economic interest to sacrifice short-term revenue for the sake of long-term longevity and popularity, and perhaps greater profits in the future.

This tension exists in other markets as well. For example, the ride-sharing company Uber faced intense opposition when it introduced surge pricing (i.e., charging a higher price when demand for rides greatly exceeds the supply of drivers in an area), and it has continually adjusted the practice to reduce customers' sense of moral umbrage. And after a hurricane, states often impose anti-gouging laws for essential goods such as food and lumber.

In concerts, Ticketmaster often assumes the role of the villain to shield performers or promoters from criticism for charging excessive prices. The infamous Ticketmaster service fee, which seems out of proportion to the service actually provided, is a way to channel revenue back to venues or promoters, and indirectly to artists, for tickets that are underpriced.[20] Part of Ticketmaster's business model is to act as a heat shield to protect artists from the reputational fallout from charging a higher price.

Even in a block party economy, market forces cannot be entirely fenced off. If ticket prices are not set with an eye toward balancing supply and demand, the result will be an empty house (if prices are set too high) or a large secondary market where resale prices are much higher than the list value (if prices are set too low). Resistance to congestion pricing, a method for charging drivers a higher price when roads are congested, has left roads from Los Angeles to New York City gridlocked with traffic during rush hour.

When asked about the tension in concert ticket pricing, Richard Thaler, the University of Chicago economist who won a Nobel Prize for his seminal contributions to behavioral economics, observed, "A good rule of thumb is we shouldn't impose a set of rules that will create moral outrage, even if that moral outrage seems stupid to economists."[21]

One indication of the distance that concerts have traveled in the direction of charging market-determined prices is the extent to which ticket prices vary within the venue, from the worst seat to the best seat. It used to be that most shows charged the same price for every seat. But this practice has broken down. As recently as the 1990s, almost half of concerts (weighted by ticket sales) charged the same price for every ticket in the house, from the last row to the front row. In 2017, less than 10 percent of shows had a uniform price.[22] Charging a higher price for a seat that is closer to the stage, just like an airline charging a higher price for a first-class seat, is a natural way to price-discriminate and extract the greatest revenue from concert attendees. When the prices vary across good and bad seats, fans self-sort into price tiers (or, equivalently, sections of the venue) based on their willingness to pay.

Artists are increasingly using innovative methods to set concert prices and extract more revenue from fans. For example, some shows have VIP pricing, where prices for the best tickets are set very high, often in excess of $500, and ticket holders are given a unique experience, such as a meet-and-greet session with the band and a photo before the show. Taylor Swift has been on the cutting edge of innovative pricing. As discussed earlier, she implemented a system of loyalty points, where fans can improve their chances of obtaining a ticket if they buy her merchandise or demonstrate their loyalty by donating time. This has proved an effective form of price discrimination—charging a higher price to fans who have a great willingness to pay.

Still, some artists resist bowing to market forces. Ed Sheeran, whose career was boosted by touring with Taylor Swift, made his views clear: "I didn't want people to pay $170 and get front row tickets and a meet and greet. I hate that shit. The moment you allow a kid with a rich father to have more things than a kid with a poor father, I think that's just shit."[23] In a similar vein, Tom Petty once remarked, "I don't see how carving out the best seats and charging a lot more for them has anything to do with rock & roll."[24]

Coming off a sixteen-year hiatus from touring, country singer Garth Brooks recently took a novel approach to selling tickets for his recent world tour, which lasted from 2014 to 2017 and encompassed 390 shows in 79 cities. He charged an affordable price, around $70 for *all* tickets, but he added more and more shows to satisfy demand at that fixed price, often performing two shows a day. Once a show sold 80 percent of its tickets, another show was added, and those in the queue were rolled over for the next show. As Brooks put it, he was "scared to death no one would show up. And then scared to death when they did." Ticketmaster called this strategy "Garth mode." Garth mode can be viewed as expanding supply to satisfy demand at a fixed price that is below the profit-maximizing price. "The whole thing was simple," Brooks said: "Make your capacity exceed your demand."[25] The strategy essentially killed the resale market, as anyone who wanted a ticket at the list price could buy one. A total of 6.3 million tickets were sold, probably the second-most ever after U2's record 360° tour (7.3 million tickets sold from 2009 to 2011). The downside of Garth mode is that the singer performed more concerts than he would have had he set a market-determined, income-maximizing price. But his fans, rather than scalpers, received the benefit of the lower price and extra performances.

Garth Brooks is the top ticket-selling solo American artist of all time. Although it is not clear whether Garth mode will be deployed by many other artists, the strategy certainly fits with Brooks's philosophy. "When we come to a city," he said, "we're not coming to play; we're coming to be invited back." Echoing a theme I have heard from many performers, from journeyman musicians to superstars, Garth Brooks added that he may feel tired while on tour but once he gets onstage, "all of a sudden you're superman. You feel 25 years old again. . . . You feel like you can fly."

One of the most successful touring bands of all time, the Grateful Dead, cut out the middleman (i.e., Ticketmaster) and sold tickets directly to their fans.[26] Over the years, the band maintained a huge mailing list of their fans, known affectionately as "Deadheads," to ensure that their most dedicated fans were able to afford a ticket. While the band performed more than 2,300 shows, each performance was unique. Not only was the set list different for almost every show, but even the same song was performed differently from show to show to create a unique experience.

Secondary Market

The secondary market for tickets has long fascinated economists. Secondary markets exist for mortgages, automobiles, and stocks and bonds: once initially originated and distributed, products can be resold. But no resale market inspires the ire of consumers quite like the secondary market for tickets for high-demand concerts and sporting events.[*] To learn more about the secondary market for concert tickets, I conducted surveys at more than thirty concerts across the United States in research with Marie Connolly, an economist now at the University of Quebec. On average, we found that about 10 percent of concert tickets are resold through scalpers on the secondary market. But that figure can easily exceed 30 percent for the hottest shows. The average ticket that is resold goes for about 50 percent above the face value, although many tickets are resold below the list price. Prices for seats in the venue are more finely tiered in the secondary market than in the primary market, and there are wide differences in prices for equivalent seats.

There are two main hypotheses for the existence of the secondary market, both of which have some merit. First, initial prices are set too low to balance supply and demand. This is especially the case for the best seats, which are more likely to be resold than seats in the nosebleed section. Second, many fans are uncertain about their plans when tickets go on sale, or are unaware that tickets are being sold, and some seek out tickets close to the date of the event. Both of these problems could be largely prevented if tickets were initially distributed in a different fashion.

Live Nation's Michael Rapino emphasized that the secondary market is created by mispricing tickets in the first place. He told the 2018 Pollstar Live! audience, "The way to solve the secondary market is to price the house better." But he also added, "Artists

---

[*] Although it should be noted that dysfunction in the secondary market for mortgages caused the entire world economy to crash in 2008.

should control ticketing. An artist should price the house how-ever he wants."[27] This is a pragmatic view, because Live Nation and Ticketmaster want to work with Ed Sheeran, Kid Rock, the Red Hot Chili Peppers, Bruce Springsteen, and many other art-ists who resist market forces in setting ticket prices. Still, it is hard to see why so much money should be left on the table for scalp-ers, who deploy an army of bots. Scalpers can take in between $1 million and $1.5 million in net revenue for a Springsteen or U2 concert.

A common view among economists, and one that I previously espoused, is that if artists misprice tickets for whatever reason, the secondary market should play a positive role by reallocating tickets to those who value them most. In this spirit, Harvard's N. Gregory Mankiw once wrote a *New York Times* column ti-tled "I Paid $2,500 for a 'Hamilton Ticket.' I'm Happy About It."[28] Yet landmark research by economists Phillip Leslie and Allen Sorensen convinced me that this view is overly simplistic. A more nuanced view is that scalpers—professional ticket brokers who have no interest in attending events for which they buy up tickets—extract whatever benefits are created from the existence of a secondary market for reselling tickets.[29] The fans who attend the events gain very little, and often are worse off, because of re-selling activity and intense competition for the initial distribution of tickets.

Ticket brokers play four economic roles: (1) they buy up un-derpriced tickets and resell them at a profit; (2) they help "price discovery" by pushing ticket prices toward a market-determined equilibrium that balances supply and demand; (3) they reallocate tickets from those who value them at a lower level to those who value them more highly; and (4) they engage in speculation and risk-taking, as they may end up with tickets that sell at a loss or do not sell at all. The first role is generally considered harmful because ticket brokers make it harder for ordinary fans to obtain tickets, while the other roles could produce economic benefits for consumers or promoters. The wasteful competition that takes place between ticket brokers deploying high-speed bots to purchase tickets and ordinary fans is analogous to the activities of high-frequency traders in financial markets, who invest millions of dollars in technology and high-speed connectivity in an arms race to complete trades a nanosecond faster than their competitors, to the detriment of ordinary investors.

Leslie and Sorensen studied fifty-six major concerts performed by the likes of the Dave Matthews Band, Eric Clapton, Jimmy Buffett, Kenny Chesney, Madonna, Phish, Prince, Sarah McLachlan, Shania Twain, Sting, and others to understand the role of ticket brokers. Ticketmaster was the sole distributor of tickets to these events. A total of 1,034,353 tickets were initially sold to the fifty-six shows. The economists hunted down information on which tickets were resold, and at what price and when, from eBay and StubHub, the two largest ticket-reselling platforms at the time. The results indicated that better seats were more likely to be resold, and that ticket reselling was most common close to the day of the event. The average markup over the list price was 40 percent, although a quarter of tickets were resold *below* their list price.

Analyzing the ticket market is complicated because the behavior of buyers in the primary market is affected by the presence of resellers, and because resellers have multiple economic roles. If ticket brokers can swoop in and buy tickets that they anticipate they can resell at a higher price, it will be more difficult for fans to purchase tickets in the primary market. There are also substantial transaction costs associated with buying a ticket on the secondary market, as anyone who has paid the StubHub transaction fee can attest. Leslie and Sorensen built a sophisticated model of consumer and broker behavior to model the effect of resale markets on consumer welfare. They reached the provocative conclusion that while the opportunity to resell tickets on the secondary market does increase the allocative efficiency of ticket distribution (which is why Mankiw felt better off for being able to buy a ticket to *Hamilton*), this benefit is partly offset by increased competition for tickets in the primary market and by transaction costs in the secondary market. When the dust settles, the big winners are the professional ticket brokers. As a whole, fans are likely made worse off by the existence of the resale market. Leslie and Sorensen conclude, "If the narrow goal is to maximize the surplus of those who ultimately attend the event, then restrictions on resale may be warranted."

In other words, it is not irrational or contrary to economic wisdom for artists or lawmakers to take steps to constrain ticket resellers and squash the secondary market to help fans. Because many artists do not want to price their tickets to market, some strange practices arise in the market for tickets that do not exist elsewhere. For example, Ticketmaster often limits purchasers to only four tickets, in a (mostly futile) attempt to restrict ticket brokers. Apart from wartime rationing or command-and-control economies like Venezuela, rationing of goods is not the norm in a market.

The most obvious way to avoid underpricing of tickets, compared to the secondary market, is to hold an auction for tickets. Ticketmaster tried this strategy for a limited number of premium tickets for hundreds of concerts in the early 2000s, but abandoned it after 2011. The auction mechanism that Ticketmaster used was a variant of the type of position auction that Google implements for keyword advertising. Research by economists Aditya Bhave and Eric Budish found that the auctions solved the pricing problem: tickets sold for about twice what their face value would have been, and at about the same price for which they could be purchased in the secondary market.[30] But the auctions proved to be cumbersome and an inefficient means to distribute tickets.

Short of setting the face value of tickets at the market-determined price, artists and ticket distributors are experimenting with alternatives to preclude scalpers—and, as shown in Figure 6.1, list prices have moved rapidly in the direction of the market price, which should erode the secondary market as well. A development that Ticketmaster has deployed to sell tickets to

Springsteen on Broadway and for presales for tours by Taylor Swift, U2, and Pearl Jam is called "Verified Fan." Potential ticket purchasers must register at Verified Fan ahead of time and receive a code that gives them the opportunity to purchase tickets. Ticketmaster "analyzes every registrant to make sure they are real people interested in going to the show."[31] Although its algorithm is secret, Ticketmaster will not verify a fan who applies for a ticket for every show date of a tour, for example. The objective of the algorithm is to prevent bots and brokers from buying and reselling tickets. Once purchased by a verified fan, tickets can be resold on Ticketmaster's platform from one verified fan to another (which generates more transaction fees that Ticketmaster can divvy up). In essence, the Verified Fan system turns fans into scalpers, so the rents from pricing below market accrue to true fans—who either attend the event or resell their tickets to other registered fans—as opposed to professional ticket brokers.

Like an airline checking in passengers, under the Verified Fan system venues check to make sure that the legitimate ticket holder attends the event. Although ticket brokers may find ways to circumvent Verified Fan, so far the procedure seems to be working as intended. Ticketmaster reports that 95 percent of fans who purchase tickets through Verified Fan do not resell them.[32] It is likely that many artists will follow this model.

Taylor Swift is a pioneer in taking Verified Fan one step further. Your chance of receiving a code that enables you to purchase a ticket is boosted if you have demonstrated your loyalty to the artist, such as by purchasing her albums or merchandise, engaging with sponsors through social media, or watching her music videos. This approach accomplishes two goals: First, it enables Ms. Swift to price-discriminate by favoring fans who purchased her complementary products with a better chance of obtaining a concert ticket. Those fans who are willing to pay the most to attend her shows, as demonstrated by buying her albums or merchandise, for example, are moved to the front of the queue to buy concert tickets. This is a brilliant and subtle approach to maximize revenue and sell more merchandise. Second, the technology enables the artist and her sponsors to interact more directly with her fans.

Taylor Swift is also experimenting with another innovation that could further clip the wings of the secondary market: slow ticketing. If an entire tour sells out in a matter of minutes, the tickets were probably grossly underpriced. Moreover, some fans who were unclear of their plans when tickets originally went on sale might decide later on that they would like to attend the show, and they might be willing to pay more for their tickets than fans who bought the moment that tickets went on sale—and they might even be more dedicated fans. Such fans have no choice but to seek tickets in the secondary market; indeed, this is one of the reasons there is a secondary market.

So instead of releasing all tickets at once, Taylor Swift released them gradually over time for her Reputation Tour. Fans were able to obtain tickets long after the initial launch. "We'd like to sell the last ticket to her concert when she takes the stage each night," David Marcus, Ticketmaster's head of music, told *Billboard*.[33] Eventually, this could also lead to more dynamic pricing, where prices vary depending on when tickets are purchased, like airplane seats. Using these innovations, Taylor Swift was able to reduce the secondary market and capture some of the revenue that would otherwise go to scalpers and ticket brokers. According to Marcus, only 3 percent of Taylor Swift tickets made it to the secondary market in her Reputation Tour, compared with 30 percent in her 1989 Tour, which used more traditional distribution methods.

Shawn "Jay-Z" Carter has also used slow ticketing, combined with more aggressive ticket pricing for upfront seats, for his 4:44 Tour in late 2017. Jay-Z sold a total of 426,441 tickets for his thirty-two-date tour, grossing $44.7 million in box office ticket sales plus another $4 million in revenue for platinum VIP tickets. The average gate was about $1.5 million per show, up substantially from his thirty-three-date Blueprint 3 Tour in 2009–10, which grossed $33.1 million from 439,540 tickets sold for an average of $1.0 million in revenue per show.[34]

One should expect more innovations in concert ticketing in the future, as the industry continues to evolve from a block party to a commercial market, and as technology enables artists to have a closer connection to their fans and to price-discriminate to maximize revenue.

Beware of Costs

One of the most insightful ideas in economics regarding how industries evolve over time is known as **Baumol's cost disease**.[35] My late colleagues William Baumol and William Bowen developed the idea. The idea is very simple. Some industries have rapid productivity growth, so more output can be produced with less labor input (think manufacturing), while other industries have slow or stagnant productivity growth (think hospitals and universities). The cost for consumers of purchasing goods or services produced in the stagnant sector will rise relative to those costs in the high-productivity growth sector over time. This dynamic can partly explain why the growth in health care and education costs is squeezing out other spending and putting pressure on families' and governments' budgets.

In their original work, Baumol and Bowen used live music as their quintessential example of a sector with stagnant productivity. They noted that it takes just as much time and effort for musicians to perform a Schubert string quartet today as it did two hundred years ago. Yet musicians are paid more today than they were two hundred years ago, because they have the option of working in other sectors, where productivity has increased. In other words, the fact that a violinist could work at General Motors has increased violinists' pay over time, even though they still are not paid very well. The higher labor costs put upward pressure on prices for live performances and make classical music relatively more expensive for consumers today than it was 150 years ago compared to manufactured goods, which can be produced with less labor. This logic can explain why TV sets and computers have seen rapid price declines, while tickets to Carnegie Hall have become more expensive.

This notion of Baumol's cost disease is fraught when it comes to practical applications in music today, however. New technologies, such as digital recording and streaming, have greatly changed the quality and quantity of output in the music industry. And new technologies, such as synthesizers and sound tuners, are continually changing the nature and quality of music produced. Even for live events, better speakers and microphones have improved the productivity of musicians.

Still, the basic insight—that one needs to be cognizant of production costs—is powerful, and readily seen in live entertainment. "Sure, concerts generate a lot of revenue," Rob Levine, a freelance writer for *Billboard*, told me, "but they also generate a lot of costs."[36] Accountant Michael Lorick told me that touring costs "add up quickly."[37] Profit is not guaranteed. Out-of-control costs can devastate touring profits. In addition, the artist's manager, agent, and business manager typically take a combined 30 percent of the artist's income. Artists have to watch their costs. A rival manager told me a possibly apocryphal (although he firmly believed it) story about a top band spending exorbitantly to prepare for a tour. The band and more than a hundred members of its crew all stayed in an expensive hotel in Florida to rehearse before the start of the tour. (Typically, the crew would be booked into a lower-cost hotel.) When it came time to hit the road, no one remembered to check the crew out, so the tour was charged with extra expenses.

Managers' incentives also affect costs. If a band does well, its manager does well. If the manager's commission is 15 or 20 percent of revenue *net of costs*, the manager, in effect, subsidizes the band's touring costs because the manager's commission is reduced if costs are higher. For this reason, the manager may resist throwing expensive after-show parties for the band while it is on the road. The manager, however, does not want to be overly vigilant in constraining the band. If a superstar band feels mistreated, it could easily find another manager. No one wants to be the person to tell Bono that a novel idea he has for a new stage design is too expensive. Several managers have told me that artists tend to be "capricious." The life of a rock and roll star comes with few guardrails.

One reason that ticket costs have been rising rapidly, as shown in Figure 6.1, is that production costs have risen rapidly. The rise in costs is mainly because staging and production for live entertainment have become more complex. Audiences have come to expect pyrotechnics, advanced videos, and stage risers. Even Paul McCartney provides such expensive extravagances in his shows.

Most of the costs incurred from putting on a performance are fixed costs, meaning that they do not rise with the number of fans in the audience. This is true for pyrotechnics, for example. As a result, given the typical 85/15 (or 90/10) split between artists and promoters, the last 10 percent of tickets sold, Cliff Burnstein told me, are pure gravy in terms of profit, as the fixed costs have already been covered.

The costs of concerts help explain why festivals have become so popular. Many of the fixed costs of a live event—including advertising, security, lighting, and setting up a stage—can be amortized over several performers in a festival. At a typical festival, the stage, for example, is used by multiple performers a day, for several days. By contrast, on tour the stage would require a couple of days to set up, be used for one show, then be disassembled, packed up, and transported to the next location.* A festival uses a stage more intensively, reducing costs per show.

My point is that controlling costs is an important economic

---

* As the 1977 Jackson Browne song "The Load-Out" goes, "Let the roadies take the stage / Pack it up and tear it down."

consideration for musicians. The idea that "you can't always get what you want" was an economics principle long before the former London School of Economics student Mick Jagger used it in a Rolling Stones song. The most effective managers look for ways to minimize expenses and negotiate lower costs without jeopardizing the quality of the art musicians produce. As an industry, the music business has to continually adapt and create new technology to avoid Baumol's disease.

Merch

Cliff Burnstein urged me to include a section in this book on merchandise, known in the trade as *merch*. He thought it so important that he arranged for me to meet with Q Prime's long-time merchandising man, Peter Lubin, for several hours in his midtown Manhattan offices.[38] Lubin is a man in his mid-sixties and, oddly enough, does not share Burnstein's enthusiasm for merchandise.

"I promise you I don't think I do anything interesting or that has mattered," Lubin was quick to volunteer. Lubin has been working with top musicians to sell merch since the mid-1970s. For a merchandising man, Peter Lubin undersells. His past clients have included Pink Floyd, The Who, David Bowie, Def Leppard, AC/DC, Billy Joel, Nirvana, the Backstreet Boys, Prince, Van Halen, and many other superstars. If Michael Jackson was the King of Pop, Peter Lubin is arguably the King of Merch; in fact, Michael Jackson was once his client. Lubin boasts of the number of times that he has been fired by famous musicians—sometimes twice by the same artist. Switching merch agents seems inherent to the business, given the short duration of merch contracts. And, he adds, artists can be capricious.

Lubin was full of economic insights. For example, not every superstar musician is a superstar of merch. Only a small number of superstars can move a lot of merchandise. As a result, merch amplifies superstar incomes for the biggest stars.[*] The challenge for Lubin is that merch is typically a small share of a superstar's total income, and it is a distraction from the artist's laser-like focus on creating innovative music. "Almost all of the acts that are big enough to make money in merch are *so* financially successful that, even though we're not an insignificant number, we are small compared with everything else they are doing," he explained. A merch superstar might make $1 million from merch sales over a couple of years, but he or she could make $20 million from touring, record sales, endorsements, and other activities.

Nonetheless, artists review and approve all of the artwork that goes into their T-shirts and other wares, and are typically vigilant about ensuring that merch products do not conflict with the band's carefully cultivated image. A band like AC/DC could review 250 pieces of art, from which it selects forty or more designs for shirts, hoodies, posters, and other products for a tour.

An artist's merch potential is measured in per capita sales. Elton John might sell $4 worth of merch per head at his concerts, while U2 might sell $15 to $20 per head, even though both have been arena headliners for decades. With few exceptions—such as Justin Bieber and One Direction—90 percent of musicians' merch is sold on tour, not through online or retail sales. It is, therefore, straightforward to calculate the amount of merchandise an artist is likely to move: once you have an estimate of merch sales per capita, you simply multiply that by the number of fans expected to attend the artist's concerts during the duration of the contract.

The artist typically receives a 70 percent split of gross revenue (net of sales tax), although, as with everything else in the music business, precise details are negotiable. Like tours and record contracts, artists receive an advance for signing a merch contract against future income. The advance is recoupable, however.

---

[*] Lubin noted that there are a small number of merch superstars who would not generally be considered superstars in the music world, such as Bring Me the Horizon or Korn. But these cases are few and far between.

Fans buy merch because they want souvenirs to memorialize the event. Artists use merch to create brand identity and loyalty, and as a source of income. The Rolling Stones' famous tongue and lips logo is an iconic image for the band's identity and for selling merch. Lubin said the demand for merch is all about "I was there." This is why T-shirts list all the cities and dates of a tour. Other items are designed specifically for one show or city, highlighting the venue, for example, to create a unique souvenir. Fans want to tell the world they were there, even as they document that they were there in Instagram and Twitter posts. To economists, this is an example of conspicuous consumption. The social aspect of merch strengthens bandwagon effects, which reinforce the superstar phenomenon.

Around forty merch items are typically available for sale at each show. This includes six staples—T-shirts, hoodies, hats, posters, programs, and mugs—which account for around 60 percent of total sales. The merchandiser will also ensure that a range of specialty items, such as lithographs or fashion clothing, is available so that fans can spend more money on merch if they so choose. It is a form of **price discrimination,** as fans with a greater willingness to pay can find items that might be more customized and appealing to them.

The quality of merch has improved over time. Lubin proudly points out that the products available on tour today are generally the best they have ever been in terms of both quality and variety.

Selling merchandise, however, is a "pull" rather than a "push" business. It is difficult or impossible to substantially increase an artist's merch sales. A great merchandising program cannot transform an average merch band into a superstar merch band. An example of a big success might be raising an artist's merch sales from $4 per head to $8 per head.

Unlike record contracts, which often seek to lock artists down for seven albums and future works (as I discuss in Chapter 7), merch contracts are of short duration. The typical merch contract lasts for an album cycle, roughly eighteen months to three years. Lubin calls it an "at once business." As a result, if an artist's career takes off, he or she will quickly be able to negotiate a more generous merch deal. Although there are not many competitors, merch margins are modest, around 10 percent of gross revenue. With tight margins and short contracts, merch companies cannot afford to carry many losers. As a result, they look for acts with steady demand or upside potential. Rock and roll bands had predictable, durable audiences. The move to pop acts, who often have more ephemeral success and fickle fans, creates more volatility for merch sellers.

There are big fixed costs associated with producing and delivering merch. "I have a store that is essentially open for two hours that moves from city to city," Lubin said, "and any dollar I don't get in a city, I never have an opportunity to get again." His economics work out only for major acts. For bands that are not arena headliners—in other words, most bands—it makes economic sense for them to produce and market their own merch. Often a tour manager or crew member takes responsibility for transporting and selling merch at shows for artists below the top echelon. Dan Ryan, who played bass for Le Loup for three years and is now principal product manager for Amazon's Alexa, told me that his band printed their own T-shirts to sell at their shows.[39] Merch income is not inconsequential for smaller bands, who often use the cash to pay for gas and meals to make it from one gig to the next.

The ideal merch client—which Lubin had in Def Leppard in 1982—is a band that is signed just before it takes off. In these cases, sales greatly exceed the amount forecasted. After Def Leppard released its *Pyromania* album in January 1983, for example, its tour expanded, and the scheduled ten theater shows in England were replaced by twenty-five arena shows, which were soon followed by a worldwide arena tour, greatly boosting merch sales. Lubin was also fortunate to be the merchandiser for Pink Floyd, Prince, and Michael Jackson "when they were having their turn as the biggest act in the world."

In the early days, merch was a cash business. Lubin regaled me with stories of flying back from concerts with hundreds of thousands of dollars, mostly in five-dollar bills, in his suitcase. Before a show, a star's manager once told Lubin backstage at the Tokyo Dome in Japan that he heard that there were bags of cash in his business. "I don't want you to get the wrong impression, I'm not asking you for a bag of money," the manager said. "But if I find out that there are bags of money and I didn't get one, I'd be really pissed."

The merch business has become much more turnkey. Venues provide concessionaires to sell merch during concerts. In a typical contract, the band pays a 25 to 30 percent commission on gross sales to the venue for the right to sell merch and for its services; the commission comes from the band's 70 percent share. This leaves the merch company 30 percent of gross sales (net of sales tax), which must cover the cost of designing and procuring merchandise, transporting goods, and policing bootleggers. To make the numbers work, Lubin aims to keep his cost of supplies below 10 percent of gross.

A typical T-shirt that sells for $40 at a show costs about $3.50 to $4 to manufacture (disregarding design and transportation costs). If sales tax is $3, then $37 in revenue is left to be divided up. The band's take (45 percent after venue commission) would be $16.65, and the venue's share would be $9.25. This leaves the merchandiser with $11.10 to pay for the product, transport it from show to show, and cover other costs. After expenses, the merchandiser is lucky to net $4 from the sale of the T-shirt.

With the ability to avoid paying band royalties and venue fees, bootleggers have a strong incentive to illegally sell unlicensed merch. This was a major problem at U.S. concerts until the mid-1980s, when a lawyer named Jules Zalon pioneered the practice of obtaining a court order to make John Doe seizures of illegal merchandise offered for sale within half a mile of the venue. Today, merchandisers and venues spend around 2 percent of gross revenue hiring off-duty police officers to prevent bootleggers from illegally selling unlicensed products. Bootlegging remains a serious problem for Internet sales, but most musicians earn most of their merch revenue from touring-related merchandise sales.

A new development in the merch market is pop-up stores. Some major artists have begun the practice of setting up a store in a city for a short period of time to sell their merch. Kanye West, for example, has been a pioneer in pop-up stores, working with Bravado, Universal Music Group's merchandising wing. Sometimes the novelty and sleekness of these shops enable them to become a flash hit.

Tour merchandising will always be a low-margin business, however. The potential for entry keeps margins low, and short-term contracts enable artists to capture the lion's share of the value of their brand. Lubin's biggest fear is a giant, deep-pocketed competitor coming in and disrupting the market. I also heard this fear expressed years ago from Ticketmaster's then CEO, Sean Moriarty, when eBay purchased StubHub and entered the ticket business. Moriarty feared that eBay could easily spend hundreds of millions of dollars in an unprofitable strategy that jeopardized Ticketmaster's viability. As Peter Lubin told me, "The only good time for us is when everyone thinks merchandise is a terrible business, and they don't want to make extravagant deals."

Despite the challenges, the future of the merch business seems bright. Disruptions in the record business that diminished royalties have made it an imperative for artists to tour to earn a living. This has elevated the role of merch in a band's revenue stream. In addition, over the last five years a growing number of retailers have been open to selling artists' merchandise in their stores and collaborating with artists. And the Internet allows artists to develop a direct relationship with their fans and sell products directly to them, without going through a gatekeeper. These developments have turned merchandise into a year-round business, even when acts are not touring, to the benefit of artists, merch companies, and fans. Peter Lubin concluded our interview by saying that despite his cynicism developed over forty years in the business, he has never been as excited about the future of merch.

Homeward Bound

"We're in an industry that prices its product worse than anybody else," Ticketmaster's chairman, Terry Barnes, observed in 2006.[40] The industry has come a long way since then, but there is still much room for improvement. Verified Fan, slow ticketing, dynamic pricing, and expanding supply (à la Garth mode) are some of the new strategies to improve the efficiency of ticket distribution. We should expect more innovation in the future, especially for the hottest stars and best seats.

While Garth Brooks labors to expand supply to satisfy demand at an affordable price, several artists—including Paul Simon, Elton John, Joan Baez, and Lynyrd Skynyrd—have recently announced their farewell tours, which is a way to limit supply and drive up demand.

Even after these rock icons retire, however, there will be plenty more first-class live entertainment to see. In his 2017 year-end business column, Barry Ritholtz wrote, "We are now in the golden age of, well, everything . . . but especially live music." He advised, "If you haven't been going out to regular live events, you don't know what you are missing."[41] One piece of advice from rockonomics research could save you some money: if you buy tickets on the secondary market, you can get the best deals by waiting until the latest possible moment to purchase your ticket. Prices tend to decline on the day of the show—after all, a ticket becomes worthless after the event is over. As long as you are not too risk averse, or if you have the option to see the show on another occasion, you can generally get the best deal if you wait to buy until just before showtime.

CHAPTER 7

Scams, Swindles, and the Music Business

As it turned out, the one thing about business is that it does have to be looked after.

—Paul McCartney

Sitting on the sofa in attorney John Eastman's office at Eastman & Eastman, located in a townhouse across the street from the Museum of Modern Art in Manhattan, it is hard not to feel in the presence of rock and roll history.[1] Eastman's first client in the music business was the soft-rock band Chicago. He also represents his brother-in-law Paul McCartney, Billy Joel, and Andrew Lloyd Webber. David Bowie was a client and friend before he died. John's younger sister, Linda, was married to Paul McCartney from 1969 until she died of breast cancer at the age of fifty-six in 1998. Despite the urban legend, the Eastman family has no connection to the Eastman Kodak company. In fact, John's father, Lee, changed his family name from Epstein to Eastman after graduating from Harvard Law School.

Back in 1968, shortly before Paul McCartney and Linda Eastman were married, McCartney asked his future father-in-law to help straighten out the Beatles' messy business arrangement with Apple Corps. Lee Eastman brought in his son to help, and the pair managed McCartney's career while the rest of the Beatles chose Allen Klein as their business manager after manager Brian

Epstein died of a drug overdose in August 1967. Their ensuing business and legal disputes were the last straw that broke up the Beatles in 1970.

John Eastman, who is nearing eighty, graduated from Stanford and earned his law degree at New York University. He told me he has never represented a record company. His two passions seem to be helping musicians gain control of their financial and creative lives (which means wrestling rights back from record companies or suing unscrupulous managers who took advantage of naive musicians) and pondering the origins of creativity in art and music.

I asked John why so many musicians have been swindled in one way or another by their managers or record labels. "The answer to your question, most politely, is cupidity and easy pickings," he said. John has had a front-row seat to an unconscionable amount of greed and avarice on the part of unscrupulous managers and soulless companies. "For each of my rock and roll clients," he explained, "I began with a lawsuit successfully removing his manager for cause and then over time restructured his affairs largely around his owning his copyrights and all that flowed from his creative output." This strategy rescued Billy Joel from financial ruin. And John and Lee Eastman managed Paul McCartney's music career so well that McCartney earned more money during his years with Wings than he did with the Beatles.

Are musicians easy prey for financial hucksters because they are capricious and not attentive to the business side of the music business? Yes, he answered, but he quickly added that it doesn't have to be that way. "I've never let a client do a deal when they couldn't sit where you're sitting right now," he said emphatically, "and with a pen and pad outline the deal on one page. And I would say, 'If you don't understand this, we're not doing it. Or we're sitting here until you do understand it.' They're smart if you just talk to them like people, for godsakes."

This seems like good advice for musicians and non-musicians alike. Business arrangements can be unfavorable to musicians because they have little bargaining power, due to fundamental supply-and-demand factors, or because the artists are hoodwinked by unscrupulous business partners. Recognizing the difference and understanding how to avoid being hoodwinked are the subjects of this chapter.

Contract Theory

My brother-in-law Jon Bick, who sometimes serves as my lawyer, once explained to me that a contract codifies in writing the understanding between the parties to an agreement. A contract is legally binding, so signing a contract is not to be taken lightly.

A well-established branch of economics called contract theory studies how parties design contractual agreements to pursue their various goals in the face of overlapping and conflicting interests, uncertain outcomes, and imperfect information. A contract works best when the parties' interests are aligned. Often, however, the parties' interests conflict, at least in part. For example, a record company makes more profit if it takes a liberal view toward counting expenses, which are deducted from an artist's royalty payments, while the artist has the opposite incentive.

Not all contingencies can be anticipated in a contract. For example, what happens when the music delivery format unexpectedly changes from vinyl albums to digital streaming and the contract does not specify a royalty rate for streaming revenue? These types of unexpected contingencies, which render contracts incomplete, can lead to lawsuits, although bad faith and distrust may be more common root causes of lawsuits.

If the parties expect to have a continuing relationship from which both would benefit, then they have an incentive to treat each other in good faith and take actions that are in each other's interest, even in the presence of unanticipated contingencies and incomplete information.

Another common concern is that one party—usually the record company—has more information than the other party. For example, contracts now typically require the record company to distribute a specified percentage of revenue from song streams and album sales to the artist. As the economist Richard Caves has noted, "From the artist's viewpoint, a problem of moral hazard arises because the label keeps the books that determine the earnings remitted to the artist."[2]

Examples of labels allegedly underreporting sales, and thus underpaying royalties to artists, are legion, as are lawsuits arising out of such allegations. The Beatles were locked in lawsuits over insufficient payment of royalties with EMI and its U.S. subsidiary Capitol Records for years. The potential for moral hazard in accounting practices leads to an obvious strategy that can be summarized as "Trust but verify." Artists benefit from having the ability to have their representatives audit their label's books. Allen Klein launched his career by uncovering multiple forms of underpayment for his musician clients. Today, I am told, there is much less financial chicanery on the part of record companies.

Record Contracts

Record contracts, like everything else in the music business, are negotiable and thus vary across labels and musicians. The typical record contract signed by a new artist with a major record label, such as Universal or Sony, lasts for four or five albums, but it could last for as long as seven albums. The contract does not guarantee that a second album will be produced; instead, the record company has the option of producing a second album. In fact, the first album may not be produced either. The commitment is to produce the first album if it meets "commercially satisfactory" standards, which means that the record company thinks it will sell.[3] Probably half or fewer of the artists who sign recording contracts do not produce a second album, and many do not even produce a first album.

In exchange for exclusive rights to the recordings made by the artist, the record company agrees to pay the artist a royalty of around 13 to 14 percent of revenue collected from streaming, licensing, and selling the artist's recordings.[*] Rates can be as high as 20 percent for established stars. The artist transfers the rights to the recordings (excluding the composition rights) to the company in perpetuity, although established artists can limit the duration of the transfer of ownership rights to a relatively short period of time. The company typically provides the artist an advance against future royalties and agrees to allocate a certain amount of money for promoting the artist's music. The artist's advance and cost of producing the recording are deducted from future royalties. The artist, however, does not need to repay the label if the stream of royalties does not exceed the sum of the advance and expenses. That is, expenses and the advance are recoupable but not refundable.

With his client Chicago, John Eastman pioneered a strategy of letting artists retain the rights to their music and leasing the rights to the record company for a period of time. This approach was also used by the Rolling Stones (although their co-manager Andrew Oldham cleverly kept many of the rights for himself) and by Phil Spector. But relatively few musicians command sufficient bargaining power to be able to negotiate such an arrangement.

An entertainment lawyer shared with me, only partly in jest, a saying in his field: "If an artist receives a royalty payment, the lawyer didn't do his job well."

---

[*] This is an oversimplification: the royalty rate can vary across distribution modes and across countries, the rate often escalates as more recordings are sold, and more popular artists can negotiate higher royalty rates. Note also that the artist's net royalty rate can be lower if producers receive a share of royalties out of the artist's share.

John Eastman had a different view. "The advance in a record contract is just expensive banking," he told me.

These seemingly opposing views are easily reconciled: a superstar band like the Beatles or Rolling Stones is better off with a small advance and a more generous royalty rate. Most artists who sign a record contract with a major label, however, will not cover their advance and expenses, and therefore never collect a dime in royalties. They are better off with a larger advance and lower royalty rate.

Record labels are increasingly trying to expand their net over artists' sources of income. For example, a standard contract offered to new recording artists by a major label often retains a slice of touring income, merchandise sales, and even fan club rights for the record company, in what's called a "collateral entertainment agreement." A handful of superstars have signed 360-degree contracts for recording and touring, sometimes with promoters instead of labels. Madonna, for example, signed a ten-year, 360-degree deal for $120 million with Live Nation in 2007.[4] These arrangements, which remain the exception rather than the rule, can make economic sense given complementarities among activities—promoting recordings also boosts concert and merchandise sales. But a real concern is that new artists can be exploited by such deals, since they have little bargaining power and may be overly eager to sign with a major music company. Given that most artists make most of their income from live performances, any musician should be wary about signing over rights to income from live performances without a full understanding of the consequences.[5]

Contracts in Practice

In an important respect, the business model for the three major record labels (Universal, Sony, and Warner) is akin to oil prospecting or venture capital businesses: a lot of investments do not pay off, so the occasional winner must generate a large enough profit to compensate for the losses from the dry holes. Only one or two of every ten records produced by a major label ends up covering its advance and expenses.[6] Thus, recording artists face long odds of ever receiving royalties. For the handful of artists who become superstars, it seems like an unfair arrangement, and they can harbor resentment toward their label. But this business model allows the labels to take chances on new artists in the first place, and to spend substantial sums of money promoting and producing their work.

Unsuccessful artists often complain about their record label as well. A top entertainment lawyer told me that musicians frequently complain that their label failed to vigorously promote their work. One record executive, he told me, responded by saying, "We managed to get your record on the air and in all of the stores. What else would you like us to do? We can't force people to buy your records."

While corruption and deception have been significant problems in the music industry, the main cause of musicians' discontentment with record labels probably stems from the *ex post* redistributive nature of the business model and the randomness of success, rather than bad faith. Even well-educated, business-savvy musicians who hire experienced legal advisers face long odds of success and unfavorable terms from record contracts, with the record label receiving most of the revenue from sales and streaming.

The business model is different for most independent labels. There are thousands of independent labels that produce and sell music created by tens of thousands of musicians. But as a group, the independents account for only about one-third of all revenue generated from recorded music.[7] Small independent labels cannot afford to have too many artists who fail to cover their costs. As a result, they tend to give artists smaller advances and pay higher royalty rates, and they often invest less in promotion. However, artists who strike it big with an independent label stand to make a lot of money because of the higher royalty rate.

A recent example of a huge indie success story is the folk band the Lumineers. The Denver-based trio signed a one-record deal with Nashville's Dualtone Records in 2011. With only five employees, Dualtone aimed for album sales of around 30,000 and offered a generous split of revenue. Lumineers frontman Wesley Schultz said that the band chose Dualtone because it offered "the best, most fair deal."[8] The Lumineers' self-titled debut album, released in 2012, sold 2.4 million copies worldwide and spent forty-three weeks on the *Billboard* 200 chart. The group was nominated for two Grammy Awards in 2013 and appeared on *Saturday Night Live*. Although details are not public, their royalties likely ran to several million dollars.

After the remarkable success of their first album, the Lumineers could have signed with a major label for a large advance, or with an independent label for a multi-album deal. Instead, they opted to re-sign with little Dualtone for another one-album deal. Their second studio album, *Cleopatra*, was released in 2016 and debuted at number one on the *Billboard* chart. Their drummer, Jeremiah Fraites, said, "We'd rather bet on ourselves and not start on some weird footing where we owe someone money."[9] That bet paid off handsomely.

Competition

Once a recording artist breaks through to become a superstar, there is a strong incentive to renegotiate the terms of the contract. But recording artists are usually locked into multi-album deals lasting several years, so they have to wait until the contract expires to seek a better deal. Few artists have the luxury of being able to negotiate the terms of their contract after each album, like the Lumineers.

In his memoir, Bruce Springsteen describes the anguish he felt renegotiating his contract with his producer, Mike Appel, in 1975, after the success of the album *Born to Run*. Springsteen's main objective was to receive what he thought was a fairer share of the money earned from the records he had already produced under his first contract over the previous five years. Appel held out a new deal as the price for retroactively redressing the terms of the earlier agreement. Springsteen concluded, "Five more years of my life against a fair shake of the five previous years of work was not an equation I'd picked up the guitar, built a life and forged a future, no matter how insignificant, to make."[10] Springsteen and Appel parted ways, and they reached an out-of-court settlement in 1977.

In economics jargon, the terms of the first contract are a sunk cost, which should have no bearing on future decision-making. Sunk costs are like water under the bridge—there is nothing you can do about them because the decisions were already made and the agreements signed. But sunk costs often matter more to individuals than economists like to acknowledge, because people care about being treated fairly. Psychologically, we often treat sunk costs as recurring costs that continually gnaw at us. As a consequence, we like to fix the past before moving forward.

But contracts are hard to break or amend. For this reason, John Eastman said he counsels musicians that there is "one term in the contract that you have to be concerned about—the term of the contract." Managers often push artists to be shortsighted and take a big advance in exchange for a longer term, he said, in part because the manager gets a cut of the advance.

Occasionally artists do find grounds to invalidate or renegotiate a contract. In the heyday of rock and roll in the 1960s, Allen Klein, who managed Sam Cooke, the Rolling Stones, the Beatles, and many others, was legendary for bullying labels to renegotiate unfavorable contracts.

More recently, after the success of his 2017 hit single "Gucci Gang," the Miami rapper Gazzy Garcia, whose professional name is Lil Pump, was able to void his contract with Warner Brothers Records in early 2018 because he was underage (only sixteen) when he signed the deal in June 2017.[11] A bidding war then ensued for the rapper among the three major labels and several independent labels, including DJ Khaled's We the Best Music Group. Taking advantage of his elevated status, Lil Pump re-signed with Warner for a much higher advance, said to be $8 million. This is an enormous improvement over the $350,000 advance he reportedly received in his initial contract, and is indicative of the kind of payment that artists face under their first record contract (although the duration and other terms of the contract may have changed as well).[12]*

The improved financial situation of record labels, due largely to the growth of subscription streaming services, has intensified competition for potential superstars. The bidding war for new talent has also been fueled by the availability of public information from YouTube and other streaming services. Multiple labels can spot unsigned artists whose music is going viral. This is especially the case for hip-hop stars, whose music is disproportionately popular on streaming services.

In the view of Tom Corson, chairman of Warner Brothers, "Anything that shows promise is being snatched up. We're definitely in the middle of a very competitive and expensive moment here with hip-hop acts."[13] *Billboard* reported that in early 2018 Juice WRLD was signed by Interscope for $3 million, SahBabii was signed by Warner Brothers for about $2 million, and 03 Greedo was signed by Alamo/Interscope for $1.7 million. In addition, Lil Xan (Columbia), City Morgue duo ZillaKami and SosMula (Republic), and Shoreline Mafia (Atlantic) were all reportedly signed to seven-figure deals. Although exactly what these figures include (advance, recording costs, promotional spending, etc.) is unclear—and one should always be a tad skeptical given the penchant of managers, lawyers, and publicists to exaggerate their clients' deals—the improved economic position

---

* Using the fact that a musician was underage when a contract was signed is not a new negotiating tactic. The Rolling Stones were able to reach a settlement with their first co-manager, Eric Eastman, in part because they were underage when they signed and thus the contract was of questionable legal validity.

of record labels, after a decade of distress, has undoubtedly intensified competition.

I asked Tom Corson whether the availability of statistical information on new artists from social media and streaming services—along with efforts by record labels to apply *Moneyball* techniques to predict future stars—has improved the odds of success (recall that historically only one or two of every ten artists signed cover their costs). On reflection, he said that perhaps the odds have increased to 2.5 in 10.[14] But then he pointed out that costs were rising given the bidding war. Thus, the fundamental business model—where winners are needed to compensate for losers, and success is difficult to predict—will likely continue to prevail. Many of today's signings will *ex post* turn out to look like folly.

Contracts Among Band Members

An often overlooked and sometimes unwritten contract involves relationships and obligations among band members. For example, the Beatles had a legal agreement to split all income evenly, *including* income that each of the four earned individually, outside of the Beatles.[15] After the band broke up, a divisive lawsuit by Paul McCartney was initiated to dissolve the legal partnership among the band members, as John, George, and Ringo had outvoted Paul. The contract could have spelled out terms once the band broke up, for continuing to split income earned individually after the breakup would have created a severe free rider problem. Why would Paul McCartney undertake the effort and trouble of touring if three-quarters of his earnings would go to John, George, and Ringo? And the same question applied to each of the others.

Jason Van Dyke, who performed with the two founding members of the Lumineers before they moved from New Jersey to Denver in 2009, has said, "I know one of the things that we didn't really do a good job of is writing up an agreement and coming up with that in a really clear manner."[16] Once the band struck it big with "Ho Hey," Van Dyke sued the Lumineers in 2014 for denying him equal partnership, copyright, and co-authorship of songs. The lawsuit eventually resulted in a confidential settlement.

Although his band Le Loup was not nearly as commercially successful as the Lumineers, Dan Ryan similarly said that a clear contract among band members would have been helpful. Some members did not participate in all of the band's songs.[17] Who is eligible for royalties if a song is sold for a television commercial—the whole group, or just those who performed the music? Not all contingencies can be anticipated, but relationships among the parties are smoother if their rights and obligations are transparent, and if the contract covers as many contingencies as possible.

Many bands, such as the Rolling Stones, Beatles, Metallica, and Destiny's Child, are formed when the members are just teenagers. In most contexts we would think it unusual if a person acquired business partners in youth and kept them for life. But that is the case for many bands. And because creating and understanding a contract is not something one would normally expect of teenagers, it's not surprising that business relations among band members are often fraught. In addition, relations among band members can become tense over decades, as teenage friends grow apart.

Financial Chicanery

Donald Passman, one of the top entertainment lawyers in the business, advises musicians, "No one ever takes as good care of your business as you do."[18]

Tom Petty's struggle with his record label illustrates the importance of understanding the music business and paying close attention to the details. Tom Petty and the Heartbreakers had already released two gold albums with Shelter Records, and they were working on a third (with Jimmy Iovine, brought in to co-produce) in 1978, when Shelter's parent company, ABC Records, sold the label to MCA. In Petty's words:

> I felt like they just sold us like we were groceries or frozen pork or something. We had a clause that said if our contract is sold to anyone else, you have to have our consent. So we went to them and said, "You're going to have to let us go." And we were pretty much told, "You just have to forget about that, and that we weren't in any financial position to fight a large corporation." This made me really mad.[19]

But Tom Petty did not back down. A key issue in the ensuing legal dispute involved the long-term agreement with Skyhill Music for the publishing rights to Petty's songs. Petty argued that he had been coerced into signing away the rights to his songs because he was told he would not be signed to a record deal otherwise. Thinking that publishing rights referred to sheet-music songbooks, Petty signed over the rights for a meager $10,000 advance. "I had no idea I'd never make money if I did that," he said in 1980.[20] Reflecting back years later, he said, "So my songs had really been taken away from me when I didn't even know what publishing was."

To pay for their legal bills, Tom Petty and the Heartbreakers went on what they called a "Lawsuit Tour." After Petty filed for bankruptcy protection, which could enable him to abrogate contractual obligations, the parties eventually reached a settlement. As part of the settlement, Tom Petty and the Heartbreakers worked with Backstreet Records, an artist-friendly label in the MCA family, and received a $3 million guarantee. And the publishing rights to Petty's songs were returned to him.

The music business has had more than its share of unethical people who take advantage of musicians.

In a useful lesson on financial literacy, Billy Joel has said that he stayed away from the business side of his career because he was sensitive to the criticism that he "was a hitmaker-meister just grinding it out for the money." But he recognizes that "I shoulda looked out for the money."[21] The Piano Man's recommendation to budding musicians is to take an accounting course—and "it doesn't hurt to know a little law, either."

Evidently a forgiving soul, Billy Joel subsequently reconciled with his former brother-in-law to the point of giving him free tickets to a show in Florida, an act that Christie Brinkley, his second ex-wife, called "mind boggling."[22]

The mellifluous pop singer Sting, a former English teacher, is another superstar who would have done well to heed Donald Passman's advice to closely tend to his business dealings. Sting's financial adviser for fifteen years, Keith Moore, reportedly embezzled nearly $10 million from him in the 1980s and early 1990s. Moore apparently transferred funds from Sting's bank account without the star's knowledge or consent and made a series of investments, including a plan to produce an ecologically friendly gearbox and create a chain of Indian restaurants in Australia.[23]

In March 1970, Lenny Hart, the original money manager of the Grateful Dead and father of one of the band's percussionists, Mickey Hart, disappeared—along with the group's money, approximately $155,000. After being found in San Diego a year later, Hart was convicted of embezzlement. The band denounced their former manager in their 1972 song "He's Gone," with the grisly line "steal your face right off your head."

It's not just superstars who are easy prey for financial scams, unknown musicians can be too. The BBC ran an exposé in 2018 on a London-based firm called Band Management Universal (BMU), which promised musicians studio sessions, gigs, help securing a record contract, and other enticements, for a fee of up to £4,000. Their services were rarely delivered, however. Dutch singer Jasper Roelofsen, for example, said a representative of BMU promised him that his band Counting Wolves would have a chance to work with well-known artists. The band shelled out £3,840, but the opportunity never materialized. "We could have used that money to do something useful for our careers, but instead we burned it," Roelofsen said.[24] The BBC interviewed more than twenty artists who complained about BMU's practices. Horace Trubridge, head of the Musicians' Union, described BMU as "the worst example of music fraud he had seen in the past 20 years."

Managing Musicians

Choosing the right manager is a tricky business for musicians. A band's manager can easily earn as much money as an individual band member. But good managers are well worth their cost. Some managers, such as Cliff Burnstein and Peter Mensch, are widely respected for their professionalism—they understand the business and can steer their clients toward financial sustainability and a long career. Others are "hometown managers"—they started with the band in the early days and are learning the business as they go, if they're lucky. Paul McCartney once lamented that the Beatles' first manager, Brian Epstein, "looked to his dad for business advice, and his dad knew how to run a furniture store in Liverpool."[25]

Elvis Presley went through a couple of hometown managers before he connected with Colonel Tom Parker, who was a former carnival barker and undocumented immigrant to the United States.[26] But Parker understood the music business and was able to raise Elvis's career to a much higher level and negotiate favorable record and merch deals. One of Parker's insights was to have Elvis appear as a guest on Frank Sinatra's television special on ABC, in his first televised appearance after returning from military service in 1960. The strategy worked and enabled Elvis to cross over to an older audience. Parker's commission rate allegedly exceeded 50 percent of Elvis's income. But in recognition of Parker's role, Elvis once said, "I don't think I'd have ever been very big if it wasn't for him. He's a very smart man."[27]

Upon achieving national or international acclaim, some superstars decide to save money by managing their own career, or by bringing management in-house. Kanye West broke with his longtime manager Izvor Zivkovic, and later with Scooter Braun, to try this strategy. Bruno Mars, Beyoncé, and Taylor Swift are pursuing similar strategies.[28] Time will tell whether they will work. But if history is any guide, it is easy for a musician to be taken advantage of, with or without a manager.

Within Your Means

Many musicians get into financial trouble because they do not live within their means or do not plan for the future. Will Smith, who performed hip-hop in the group DJ Jazzy Jeff & the Fresh Prince before being cast in *The Fresh Prince of Bel Air*, is a textbook example. The duo won the first Grammy Award given out for Best Rap Performance for their hit "Parents Just Don't Understand" in 1989. Their first album went triple platinum. Thinking that the good times would continue, Smith spent extravagantly. His second album, however, was a flop. Smith jokes that it went "double plastic." He neglected to pay his income taxes, and the Internal Revenue Service repossessed Smith's car and motorcycle, assessed him with a $2.8 million tax debt, and garnished his income. "Being famous and broke," Smith recalled, "is a s****y combination, because you're still famous and people recognize you, but they recognize you while you're sitting on the bus."[29]

On the verge of bankruptcy, Smith caught a break. A chance meeting led to an impromptu audition at Quincy Jones's mansion in Bel Air, and the rest is history, as Smith went on to become one of Hollywood's biggest stars.

Musicians are not so different from many Americans when

it comes to making financial decisions, but the unpredictable nature of their income, the high rate of self-employment, and the laser-like focus on their art often makes their financial situation more perilous. Because musicians typically earn their income as independent contractors, they do not have an employer who withholds income from their pay for taxes. Like Will Smith, many musicians fail to set aside income for tax purposes, and run into trouble with the IRS.

Many musicians have also been aggressive in trying to avoid tax payments. The pop singer Shakira, for example, came under investigation for possible tax evasion in Spain.[30] And some musicians have gotten into trouble because their business manager or tax adviser set up a scheme to evade taxes—for example, by booking income through a third party in a tax haven—that caused the musicians to lose control of their income.

But it is excessive spending—leaving too little to live on after their career is over and neglecting to provide for children's college tuition and other needs—that is a problem for many musicians, and millions of Americans. Earning a lot of money is not a foolproof barrier against financial insolvency and bankruptcy.

A study of National Football League players drafted from 1996 to 2003 found that 16 percent had filed for bankruptcy within twelve years of retiring.[31] The median player earned $3.2 million (in 2000 dollars) over his career, and the median career lasted six years. Moreover, players who were better-paid or had a longer career were not less likely to fall into bankruptcy. This suggests that spending beyond their means is the problem, not inadequate income.

The life cycle model in economics presumes that people will save when their incomes are the highest, putting aside money for periods when income is low and for retirement. But as economists have documented, many people have a tendency to overspend out of their current income, either because self-control problems cause them to make impulse purchases or because they excessively discount the consequences of their actions for their future financial health, a phenomenon economists call *hyperbolic discounting*. Another explanation was frequently mentioned by managers who worked with superstar musicians: many failed to appreciate that their stratospheric earnings could turn out to be ephemeral. Will Smith, for example, seemed genuinely surprised that his second album bombed and his income failed to keep up with his spending habits.

To help musicians take charge of their financial lives, career coach Astrid Baumgardner gives them seven sensible rules to follow.[32] First, "articulate your challenges," including spending too much money and overcharging credit cards. Second, "gain basic financial literacy" so you will understand how to handle your finances throughout your life. Third, "think expansively about revenue streams," as musicians often piece together a living through gigs, teaching, publishing, and other sources of income. Fourth, "budget wisely": review your income and expenses to ensure that you are living within your means, being paid what you're owed, and not being overcharged. Fifth, "avoid debt," including credit cards and other sources of debt with high interest rates. Sixth, "save now," as income will fluctuate; you will be grateful for those savings when you hit a rough patch or retire. Seventh, put money aside for taxes that you will owe Uncle Sam, and record your expenses so you can deduct them from your income for tax purposes.

Brand-New Day

At one level, all of these rules boil down to understanding your costs, planning for the future, and living within your means. Excessive costs are deadly for businesses and personal finance. Artists who spend a fraction of their time monitoring where their money is going to and coming from will be more financially secure and able to pursue their passion throughout their lives, whether they are journeymen musicians or arena headliners.

CHAPTER 8

Streaming Is Changing Everything

Technology always wins. But what if you can make a better product than piracy?

—Daniel Ek, co-founder and CEO of Spotify

*T*he year Napster was launched in 1999 also marked the peak year for recorded music revenue. Revenue from recorded music fell by more than half from 1999 to 2015, from $14.6 billion to $6.7 billion in the United States, even before adjusting for inflation.* The reason for the decline? The switch to digital music enabled piracy and illegal file sharing to explode. It is only with the advent of streaming that there has been a rebound. From 2015 to 2017, revenue increased by $2 billion, erasing the last ten years of declines and providing a much-needed boost to the music industry.[1]

A mind-boggling total of one trillion songs were legally streamed in the United States in 2017, and that figure could double by 2019.[2] The advent of streaming services has changed the economics of the music business. Music streaming services provided on platforms such as Spotify, Amazon, Apple Music, Deezer, QQ, Tidal, Google Play Music, Internet radio, and YouTube are rapidly transforming music from a durable-goods/ownership

---

* In inflation-adjusted dollars, revenue from recorded music fell by 68 percent from the peak in 1999 to the trough in 2015.

market to a service/leasing market. Streaming is expanding the amount of time people spend listening to music, and helping reduce music piracy around the world by providing a more convenient service for consumers at an affordable price. Daniel Ek, who co-founded Spotify in 2006, correctly predicted that if he built a better, more convenient service, consumers would be willing to pay for music.

The music industry has been upended by new technology about once every decade. Faster-playing 78s gave way to long-playing (LP) albums and 45s in the 1950s and 1960s; cassettes and eight-track tapes proliferated in the 1970s, and those gave way to the Walkman in the 1980s, followed by CDs. MP3 players and digital downloads emerged in the 1990s, and the iPod in the 2000s. Today streaming is surging. You can mark the rate of technological progress by the old devices that you discard, or that pile up in a drawer or a closet, never to be used again. We are likely in the early days of the streaming revolution, and the music distribution business is sure to morph again in the future. Nonetheless, the current state of music streaming provides a clear lesson on how economics is tied to technology, and how economic incentives and technology shape our culture.

Mapping Streaming

As recently as 2008, two-thirds of the revenue from recorded music came from the sale of physical products (mainly CDs), and 30 percent came from digital downloads (mainly tracks sold through the Apple iTunes store).[3] Today, streaming accounts for two-thirds of recorded music revenue, and physical products and digital downloads each account for about 15 percent. Vinyl records survive mainly as novelty items, although demand is growing again among aficionados. The main driver of demand propping up CD sales is the stock of old cars still on the road. Older vehicles have CD players in their dashboards.[4] Once these aging vehicles are phased out, however, CDs could well go the way of eight-track tapes.* "I definitely believe the next decade is going to be streaming plus vinyl—streaming in the car and kitchen, vinyl in the living room and the den," Jack White, singer and founder of Third Man Records, recently told *Rolling Stone.* "Those will be the two formats."[5]

Given that vinyl is expensive and much less portable than streaming, I suspect it will remain popular only among a relatively small set of enthusiasts. Streaming is the present and future distribution mode for music. And streaming is changing everything in music.

Streaming comes in a variety of forms. One important distinction concerns interactive versus non-interactive services. With interactive services, consumers can choose which artists, albums, or songs to play. In non-interactive services, music is pre-programmed, similar to a radio broadcast. Another important distinction concerns ad-supported streaming services, where the listener pays nothing but the content is occasionally interrupted by advertisements, and subscription-based models, where the listener pays a monthly fee for ad-free content. Some platforms, such as Spotify and Pandora, provide both ad-supported and subscription plans.

As far as artists and record labels are concerned, paid subscribers offer a better deal for them. Royalty payments per song are greater for music streamed via subscriber services than in free ad-supported services, as subscription revenue greatly exceeds ad revenue.

Paid subscriptions have grown exponentially in the United States in recent years. It is growth in paid subscriptions that is driving the increase in recorded music revenue. From 2013 to 2017, the number of paid subscriptions increased almost sixfold, from 6.3 million to 35.3 million.[6] Revenue received by artists

---

* One exception to this prediction is Japan, where CDs are still king. See Chapter 10.

and record labels from paid subscription services increased at an even faster rate, rising from $0.6 billion in 2013 to $4.0 billion in 2017. Revenue from ad subscriptions grew as well, but at a slower pace and from a lower level, rising from $0.22 billion in 2013 to $0.66 billion in 2017.

Several large streaming platforms are engaged in fierce competition for listeners and subscribers. Spotify and Apple Music both had more than 20 million paid subscribers in the United States as of mid-2018, and Amazon is not far behind.[7] Amazon's unlimited service doubled its subscribers in the last six months of 2017, according to CEO Jeff Bezos, and is available in forty countries. Worldwide, Spotify has 157 million active users and 71 million paying subscribers. Apple has an estimated 45 million paying subscribers worldwide; it does not offer a free ad-supported service. Pandora has 75 million active monthly users but only 5.5 million paying subscribers. Sirius XM Radio has upward of 33 million paying subscribers in North America. Chinese Internet giant Tencent's streaming platforms reach the most ears worldwide, with more than 800 million monthly listeners who are overwhelmingly using their free ad-supported service.

Today there is a great deal of optimism about the future of the music industry, because streaming is not close to reaching its saturation point. If one uses cellphone penetration or the adoption of subscription video services such as Netflix as a guide, the number of music streaming customers could easily experience double-digit annual growth rates in coming decades. William Morris's Marc Geiger has predicted that the number of worldwide paid subscribers will grow from around 100 million today to 1 billion over the next fifteen years.[8] And he foresees an even larger number of ad-based listeners.

The Muddy Waters of the Streaming Business

Streaming creates a new and different type of product that is not directly comparable to physical album sales or digital downloads. Physical records, such as CDs, are durable goods, which individuals purchase and own; they can listen to the songs recorded on those CDs an unlimited number of times in the future. Streaming uses the output of the recording industry, recorded masters, to create a service: a vast catalog of audio streams that consumers can access whenever they want, wherever they want, as long as they pay the monthly fee required for the service (or endure ads) and have a device that can stream music. The service entails playlists, curated recommendations, on-demand song, album, and artist choices, and other features. Although from the listener's perspective streaming has something in common with the old durable-goods model, it is quite different, and attempts to shoehorn streaming metrics into album sales have been ad hoc at best.

Streaming is like leasing rather than buying a car. People who lease a car tend to drive it more and take less care of it than if they owned the car, because they are less concerned about the wear and tear on a leased car. Because a streaming subscription puts the entire music catalog at the listener's disposal, streaming is equivalent to having a whole fleet of cars— sports cars, station wagons, SUVs, trucks, and so on—at your disposal, whereas owning a CD gives you access to only one particular car.

Because it is a new product in a less-than-transparent industry, there is a lot of confusion concerning the business model underlying streaming. Streaming services such as Spotify typically pay 65 percent to 70 percent of their revenue in royalties to music rights holders (record labels, artists, publishers, and songwriters).[9] Payout rates are confidential and are negotiated between record labels and streaming platforms. The calculation of the exact amount paid by streaming services is more complicated in practice, but assuming a fixed 65 percent to 70 percent ratio is a reasonable approximation.[10] After the payout ratio is set, royalty payments are apportioned to song rights holders according to their share of streams on the service.

To take a hypothetical example, suppose a streaming platform has 100 billion songs streamed in a year, collects $600 million in revenue from paying subscribers, and pays two-thirds of its revenue ($400 million) to rights holders. If a hit song accounts for 100 million streams on this service (which equals 0.1 percent of total streams), the payout to the rights holders of that song will be 0.1 percent × $400 million = $400,000. If an on-demand audio streaming service such as Spotify has more paying customers, and therefore more revenue, it will pay out more money to rights holders. Revenue collected from advertisers is also apportioned to rights holders according to their share of streams.

This analysis oversimplifies the revenue issues, however. In practice, more is negotiated between the streaming platforms and record labels than just the payout rate. A confidential and murky feature of the streaming business is that record labels sometimes implicitly compensate streaming platforms to undertake campaigns to promote their artists. Promotional campaigns are sometimes obvious. For example, Spotify pushed Drake's hit album *Scorpion* so pervasively that many fans complained on social media. *Scorpion* was featured in multiple Spotify playlists, and Drake's picture was displayed on playlists that were unrelated to his music, such as "Best of British," "Massive Dance Hits," and "Happy Pop Hits." Apple Music also heavily promoted the album, creating a website where users could create their own Drake album cover art and prepping Siri with answers about Drake. This effort was highly successful: *Scorpion* broke Spotify's one-week U.S. streaming record in its first three days, and Apple's single-day streaming record.[11] And *Scorpion* occupied the number-one slot on the *Billboard* Top 200 chart longer than any other album in 2018.

A less well-known practice is that labels and platforms can also tie promotional efforts for new artists to their deals with streaming services. And Spotify has experimented with paid sponsored songs on its ad-supported service.[12] These marketing efforts raise questions of whether negotiated promotional tie-ins cross a line into payola, the now-illegal practice of record labels paying radio stations to play their artists' music.

Streaming services compete with one another on a number of dimensions. Although the major platforms all have a similar catalog of music available for premium subscribers, they design different playlists and have different features, such as voice interaction. Unlike broadcast radio, streaming services collect voluminous information on the history of individual listeners' music choices and use this information to make personalized listening recommendations. And the free-form nature of voice-interactive services enables Amazon Echo Dot and Google Home to collect different types of information (e.g., users' interest in dinner music) than the more regimented screen-based streaming services; they can use this information to create customized playlists and recommendations for users. Furthermore, streaming services invest in metadata to code different features of songs, to better match music selections with listeners' preferences.

One aspect of such personalized service is that information becomes an asset for streaming services. This asset creates "individual-specific match capital," in that a streaming service is able to provide a more customized service for its clients than a rival streaming service could without that listener's history. The better that platforms become at delivering personalized services, the less likely subscribers will be to move to another platform, and the more scope streaming services will have to raise prices for long-standing customers.

Some streaming platforms provide complementary services and have created complementary products from their activities. For example, Spotify offers recording artists a dashboard of data on their streaming performance, which they can use to draw insights about their fans, target audiences, and select touring locations. Apple provides a similar service, and Amazon has promised to follow suit. And Spotify together with Songkick provides information about concerts based on listeners' interests. Some services also have links to merchandise for sale.

Streaming platforms gain many advantages from scale. They are in a stronger position to bargain with labels if they are larger, and they can provide better service to listeners and artists if they have data on a larger number of users' preferences. And even though the platforms pay a more or less constant share of revenue in royalties, some costs are fixed (e.g., developing a web platform and recommendation algorithm) and therefore do not rise as more customers are added. As a result, there is intense competition among the various streaming services to grow and expand to new regions of the world, such as India and Latin America. Just as scale and uniqueness create superstars in music, conditions are ripe for a handful of streaming companies to dominate the music market in the future.

A final aspect of the business model worth noting is that streaming services are beginning to price-discriminate to maximize revenue and increase their number of users. Although the most common subscription price is $9.99 a month, prices vary depending on class of service and number of devices or family membership. Amazon currently offers its Prime members a limited catalog (two million songs) for free and an unlimited catalog for $7.99 a month ($3.99 a month to use the service specifically on one Echo Dot device), and a family plan for $14.99 a month where the unlimited category can be streamed by up to six family members. Spotify has a free on-demand service with ad interruptions and a premium individual and family subscription plan without ads. Apple Music does not offer a free service but has an individual plan for $9.99 a month and a family plan for $15 a month for up to six family members. YouTube, which is overwhelmingly an ad-supported platform, recently started to offer ad-free music for $11.99 a month and a family plan for $17.99 a month.[13] Many platforms offer lower prices to students. The goal of these pricing strategies is to charge a higher price to consumers who are less price sensitive, in order to increase revenue and increase market share.

The Economics of Streaming

A useful approach for understanding the economic impacts of any innovation is to consider the effect of the innovation on the *size of the pie* (i.e., whether the total amount of income rises or falls) and on the *distribution of the pie* (i.e., how large a slice of the pie various parties get). The advent of paid streaming services has undoubtedly increased the size of the pie. More money is being spent on recorded music because of streaming over the last few years, and this is to the benefit of musicians and labels as a whole. The anticipated growth in the number of streaming subscribers should increase the size of the pie further in the future.

The distribution of the pie is more complicated, and depends on the contracts that particular artists have with their labels. Nonetheless, it is clear that some genres have benefited more from streaming than others. For example, hip-hop and R&B represented 15.5 percent of total album sales and 36 percent of total on-demand music streams in the first half of 2018, according to Nielsen.[14] Dance and electronic music also represented relatively more on-demand streams than album sales. The fact that hip-hop, R&B, and EDM outperform their album sales on streaming services is largely a reflection of the relatively young and urban customer base that is using streaming services.

Streaming is also giving a second wind to older songs, known in the trade as the back catalog. Publishing and performance royalties are an annuity, and a vibrant financial market has developed to securitize and sell shares in artists' royalties. This development was foreshadowed by David Bowie, who securitized the royalties from twenty-five of his albums to raise $55 million in eponymous Bowie Bonds in 1997.

Many new artists, however, may receive a smaller slice of the pie with streaming compared with physical records or digital downloads, at least initially. The reason is that when music was a durable good that was purchased and then listened to later (often multiple times), new releases were more likely to be purchased than older releases. Emerging artists, who tend to release more new music, therefore are initially receiving less revenue with the transition to streaming. It is possible that the size of the pie will grow large enough that new artists are eventually better off with streaming as well, if one considers the present value of royalty payments under streaming compared with the previous state of the record industry.

Three Misconceptions

Because streaming is a new product with a different business model, there are three mistakes that people commonly make concerning the economics of streaming.

First, it is common for industry insiders to view streaming as a zero-sum game. The logic is that if one artist's streams rise, that artist's share of total streams will rise, and the share earned by other artists' will necessarily fall. In other words, instead of vying individually to sell more records, artists are now viewed as competing against one another to earn a larger share of the pie. This logic holds in a static world but not in a dynamic one, as the number of paying customers can increase the size of the pie over time. And even in a static world, the size of the pie is so large that the quantity of one artist's streams does not meaningfully affect the share accruing to any other artist.

Consider the following calculation. With 2.3 billion streams across audio platforms, the Canadian rapper Drake was the most-streamed musician in the world in the first half of 2018.[15] His streams accounted for 1.7 percent of all songs streamed in that period. If Drake had decided to become a lawyer instead of a musician and his catalog of songs was never produced—and nothing else had changed—by how much would Kendrick Lamar's share of streams have increased? The answer is: not much. If we remove Drake's streams from the total, Kendrick Lamar's share of streams would only increase from 0.50 percent to 0.51 percent. The benefit for Cardi B is even smaller, as is the case for every other artist who was streamed less frequently than Kendrick Lamar, given the nonlinear effect of shaving the denominator. And removing artists with fewer streams than Drake would have even less effect on other artists' shares. Thus as a practical matter, even in a static view of the world, there is little zero-sum aspect to competition among artists with streaming.

Furthermore, the fact that streaming is not yet close to reaching its maximum number of paying customers is another reason streaming is not a zero-sum game; the sum will grow larger if more hit songs cause more customers to sign up. And even when the number of paid subscribers levels off, the size of the pie could still continue to grow if monthly subscription fees increase, or if subscription fees are further tiered to take advantage of price discrimination.

A second common misperception is the belief that the amount an artist earns *per* stream from a platform such as Spotify or Tidal is a meaningful indicator of the generosity or contribution of the streaming service to a musician's income. Music blogs, the *New York Times*, *Forbes*, and other news outlets have presented artist payments per stream as a measure of streaming services' generosity.[16] In a subscriber-based streaming market, however, the parameters that determine income from recorded music depend on the platform's payout rate, the fee that subscribers pay per month, and the number of subscribers. The number of streams is irrelevant. To see this, suppose there are two platforms, A and B, and both charge $9.99 a month. Each has one million paying subscribers, and each pays 70 percent of its revenue to rights holders. Suppose service A's subscribers stream twice as much music as service B's subscribers, because service A does a better job of recommending music that subscribers like. In this example, the amount paid per stream would be half as much for service A as for service B. But service A is clearly better for the music industry, because it does a better job recommending music, makes listeners happier, and pays out just as much money to rights holders as service B pays. This example makes clear that the amount paid out per stream can be a misleading indicator of which streaming service is better for artists and the rest of the music community. In fact, all else being equal, more successful services can be expected to pay less per streamed song than less successful ones.

This is not to say that there is not a "value gap" when it comes to certain streaming services. YouTube is a prime example of the value gap. YouTube, which has only a small subscription service, pays a smaller share of its revenue out to rights holders (as I explain in Chapter 9, this is a result of a quirk of the Digital Millennium Copyright Act of 1998). The other services are fairly similar in their payout rate and monthly fees. Services that rely relatively more on ad-supported customers than on paying subscribers, however, have less revenue to pay out, because ads generate less revenue than subscribers. So the fact that Apple Music pays out more per stream than Spotify may be an indication that Apple subscribers spend less time listening to music than Spotify subscribers (as well as the fact that Spotify is more reliant on ad-supported customers). And the fact that Spotify's payments per stream have declined over time is a sign that Spotify's growing number of subscribers are spending more time listening to more songs, which is good for the music industry.

A final misconception is that there exists a metric to convert the number of streams to album sales equivalents. There is a natural desire to try to measure the popularity of artists or albums, because music is a social good. This has led to a controversial and fraught search for a simple way to combine album sales, digital downloads, and streams into one overarching measure of popularity. *Billboard*, for example, counts 1,500 song streams from one album as the equivalent of one album sale in its influential *Billboard* 200 chart.[17] But combining a certain number of streams with the number of albums sold to measure popularity is as sensible as using horsepower as a metric to gauge the combined popularity of automobiles and horse and buggies. Streams and album sales are different products, and the yardstick used to combine them is arbitrary. Streaming increases the variety of songs available and reduces the marginal monetary cost of listening to music to zero, so more music is consumed with streaming. Another difference is that albums necessarily bundle songs, while with streaming songs are unbundled (as explained further later).

From à la Carte to an All-You-Can-Eat Buffet

From the music consumer's perspective, streaming converts recorded music from an à la carte menu to an all-you-can-eat buffet that is more convenient than downloading pirated music from unauthorized websites. Once the monthly subscription is paid, the marginal pecuniary cost of consuming music is zero. And as with an all-you-can-eat breakfast, consumers tend to consume more when there is no extra cost of consumption. The main constraint on the consumer's side is time.

It has become clear that many consumers are willing to pay for convenience. Spotify was designed to be quicker and easier to use than the free file-sharing services provided by LimeWire, Pirate Bay, and the profusion of other pirate music sites that followed Napster and the BitTorrent wave. The model has worked. In its public filing, Spotify forecasted that it will have ninety-six million paid subscribers, paying a combined $6.5 billion, by the end of 2018.[18]

Users tend to sort into a streaming plan that matches their preferences and situation. Individuals with a high opportunity cost of time and more disposable income are more likely to pay for ad-free premium services. Young and low-income listeners are more willing to endure ads that come with "freemium" service. As with lunch, however, there really is no such thing as a *free* streaming service.

The Demand for Ad-Supported Streaming

With primarily ad-supported streaming services such as Pandora or the gigantic Chinese platform QQ, the cost of listening to music is the inconvenience of having to hear (or watch) paid advertisements. Pandora listeners are interrupted by roughly one or two ads every fifteen minutes, amounting to about three minutes of ads over an hour of listening.[19] Ads are targeted to the demographics and geography of listeners. Some are entertaining and play to the medium. Nonetheless, ads impose a cost on the listener—they pay with their time spent listening. (Economic tools can be applied even when money does not change hands.)

In one of the clearest demonstrations of the existence of a downward-sloping **demand curve,** Pandora conducted an unprecedented large-scale experiment to measure the extent to which listeners' demand for music—and for Pandora itself—declines as the volume of ads rises. Between June 2014 and April 2016, nearly 35 million listeners on Pandora radio were subjected to varying amounts of ads.[20] The listeners were randomly assigned to one of nine treatment groups, which varied the number of ads and frequency of interruptions that listeners were exposed to over the next twenty-one months. A tenth group formed a control group, which heard the normal number of ads (approximately three minutes per hour). The group with the most ads received more than twice as many ads as the group with the fewest ads. This is an example of the type of A/B experiment that many Internet companies routinely conduct on unsuspecting users without publicly disclosing their research results. The experiment was so vast that economist David Reiley left academia to lead the Pandora research team. His findings illustrate the power of applying economic analysis to the music business.

Consumers responded to advertisements the same way they typically respond to higher prices: they demand less of the good (in this case, streams) if ads impose greater nuisance costs. Figure 8.1 documents that over the course of the experiment, time spent listening to Pandora declined for the group exposed to the most ads relative to the control group, while listening increased for the group exposed to the fewest ads. Listening time fell as the number of ads increased because users listened for fewer days or dropped the service altogether. This creates a fundamental trade-off for Pandora and other ad-supported streaming services: they can charge corporate clients higher rates for advertisements if they attract more listeners, but they lose listeners if they increase the number of advertisements. Interestingly, Pandora's experiment suggested that the company's revenue could be increased if more ads were delivered. That is, although Pandora would lose some listeners and therefore advertising fees would fall if ads were aired more frequently, this would be more than offset by the extra revenue gained from selling more ads.

Pandora's experiment yielded another important finding. Pandora offers both free ad-supported radio and paid ad-free subscription services, although the company earns 80 percent of its revenue from the ad service.[21] For $4.99 a month, listeners can receive an ad-free personalized radio experience. The free ad-supported service and subscription service are substitute goods. As the inconvenience of the free service increased, listeners switched to the paid service. The chance of someone signing up for a paid subscription increased by 0.14 percentage point for every additional ad played per hour. More listeners dropped the service altogether, however. For every user who signed up for the paid service, three stopped using Pandora. Older listeners

Figure 8.1: Average Hours Listening to Pandora for Low-Ad Group and for High-Ad Group, as a Percentage of Control Group

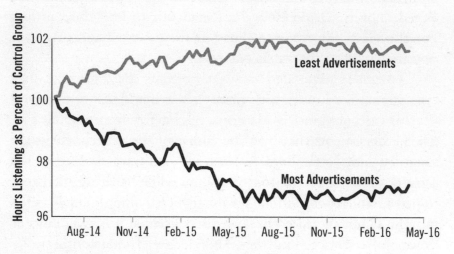

Source: Jason Huang, David Reiley, and Nickolai Riabov.

were more likely to pay to avoid the inconvenience of ads, while younger listeners were more likely to drop the service, probably to switch to an alternative free streaming service, such as YouTube.

Music Discovery

Although radio remains an important source for discovering new music, especially in the Midwest, streaming is rapidly becoming an important source of music discovery as well. In its public filing with the Securities and Exchange Commission in 2018, Spotify reported that 31 percent of listening time on its platform occurred through its playlists, up from 20 percent just two years earlier. A playlist is a set of songs selected by human curation or a computer algorithm (e.g., machine learning), or a combination of the two methods. Playlists can be created for a mass audience, such as Spotify's "Today's Top Hits," or personalized for an individual. Spotify offers more than thirty-five million tracks for listeners to choose from, so it is obvious that some sort of mechanism is necessary to simplify song selection. Spotify's public filing noted, "Given the success of our playlists in driving music discovery, they have become one of the primary tools that labels, artists, and managers use in order to boost artists and measure success."

In fact, playlists are becoming the new gatekeepers for music. The economists Luis Aguiar and Joel Waldfogel examined the effect on the popularity of a song of having that song included on one of Spotify's playlists.[22] Using a variety of statistical methods, they concluded that playlists can wield significant influence over song discovery. For example, here is one of their findings: "Being added to Today's Top Hits, a list with 18.5 million followers during the sample period, raises streams by almost 20 million and is worth between $116,000 and $163,000." Not surprisingly, labels vie to have their songs included on playlists to promote their artists.

Even with the advent of individualized playlists, listening to music remains a social activity. Spotify and other streaming platforms have built-in social features, where users can share their music recommendations with others in their network. Facebook also allows users to share their musical tastes with friends. And playlists that recommend a small set of songs to millions of listeners tend to magnify superstar effects. These features reinforce bandwagon effects and strengthen cumulative advantage benefits for star recording artists. As discussed in Chapter 4, there is little sign so far that streaming has moved music away from a superstar market, where a relatively small number of performers garner the lion's share of the rewards.

The Long Tail

Although the long tail of recording artists who soldier on with little recognition or reward is likely to remain long and lonely, the Internet and digital technology are changing the way that new superstars are discovered and how everyday musicians do their work. In the right hands, a laptop computer armed with GarageBand or Logic Pro software could have as much recording capability as the Abbey Road Studios. It has never been easier for undiscovered musicians to produce high-quality pilots and demos and to make them widely available. This makes it possible for superstars to emerge without the traditional A&R nurturing and search process. Justin Bieber, for example, was discovered after posting his music videos online, as was the multi-talented Jacob Collier. The highly skewed shape of the distribution of successful musicians is unlikely to change because of streaming and digital technology, but the means by which artists move from one end of the distribution to the other has already changed.

And digital technology is encouraging more music to be produced than ever before.[23] In 2018, for example, some 18,000 new releases were added *per month* to the online music encyclopedia MusicBrainz, more than twice the amount (8,400) added monthly in 2004.[24]

It is often said that streaming makes it possible for many musicians to make a little money but difficult for any to make a lot of money. The data bear this out. The 2018 MIRA Musician Survey found that 28 percent of musicians earned some income from streaming, but the musician in the middle of this group earned only $100.

If more opportunity does come about for members of the long tail, it will probably be through platforms such as Patreon, which enables artists to directly collect subscription fees from their patrons (see Chapter 2), or other start-up companies that give unknown "bedroom" artists a platform to directly promote and stream their music over popular services.

One such company is Rehegoo Music Group, founded in 2014 by Italian entrepreneur Marco Rinaldo. Rehegoo's model is artist friendly compared with traditional record companies. Artists are signed to a short contract (e.g., one year), which can be exclusive or non-exclusive. Artists typically record their music at home or at a local studio and upload it to Rehegoo. Rehegoo then remixes the music, creates compilations and albums, arranges for the music to be available on major streaming services around the world, and promotes the music to target audiences. Their artists include Lynn Samadhi, who creates meditation music; Marcus Daves, who composes and records jazz tunes; Luna Blancos, who makes New Age music; and hundreds of others. For songs that are exclusively provided to Rehegoo, royalties are split fifty-fifty. Rehegoo's songs are being streamed more than four billion times a year, and the company is growing exponentially.[25]

Rehegoo has offices in New York, Los Angeles, and London, but the heavy lifting is done in a converted century-old brick textile factory in Bielsko-Biala, Poland, which I visited in June 2017. One could literally see the old industrial economy transformed into the modern service sector in Rehegoo's hulking facility. Rooms that previously housed looms and spindles in the 45,000-square-foot factory had been transformed into soundproof recording studios with state-of-the-art equipment, open offices for marketers, publishers, and graphic designers, and spaces for chilling out, with foosball and ping-pong tables for entertainment. Rehegoo is a microcosm of the industrial transformation taking place in America and around the world.

Rehegoo shared with me proprietary data on the net monthly earnings from streaming and digital downloads received by each of the top thirty artists on its platform from January 2015 to March 2018. Figure 8.2 shows that earnings have been growing across the board, but especially for those at the top. The top five performers earned an average of $57,800 over the most recent twelve months, compared with $13,500 in 2015. The fanning out of the spaghetti-like lines indicates that variability in earnings across artists is growing over time. Notice also that, except for the top five earners, it is rare for an artist to make a large jump ahead of his or her peers from one month to the next. Nonetheless, the bulk of musicians have increased their earnings over time. The thirtieth-ranked artist saw income rise from around $100 a month in 2015 to over $1,000 a month two years later.

Figure 8.2: Top 30 Artists' Monthly Streaming Income from Rehegoo (U.S. Dollars)

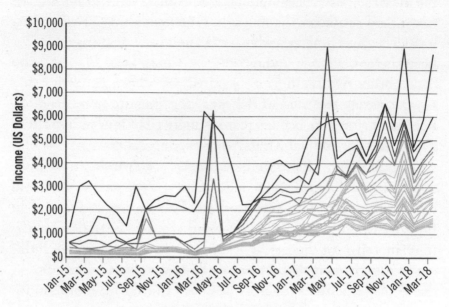

Source: Author's calculations with data supplied by Rehegoo.

If this trajectory continues, and if these results can be replicated on a wider scale for more artists, Rehegoo may indeed realize its goal of making "the world a better place for the people who create music."

"Swish, Swish": Music Responds to Incentives

The economic incentives imbedded in streaming are changing the nature of the music that is produced and heard. With a tap on a screen or keyboard, listeners can instantly skip through songs. To qualify as a "spin" that counts toward royalties and chart tallies, a song must be streamed for at least 30 seconds. According to Marc Hogan of *Pitchfork*, "That's why, while how a song starts has always been important in pop, with streaming it's more crucial than ever. Catchy bits come early and at a quick clip."[26]

Hogan cites Katy Perry's single "Swish, Swish," which features Nicki Minaj, as an example of a song that devotes much of its first thirty seconds to sampling familiar-sounding British house music, because listeners tend not to skip over songs that they have heard before.

Another trick is to have the most popular member of a collaboration appear in the first thirty seconds of a song, and the less famous member(s) later on. Looking at the *Billboard* Top 100 songs in 2016 and 2017, there is ample evidence of this strategy.[27] The median rank (in terms of streams) of singers who appear in the first thirty seconds of a Top 100 song in 2017 was 72, while the median rank for those appearing in the rest of the song was 129. In 2016 the difference was even starker: the median rank for singers appearing in the first thirty seconds was 59, and for those who make their appearance later in the recording, their ranking was 129. An example is Post Malone's "Congratulations" (featuring Quavo): Post Malone's familiar voice appears at the start, and Quavo's vocals can be heard after thirty seconds.

The demise of the album is an even more dramatic change in music production wrought by streaming incentives. An album, of course, is a compilation of songs that are sold together. In economic terms, albums are bundled songs. Bundling requires consumers to buy songs that were not necessarily their top choice, which facilitates price discrimination and provides benefits for record labels and artists. Digital downloading and streaming enable albums to be unbundled (although streaming subscriptions can be viewed as bundling the entire catalog of music).[28] You can buy or stream individual tracks. J. R. Rotem, the acclaimed songwriter and record producer who has worked with Rihanna, 50 Cent, Gwen Stefani, and other stars, readily acknowledges that streaming is changing the way he approaches songwriting. "For the most part, it seems the concept of making an amazing album as a full body of work seems to be less important than making a song," he told *Music Week*. "The way people consume music, people are switching from one song to the next, they're listening to 30 seconds of one to another."[29]

Whether artists and producers consciously respond to incentives or the Darwinian selection process that governs popularity and economic success under streaming incentives leads to changes in music is, in some sense, irrelevant. The fact remains that music is changing in response to the incentives embedded in streaming.

Taylor Swift: Economic Genius

Artists have pursued different strategies in response to the emergence of online streaming platforms. Most have allowed their labels to negotiate deals for streaming services to include and promote their songs in their enormous catalogs. Jay-Z and a coalition of other top artists acquired the company that owns the fledgling streaming service Tidal in 2015, and promised artists higher royalties for their music in exchange for exclusivity.[30]

Another artist who stands out is pop star Taylor Swift. The twenty-eight-year-old singer and songwriter is already one of the most successful musicians of all time. As we saw in Chapter 6, she has pioneered Verified Fan, slow ticketing, and loyalty points, boosting her revenue and selling more complementary products (merch) in the process. She has also pioneered a bold strategy in music streaming, producing beneficial results for herself and other recording artists: strategically withholding her music from Spotify, Apple Music, and other streaming services from time to time.

Disappointed by the low compensation available from Spotify's free ad-supported service, Swift removed her music from Spotify in late 2014, signing an exclusive deal with Apple, which only offers a paid subscriber service. She placed her music back on Spotify three years later, after Spotify and Universal Music Group, Swift's label, agreed to allow artists to stream their albums only to paid subscribers in the first two weeks after release.* When she released her sixth album, *Reputation*, she kept it off all streaming services during the first week after it was released. Fans could only purchase CDs or digital downloads of the album— and they bought 1.2 million copies that week.[31] The economic logic of the strategy implicitly involves segmenting markets to price-discriminate: customers with a higher willingness to pay are impatient and will purchase her album when it is not available on streaming services. And more revenue is available from paid subscription-supported services than free ad-supported services. The bottom line is that this aggressive strategy enabled Swift to sell more digital downloads and CDs, set more album sales records, and earn more streaming royalties.

A risk for an artist is that segmenting the market in order to price-discriminate and maximize revenue can jeopardize the artist's popularity—the artist can be viewed by fans as "in it for the money, not the art." Part of Taylor Swift's genius is that she has managed to pursue economic strategies to maximize her revenue while putting herself on the side of the angels and doing minimal, if any, damage to her reputation. In 2014, for example, she penned a *Wall Street Journal* op-ed standing up for recording artists, arguing: "Music is art, and art is important and rare. Important, rare things are valuable. Valuable things should be paid for."[32] While one could question how rare music actually is as an economic proposition, the op-ed cleverly positioned Swift as a defender of art, not profit.

Taylor Swift has also used her might to pressure Apple to pay artists for music that was streamed to new members during the free three-month trial periods that Apple offered potential subscribers.[33] In 2015, Swift threatened to withdraw her music from Apple unless artists were explicitly compensated for music streamed during the trial period. "Three months is a long time to

---

* The day she returned her music to Spotify also happened to coincide with the release of rival pop star Katy Perry's album *Witness*.

go unpaid, and it is unfair to ask anyone to work for nothing," she wrote in an open letter to Apple.* Apple immediately backed down. "When I woke up this morning and I saw Taylor's note that she had written," Eddy Cue, Apple's senior vice president, conceded, "it really solidified that we needed to make a change."

A Stream Runs Through It

The music industry is probably not yet midstream (pardon the pun) in the streaming revolution. Streaming is the present and future technology of music. But the distribution business model will likely evolve and change directions for years to come. According to Steve Boom, vice president of Amazon Music, we have only scratched the surface of what the technology can deliver.[34]

Spotify has demonstrated that it can draw tens of millions of paying customers away from pirate music sites. Spotify's successful and novel initial public offering (IPO) valued the company at more than $25 billion. Yet Spotify has lost money in each of the last three years. In 2017, Spotify's loss was $1.4 billion on $5 billion of revenue. To become profitable, Spotify will have to control costs, raise monthly subscription fees above its competitors' rates without losing subscribers, or generate additional revenue from creating complementary products (such as merch sales). Spotify could also attempt to compete with record labels by directly signing artists. Indeed, Spotify's partnership with DistroKid, a service that allows artists to directly upload music to streaming services and online stores for a fee, could be a step in this direction.

Spotify's long-run existential challenge is exacerbated by the fact that Amazon Music and Apple Music can sustain losses be-

---

* In the company's defense, Apple's Eddy Cue noted that the company "had originally negotiated these deals based on paying them a higher royalty rate on an ongoing basis to compensate for this brief [trial] time." Apple agreed, however, to compensate artists during the trial period and keep the royalty rate at the previously negotiated level.

cause they generate large complementary benefits for their parent companies, and because YouTube is a close substitute that can operate under different rules (see Chapter 9). Apple is a hardware company that makes money from selling devices, such as iPhones and iPads. If Apple Music drives more iPhone and iPad sales, the company can happily withstand losses from Apple Music. And Amazon makes money from selling merchandise over the Internet. If the Echo Dot and Alexa prove to be popular portals that draw millions more customers to buy sneakers and other goods from the Amazon retail site, Amazon would be willing to sustain losses from Amazon Music.

A similar dynamic is taking place elsewhere in the economy. Google, together with its subsidiary autonomous car development company, Waymo, for example, is challenging traditional automobile companies, such as Ford and General Motors. Google's combination of technological prowess, deep pockets, and complementary activities poses a formidable threat to standalone car companies. Some banking functions could be similarly challenged by Apple Wallet.

This raises the question of whether Spotify can be sustainable as a stand-alone company. Spotify could be absorbed by a company that might realize complementary benefits from having Spotify under its umbrella, such as Google, if Google Play does not succeed, or Chinese e-commerce giant Alibaba, if it wants to challenge Amazon in the United States, or some other Internet behemoth. Another possibility is that the major record labels—which already hold an equity stake in Spotify—could take over the company if it fails, although that would create an obvious conflict of interest, as they would have an incentive to promote their own music over that from independent labels. (The majors held about a combined 10 percent stake in Spotify before its IPO. They reduced their stakes after the IPO and shared their capital gains with their artists and independent labels.)

Amazon's Steve Boom thinks streaming is not a winner-take-all technology, and that multiple streaming companies can co-exist without a single dominant player (that is, unlike Facebook in social media and Google in search engines).[35] Such an assessment is correct only if the companies can distinguish themselves, perhaps by exploiting their monopoly on users' listening histories to provide personalized service and other unique benefits to their customers.

Marc Geiger conjectures that in the future streaming services will bundle movies, music, and other content.[36] Currently, Spotify and Apple provide music streaming for monthly subscription payments, and Netflix provides movies for subscription payments; it would be more convenient for consumers if these separate streams merged. Geiger predicts that Netflix will buy Spotify and provide one-stop shopping for all entertainment needs. Amazon Prime is already in both the movie and music businesses and could become, well, the Amazon of bundled entertainment streaming. Others, such as Facebook and Google, could also compete in Geiger's "bundled services revolution." A key question for Geiger and his clients is how the revenue will be divided if we do see bundling of movies, music, and other entertainment services.

Another development to watch is that streaming companies can attempt to compete with traditional record labels and publishers, much as Netflix has done with movie studios. Spotify has encouraged artists to post music on Spotify directly, without a label, and has built a recording studio in its New York City office. Amazon is also recording some music that is not copyright protected. With their informational advantages, streaming companies have unique insights into the most profitable types of music to mimic and supplant (e.g., "Happy Birthday" and other children's music). And Apple has launched its own music publishing company.

Yet another area that is sure to change involves audio technology. The innovative company Sonos, for example, has created a highly successful line of smart speakers. A new generation of smart speakers could displace Google Home, Amazon Echo Dot, and other devices that are currently being used to stream and listen to music.

Amazon's founder and CEO, Jeff Bezos, once told me that he is often asked, "What is going to change in the future?" But he is rarely asked, "What is *not* going to change?" "That second question is actually more important than the first," he said, "because you can build a strategy around it."[37] That seems like the type of perspective that enabled Bezos to become the wealthiest businessperson on the planet. When it comes to music streaming, and media more generally, it seems to me that customers are always going to want convenience, affordability, wide variety, and good listening recommendations. Streaming services that can deliver on those priorities are likely to be among the handful of platforms that survive and thrive in the twenty-first century.

Outro

We are likely in the early stages of the streaming revolution. The multitude of streaming services will surely face a shakeout in the future, and it is unclear what form successful business models will take. Streaming companies may displace record labels, or they may be absorbed by labels. A handful of streaming platforms may survive as stand-alone companies and dominate the market. Or streaming platforms may all become—or, in the case of Amazon Music, Apple Music, and Google Play, remain—subsidiaries of dominant Internet companies that benefit from complementarities. New players, such as Netflix and Facebook, may become competitors or strategic partners for streaming companies. And new devices, such as future generations of smart speakers, may significantly alter the contours and possibilities of streaming.

All of these possible developments—and more that cannot currently be predicted—can significantly change the incentives that affect music production and music discovery. Twists and turns in the streaming landscape will continue to affect the size and division of the music pie. The only thing that is certain is that the future of streaming will pose many intriguing issues for musicians, managers, labels, publishers, performing rights organizations, policy makers, and others that can be studied with the tools of economics. Rockonomics will be an active field for decades to come.

CHAPTER 9

Blurred Lines: Intellectual Property in a Digital World

Music fans cannot expect their favorite musicians to continue to produce quality albums if they are not willing to pay. People, including musicians, expect to be rewarded for a job well done. It's all about supply and demand. If there is not demand, there will eventually be no supply.

—Sheryl Crow

Sitting for a deposition early in the afternoon on April 21, 2014, Pharrell Williams looked uncomfortable answering questions. In fact, he said so on several occasions. The deposition was part of a landmark trial to determine whether Pharrell Williams and Robin Thicke's hit 2013 song "Blurred Lines" crossed a legal line and infringed the copyright of Marvin Gaye's 1977 song "Got to Give It Up."

After a weeklong trial and two days of deliberation, the jury ruled in favor of Marvin Gaye's family. Williams and Thicke appealed to the Ninth Circuit, which covers the western region of the United States, but lost a split 2–1 decision in March 2018. They and their publisher were ordered to pay the Gayes $5.3 million in damages and share 50 percent of future songwriting and publishing royalties. In rejecting Williams's argument, the court held that "musical compositions are not confined to a narrow range of expression."[1] In her dissenting opinion, Judge Jacqueline H. Nguyen wrote, " 'Blurred Lines' and 'Got to Give It Up' are not objectively similar. They differ in melody, harmony, and rhythm. Yet by refusing to compare the two works, the majority establishes a dangerous precedent that strikes a devastating blow to future musicians and composers everywhere."

The theatrics of the trial aside—and there were many—the case of *Williams v. Gaye* illustrates the difficulty of determining copyright to a song, and the stakes involved.[*] The Copyright Act of 1831 extended copyright protection to original musical compositions. When I listen to "Blurred Lines" and "Got to Give It Up" with my untrained ears, I don't hear enough similarities to conclude that Williams plagiarized Marvin Gaye. And since the legal case was confined to the composition, not the recorded performance, the similarities are even less apparent if you strip out the rhythmic cowbell tones and falsetto singing that both songs have in common. Williams lost not because he copied Gaye's expression, but because he was inspired by the feel and groove of Gaye's music. Listen to the songs when you have a chance, and see if you agree with the ruling.

It is unclear whether the case will set a precedent for future cases and other jurisdictions. But it is likely that more claims will be brought and settled out of court, rather than risk an embarrassing trial and uncertain verdict. Even before the verdict in *Williams v. Gaye* was reached, Sam Smith chose to share credit for his Grammy-winning "Stay with Me" with Tom Petty and Jeff Lynne, after Tom Petty said it sounded a lot like his 1989 hit "I Won't Back Down."[2] And Mark Ronson settled two copyright challenges to his 2014 hit with Bruno Mars, "Uptown Funk"; a third challenge is ongoing.[3] Another high-profile case, in which it was initially ruled that Led Zeppelin's "Stairway to Heaven" did not plagiarize its iconic opening from Spirit's instrumental "Taurus," will be retried as a result of an appellate court ruling, and could set a precedent that expands or narrows copyright protection, depending on the outcome.[4]

---

[*] In his deposition, Robin Thicke disclosed that he was under the influence of alcohol and Vicodin when he recorded "Blurred Lines," and that Williams "wrote almost every part of the song."

It is an understatement to say that the lines between legitimate inspiration and illegal copyright infringement are blurred. Quincy Jones told me that the amazing thing about music is that it all involves "the same 12 notes being played over and over again," so some overlap is inevitable.[5] There is no Shazam-like app, however, that can tell a composer or a judge whether a song infringes another song's copyright (although maybe there should be). Mark Twain was on to something when he quipped, "Only one thing is impossible for God: To find any sense in any copyright law on the planet."

Copyright assigns a legal right to allow authors to exclude others from using their original work for a period of time. Copyright law as applied to music is even more complicated and confusing than it is for books and other written works. There are *two* copyrights to music: a right to the sound recording and a right to the underlying composition and lyrics.[6] The rights that must be secured to use a song depend on the particular use, such as a movie soundtrack, streaming platform catalog, videogame sound effect, phone ringtone, or terrestrial radio broadcast. The fees for obtaining the relevant rights vary as well, depending on the use of the work. Access to the rights for some uses is compulsory (i.e., no permission required) at a preset price, while the rights and fees for other uses must be negotiated on a case-by-case basis.

The goal of copyright law is to grant a temporary monopoly to creators so they have a financial incentive to create new music, books, or other works. Copyright protection makes particularly good economic sense when the cost of producing a new work is high but the cost of producing subsequent copies is low. "Drawing the line of copyright infringement too short will fail to give the original author his due," writes Stanford Law School's Paul Goldstein, "but extending it too far will make it hard for other writers to earn theirs."[7] As the dispute between Pharrell Williams and Marvin Gaye's heirs indicates, the line must be drawn between different creators. Copyright must also strike a balance between copyright owners and copyright users—that is, between those who create music and those who broadcast it or listen to it. Similar issues arise with other forms of intellectual property rights, from iconic photographs to scientific patents.

The music copyright system was originally developed for rights involving sheet music in the days of player pianos. An elaborate legal and administrative system has evolved over more than a century to (1) determine the rights that must be secured to use music, (2) set royalty rates, and (3) collect and distribute payments to rights holders. Not surprisingly, such a system is antiquated in the digital era. Any normal human being's head spins faster than a turntable when confronted with the varying rights, collection agencies, and processes that determine fees for the myriad different uses of music. In this chapter I sample some of the key economic issues that arise in copyright protection in a digital era.

Digital technology reduces the cost of sharing identical copies of already-produced copyrighted material to essentially zero, and accelerates the speed and cuts the cost of creating and distributing new music. Neither economics nor any other field can provide complete or unambiguous answers to fundamental questions about where copyright lines should be drawn, but economics research can help frame the questions and provide insights into the various trade-offs involved.

The Useful Arts

Intellectual property protection is so important that it is enshrined in Article I of the United States Constitution. Specifically, Section 8, Clause 8, gives Congress the power "To promote the Progress of Science and useful Arts, by securing for limited Times to Authors and Inventors the exclusive Right to their respective Writings and Discoveries." Popular music surely falls into the "useful Arts."

Songwriters are creators. Without lyricists and composers, there would be no music. Once a song is written or recorded, however, it is what economists call a *non-rivalrous good*, meaning that one person's consumption does not diminish another person's opportunity to consume the good. If you listen to or perform a song, I can listen to or perform the same song too, without diminishing your experience. By contrast, if you eat a ham sandwich, I cannot consume that same sandwich. Other examples of non-rivalrous goods are television and radio broadcasts, patented ideas, fashion designs, and architectural plans. There is a strong incentive for free riding when it comes to non-rivalrous goods—that is, for people to consume the good but avoid paying for it. James Madison and the other framers of the Constitution recognized that it is necessary to establish a property right to intellectual property, such as writings and inventions, in order to prevent free riding and encourage investment in the development of new writings and discoveries. This is the foundation of copyright and patent law.

By establishing a limited property right—the legal authority to exclude others from using a creative work for a period of time—copyright law seeks to strike a balance between the interests of creators and the interests of consumers.[8] And while in pre-Internet days one could plausibly argue that bringing a new book or song to market first provided protection against copiers and imitators—as a young Stephen Breyer once argued before he was named to the Supreme Court—that argument clearly does not hold water in the digital era, when perfect copies can be made and distributed throughout the world almost instantaneously.

Property rights are essential in an economy. How can you trade something if you do not know who owns it? Why would you invest in something if you were unsure of whether you could share in the returns? One of the basic insights of economics is that well-defined property rights are necessary for a market to function well. This applies both to intellectual property, such as songs, and to physical property. The lack of copyright protection for music until recently in China is one of the reasons the most populous country on earth has produced such little indigenous music. But where should the lines be drawn? How long should copyright protection last? How should access to copyrighted songs be restricted? How should royalties be collected when there are more than two billion streams a day? And, in practice, how does copyright protection actually affect the total quantity and quality of music produced?

Napster: A Case Study in Destructive Creation

The advent of the file-sharing service Napster and other websites that made unauthorized, pirated digital music available on a mass scale laid bare the centrality of copyright protection for the music industry, and the fragility of the system. In principle, the availability of illegal file-sharing websites could have several effects on authorized sales of music. First, and most important, potential buyers could substitute unlawful downloading for purchases of legitimate recordings that they otherwise would have made. Second, file-sharing services could increase customers' exposure to new music, and increase their purchases of such music as a result or increase their demand for live performances (i.e., file sharing could act like advertising). Third, those who listen to music on unlawful file-sharing sites could inform others in their network about the music, and those others might purchase it. The evidence overwhelmingly points to the dominance of the substitution effect: why buy music if you could obtain it for free?

Music has always been subject to illegal copying. Before he was chairman of the Federal Reserve Board, Alan Greenspan conducted research for the Recording Industry Association of American that concluded, "From the available data, it appears that roughly half of the taping from borrowed records or tapes would have generated record or tape purchases had home audio taping not been possible. . . . This represents lost sales of approximately 32 percent of the total volume of record sales in 1982."[9] Even discounting the interest of the sponsor, this suggests a lot of illegal copying. The record business was growing at a healthy clip in the 1980s, so piracy was not considered an existential threat. Some bands, like the Grateful Dead, even encouraged their fans to record their concerts, which likely cannibalized album sales (but increased demand for their live shows and fostered fan loyalty).

Napster and its ilk, however, did represent an existential threat to the incomes of recording artists and record companies. As I noted earlier, record company revenue and musicians' royalties plummeted because of digital piracy after Napster was launched in 1999 (see Figure 2.2). Napster provided much greater ease and wider access for users to obtain music without paying for it than homemade cassette tapes ever afforded. After the band Metallica successfully sued Napster for copyright infringement, the file-sharing site filed for bankruptcy and closed in 2001.[10] (The streaming service Rhapsody was rebranded as Napster in June 2016.)[11] A host of other file-sharing and torrent services subsequently moved into the space, including Gnutella, Freenet, Kazaa, LimeWire, Scour, Grokster, eDonkey2000, and Pirate Bay—some of which were also challenged for copyright infringement.[12] Only in the last few years have legitimate streaming services offered an effective alternative to piracy.

Economist Joel Waldfogel used the unprecedented growth of pirated music in the 2000s that was ushered in by Napster as a natural experiment to examine the effects of weakening copyright protection on the quantity and quality of music produced. After looking at a variety of measures of the quality of music produced each year (e.g., critics' ratings, comparison of one vintage of music against another in terms of airplay or sales), he reached the surprising conclusion that "the quality of new recorded music has not fallen since the introduction of Napster."[13] And the total volume of music produced actually increased, rather than decreased.

Why didn't the erosion of copyright protection lead to a reduction in the quantity and quality of creators' output? Is Sheryl Crow wrong that it is all about supply and demand, and that musicians would not create quality albums if consumers were unwilling to pay for them?

Maybe copyright protection is overrated because musicians

would continue to create high-quality music even absent copyright protection.

There are two reasons to doubt this conclusion. First, Napster did not occur in a vacuum. The technological improvements that enabled Napster and led to rampant illegal file sharing also coincided with a rapid decline in the cost of creating and distributing digital music. The lower costs of creating and distributing music apparently overwhelmed the adverse effect of rampant copyright infringement on creative output. As Waldfogel noted, "Absent the weakening of effective copyright protection, the other changes in technology might have ushered in an era of even greater creative output." Second, a decade is a short period for a major occupational transition to take place. Had Napster been allowed to operate in wanton disregard of copyright requirements for several decades, the supply of quality music may have eventually declined, as Sheryl Crow predicted.

The strongest empirical evidence that copyright protection encourages greater musical output and higher quality comes from a historical study of Italian operas. The economists Michela Giorcelli, of the University of California, Los Angeles, and Petra Moser, of New York University, exploited the fact that the timing of Napoleon's military victories created something of a natural experiment for studying copyright protection, because Italian states that came under French influence by 1801 adopted French copyright laws (copyright for the duration of the composer's life plus ten years), while states that came under French influence after 1804 did not adopt copyright laws, because by then the French parliament had adopted its civil code, which did not protect copyright.[14] So composers in Lombardy and Venice had copyright protection, while composers in Sardinia did not. Piracy was rampant in regions without copyright protection.

Professors Giorcelli and Moser found that the number of operas produced increased by 150 percent in states that became covered by copyright protection, compared with states that did not benefit from copyright protection. Gioachino Rossini is an example of a popular and prolific composer who benefited from copyright protection in Venice and Milan early in his career.

Composers also produced higher-quality operas, as judged by their popularity and longevity, if they were covered by copyright protection. A good example is Giuseppe Verdi, who apparently substituted quality for quantity. Verdi's publisher even hit upon the idea of using **price discrimination** to maximize the amount of revenue that could be generated with copyright protection. In a letter he advised Verdi, "It is more advantageous to provide access to these scores for all theaters, adapting the price to their special means, because I obtain much more from many small theaters at the price of 300 or 250 lire, than from ten or twelve at the price of a thousand."[15]

Complicated Lines

The connection between copyright protection and incentives for musicians to create innovative, high-quality music in modern times is more complicated than the framers of the Constitution imagined, for several reasons. First, there is no recipe for creativity. The precise factors that lead to new discoveries are hard to predict and even harder to incentivize. In his book *Creative Quest*, Questlove writes, "We take our ideas where we find them and largely we find them in the works of other artists."[16] On The Roots' 2013 album with Elvis Costello, *Wise Up Ghost*, Questlove says, "I'm drumming on it as Steve Ferrone," an acknowledgment of creativity's inevitable blurred lines.

To be creative in whatever we are pursuing, Questlove advises, we should *unfocus* and "refuse to keep things out," participate in a collaborative environment, "make a point of hanging out with people from different disciplines," and engage in curatorial thinking. This list is not easily incentivized by copyright protection.

John Eastman told me that innate, intangible talent separates great musicians from the rest:

> Beethoven studied with Haydn, and his first two symphonies are almost pure Haydn; his genius broke out in his third and then reached his intellectual apex with his late quartets. And while the Beatles did not study academically like Questlove, they were immersed in the rock 'n' roll greats who came before.
>
> What differentiates Beethoven and the Beatles, the greatest musical composers, from the just very good is an innate talent, without which one's work cannot be part of the pantheon of musical greatness. It is this intangible which gives the greatest composers their unique place in the brilliant spine of music.[17]

Economics research has looked extensively at patent innovation, where it is easier to define and measure creative contributions than in music. After surveying the literature, Petra Moser reached the provocative but probably correct conclusion that "historically, the great majority of innovations have been created outside of the patent systems."[18] Creativity is hard to incentivize in science and music. Perhaps the best insight economics has to offer is a simple one: if there are more people looking to make a new discovery, the more likely it is that a new discovery will be found.[19]

A second complicating factor in the chain from copyright protection to incentives to create is that music today is a superstar market, with a few stars whose songs strike it rich and numerous others who earn a small amount. As I explained in Chapter 5, luck, timing, and many unpredictable factors matter for popularity, in addition to the intrinsic quality of a song. Even superstars write songs that turn out to be duds. And seasoned professionals at major record labels often cannot predict which songs will be successful. Warner Brothers, for example, chose "The Way I Are (Dance with Somebody)" as the lead single of Bebe Rexha's third

EP. Fortunately for Ms. Rexha, streaming provides fast feedback: Warner quickly noticed that another song on the album, "Meant to Be" (featuring Florida Georgia Line), was doing well. They never anticipated that "Meant to Be" would be streamed more than one billion times and spend over half of 2018 as the number one song on the *Billboard* Hot Country song chart.[20] Very little in music success is "meant to be"; it just happens when the stars align.* The unpredictability of payoffs makes the link between copyright protection and incentives to create indirect at best.

Composer Raney Shockne alluded to the arbitrariness of the incentives in his business. Shockne, a cousin of the Beach Boys' Brian Wilson, hit the jackpot composing for the television series *Anger Management*. In addition to scoring the music, he whistled on the theme song, which earned him performance credit as a voice actor as well as composer royalties. With the show in syndication, he has earned more than $1 million for his efforts. "It is so arbitrary," he said. "It is such a bizarre thing. I've been paid $500 for the same type of piece of music that fetches $5,000 or $50,000, for that matter. It is so all over the map. We do it for the love of it. We do it for the prestige of it. . . . And we do it at every capacity for, 'Oh my God I'm making money from playing music.'"[21]

If copyright protection does not provide much of an incentive for additional creative output, why have it? I think there are three important arguments in support of copyright protection beyond the incentive effects that have occupied most of the economics and legal debate: fairness, artistic credit, and creative control. First, copyright infringement is unfair. I have already argued that music is the best deal in the economy. Americans spend relatively little money on music yet enjoy countless hours of entertainment. Musicians are not rewarded fairly for their services compared

---

* "It just happened that way" doesn't make for good lyrics in the same way as "If it's meant to be, it'll be," but it often provides a more accurate explanation of the music business.

with others in the economy. Copyright protection helps musicians earn a reward for their contributions, regardless of whether they would have done the work for free.

Credit is also an issue. Part of the reward for creativity is recognition for one's efforts. Copyright establishes a legal basis for musical contributions. Desire for recognition for creative contributions is not unique to musicians. Academics, for example, sometimes bring plagiarism charges when no money is at stake.

On a related issue, creators deserve, and currently have, a right to some degree of creative control over their works. A songwriter can deny a filmmaker the right to use his or her music in a movie if the songwriter objects to the context in which the music will be used. David Bowie, for example, refused to allow director Danny Boyle to use "Golden Years" in the outlandish toilet scene in the movie *Trainspotting*. And he later refused to license his music to the Academy Award–winning director for a planned Bowie bi-opic, which Boyle scuttled as a result.[22]

When General Motors approached the singer Brandi Carlile to use her song "The Story" in an ad campaign, she initially turned them down. But the singer later agreed once they offered to use the song in a campaign promoting hybrid vehicles and biofuels during the summer 2008 Olympics. The popular commercial helped launch her career. She later announced that her band would donate the money they earned from the ad campaign to environmental organizations supporting alternative energy sources.

Because of the historical development of copyright law, however, music creators do not have the right to control the use of their music on terrestrial radio or in cover songs. Those licenses are compulsory, meaning that a radio station can broadcast any song as long as it pays the relevant fee, and a cover band can record its version of a song as long as it pays the relevant fee. Hit singer-songwriter Aloe Blacc has passionately criticized the lack of creative control afforded to songwriters under the law:

A sculptor, let's say, has the opportunity to choose where and when and how their art is consumed. If the sculptor makes their sculpture at Venice Beach, well, you have to be at Venice Beach to see it. And he could probably mask it so that it could only be seen from 5 p.m. to 8 p.m. if he wanted.

If I wanted to do that for my music, I couldn't. There is no freedom for me to say, this song that I wrote about beautiful mornings can only be consumed at morning time from my website. I don't have that right, because anyone in the world can cover it and play it anytime they want, and once it's available, radio and other forms of radio (like Pandora) have the right to play it, and I don't have the right to tell them not to. . . .

It should be fair. . . . A lot of artists, the majority of them, are one-hit wonders. Give them that one year to exploit it in full with no competition to diminish the value of their copyrights. Think about all the terrible covers of Beatles songs you've heard.[23]

Political events present another set of legal challenges for artistic control. Politicians can license music even if the composer objects because the license is compulsory, but the composer can sue to prevent usage on other grounds, such as by arguing that use of his or her music creates the impression of a false endorsement. These cases are not always easy, however. A lawyer representing Steven Tyler of Aerosmith, for example, sent two letters to Donald Trump's campaign requesting that the candidate cease and desist from using the band's song "Dream On" at campaign events, to no avail. The singer, a registered Republican, later objected when President Trump used his "Livin' on the Edge" at a rally in Charleston, West Virginia.[24] Tyler later tweeted: "I do not let anyone use my songs without my permission. My music is for causes, not for political campaigns or rallies. Protecting copyright and songwriters is what I've been fighting for even before this current administration took office."[25]

Artistic control was also the issue that sparked Metallica's landmark lawsuit against Napster in 2000. Having discovered that an unauthorized copy of an unmixed demo track of theirs was available for download on Napster, and being played on the radio as a result, the heavy metal band was rightly outraged. "Napster wasn't about money," drummer Lars Ulrich subsequently explained. "It wasn't about commerce. It wasn't about copyright. It was literally about choice. Whose choice is it to make your music available for free downloads? We were saying, 'Hang on. It should be our choice.' "[26]

Protecting Mickey Mouse

A key parameter of copyright law is the *duration* of copyright protection. Set the term too long, and creativity is stifled. Set it too short, and creators do not receive their due. Over the last century, the duration of copyright protection has increased markedly in the United States and many other countries.

The 1998 Copyright Term Extension Act—also known as the Sonny Bono Act, after the then-congressman and former member of Sonny and Cher—extended copyright protection for new works from the life of the author plus fifty years to the life of the author plus seventy years. A distinguished group of economists, including George Akerlof, Kenneth Arrow, and Milton Friedman, wrote an amicus brief to the Supreme Court arguing that this twenty-year extension, coming long after the death of an author or composer, would have virtually no impact on the economic incentive for creative output. "Because the additional compensation occurs many decades in the future, its present value is small, very likely an improvement of less than 1 percent," the economists wrote.[27] They further warned that extending protection raises costs for consumers and reduces "the set of building-block materials freely available for new works [and therefore] raises the cost of producing new works and reduces the number created."

Another, even more economically questionable feature of the

1998 act is that it extended the copyright term for works created after 1923 that were still under copyright protection. This feature led the law to be derisively nicknamed "the Mickey Mouse Protection Act" because it delayed Mickey Mouse's entry into the public domain until 2024. Winnie the Pooh's copyright was extended as well. As the team of economists wrote, "Term extension in existing works provides no additional incentive to create new works and imposes several kinds of additional costs." The costs are higher prices for books, cartoons, T-shirts, costumes, and other products related to Mickey Mouse or Winnie the Pooh. Not surprisingly, owners of valuable copyrights have lobbied strongly for term extensions around the world, an activity that economists refer to as "rent-seeking." Rent-seeking is an attempt to extract greater compensation without creating additional value for society. In other words, rent-seekers expend resources to obtain a larger slice of the pie, while doing nothing to increase the size of the pie.

There is little evidence that copyright term extensions produce beneficial effects. Even Giorcelli and Moser, the economists who found that enforcing copyright protection increased the quality and output of Italian operas, concluded that increases in the duration of copyright protection did not improve output.

A resourceful study by Megan MacGarvie of Boston University and co-authors approached copyright duration from the opposite perspective: they examined what happened when recording copyrights for artists who were popular in the United Kingdom in the 1960s expired. Analyzing data on 11,639 tracks recorded by 135 artists, they found that re-releases increased threefold once copyrights expired. Interestingly, after a song's copyright had expired, the artist who originated that song was less likely to perform it at live events, suggesting that artists kept these songs on their set lists to increase record sales or downloads while they were covered by copyright protection. "These results suggest that copyright term extensions may lead to fewer re-releases," they concluded.[28]

Not only are copyright terms that long exceed the life of song-writers hard to justify on incentive grounds, they are also hard to justify on grounds of artistic control or where apportioning credit are concerned. One also could argue that it is unfair to consumers and other creators to extend the term of copyright for owners of works that were created long ago under copyright terms that were established at the time.

Dan Wilson: A Series of Magnetic Yeses

Dan Wilson has achieved just about everything one can aspire to in the music business, including recording, touring, songwriting, and producing. He was the frontman of Semisonic, known for their hit "Closing Time." He has shared songwriting credit with Carole King, Taylor Swift, Halsey, John Legend, and more than one hundred other collaborators. He won a Grammy for Album of the Year for contributions to Adele's *21* and for Song of the Year with the Dixie Chicks for "Not Ready to Make Nice." I interviewed Wilson about the arc of his career, which brought him from Minneapolis to Harvard and the Grammys, on June 29, 2018.

When did you know you wanted to be a professional musician?

Around age ten or eleven I would walk home from school and concoct a way to sing that I had decided was going to be my trademark when I was a professional musician. I took piano lessons from age eight until eighteen from a smart lady who focused on theory, the circle of fifths and the structure of harmony, which is not common for a piano teacher for beginners. I studied classical and jazz music in my late teens, and learned composition from studying jazz. I tried to be in bands all through high school. I played in bands that would play at backyard parties and basement parties. When I went to Harvard I basically started in earnest and was always in a band playing somewhere in Boston.

Then I quit music for three or four years to try to be a painter. But I continued writing songs and eventually my brother asked me to join his band, Trip

Shakespeare. And I learned all the second guitar parts to their songs. I hadn't really been much of a guitarist until then. We needed to make enough money to live at that time, but we lived super cheaply in dangerous parts of town.

I did three albums with Trip Shakespeare and an EP. And then the band did kind of a soft split. I formed Semisonic with Jacob Slichter and John Munson.

How do you think about the progression of your career?

Well, from within, I can sort of make a story out of my career, but from within I don't experience it as a story or a progression. It's kind of a sequence, but not exactly a progression.

I had a math teacher in junior high who, speaking of me, told my parents that if you have a handful of clay and squeeze the clay, it's going to come out from between the fingers. And he said that your son is like that too, "You don't know what direction his talent is going to come out, but there's too much talent and it's going to come out." He thought that genius was omnidirectional in some cases. He thought I was a good mathematician, but he didn't think that's where I was going to excel. I know a lot of people like that: if they're songwriters now, they could have been filmmakers too, or they could have been painters. A lot of the path in life has to do with the sequence of yeses that come down from the universe to the artist and then it looks to all the world like you charted a path. But instead you just followed magnetically from one yes to the next. I feel in a way that that is what I do.

When Semisonic was doing its very best work, my first daughter was in the hospital for a long, long time. When she came home she required twenty-four-hour nursing and a ventilator, and this continued until she was three. It became obvious that her issues in life were going to be profound for a long time. I don't think it was a completely conscious decision for me, but the thought of being away for two hundred nights a year touring seemed less and less sustainable. So I applied a lot of creativity to try to figure out how to write songs for other people. That was a conscious decision in a way. The fact that it worked out so stupendously well definitely has affected how many gigs I do. If the writing had not gone well, I might have been a music teacher as well.

You still do some live performances and tour. Why?

I like performing for a couple of reasons. I love interacting with other musicians, so if I get to perform with other musicians, it's where the stakes are highest and most immediate. The rush of channeling something is more intense when it is in front of an audience because you can feel the validation of the audience's emotion. Also, I like making people laugh.

What led you to produce music?

When I first thought about being a songwriter, the model in my mind (because of my parents listening to soft rock and folk music) was Carole King, who wrote tons of songs for other people and performed a bunch of songs herself. She was incredibly flexible as a songwriter. Her genius was to me a kind of gold standard.

When I was coming up, we were beginning an era that you had to play an A&R person a fully finished record to make them understand that it might be a hit. And because home studios were more and more available, the expectations of demos to be perfect presentations of hit-sounding prototypes of records changed; it wasn't even a demo anymore, it was literally either the record or the prototype for the record. The pressure to be able to make a record out of the song was very high. I realized I had to teach myself how to produce records.

I went on kind of an expedition for part of 2002 or 2001 and I wrote a bunch of records with pop producers in Europe for myself. My observation was that people who worked in digital media would always tell you all their tricks, whereas the analog recording tradition was shrouded in secrecy and black boxes. The digital producers I worked with taught me a massive amount about how to make a record sound great. I really do enjoy producing records.

Everybody has a studio at home, because everyone can do whatever they want now on a laptop in their living room. I have musical instruments and the capacity to record things at home, but I use studios in LA if I want to record a big project.

What is the impact of home studios and computer technology on musicians?

Computers have made music a lonelier process for lots of people, especially beginners. But music is a social activity. The people who do the best are generally people who can play the hell out of their instrument and make the people around them feel great about themselves.

A musician's natural perfectionism will lead them to labor alone until something is perfect or right. That's already an isolating factor. Now, if you have an entire studio and samples of all the great violinists in the world, and everything on your laptop, it is just one more avenue to keep you isolated from other musicians.

Did your label know from the beginning that Closing Time *would be a hit and garner a Grammy nomination?*

No. They rejected the album as having no singles and gave us the opportunity to make more songs.

Our manager, Jim, said, "You'll write several new songs, they'll give you a budget, you'll go back to the sandbox and make a few more songs and add them to the batch. When you've done three more songs for the label after they rejected your album, which songs are they going to choose as a single?" I said, "The new ones of course, because they commissioned them." Jim said, "That's right. So, here's the question: can you guarantee me that the three new songs that you're going to write are going to be better than 'Closing Time,' 'Secret Smile,' and 'Singing in My Sleep,' the three that we identified as singles?" I said, "No, those are great songs. I can't guarantee beating those songs." He said, "So you're saying you want to go back to the studio to replace those three songs with songs that are very unlikely to be better and have those be the singles for the record." So, we ignored the label for weeks when they called to try to convince me to do more songs. Finally, they got a new person at radio promo, who said, "I'll take a risk on this." And, the president of the label called my manager up and said, "Well, it's your funeral for putting out a record like this."

Those were some magnetic yeses.

Washington Gently Weeps

A key principle of economics is that commercial policy should be neutral—neither favoring nor disfavoring one technology or company over another. This principle makes sense because governments are not good at picking winners or losers, and powerful companies are able to lobby the government for special treatment, even if they do not provide the best service or prices to customers. Moreover, the path of technology is often unpredictable. George Washington eloquently endorsed the neutrality principle in his Farewell Address in 1796, arguing, "But even our commercial policy should hold an equal and impartial hand; neither seeking nor granting exclusive favors or preferences; consulting the natural course of things; diffusing and diversifying by gentle means the streams of commerce, but forcing nothing."*

Current U.S. policy, which authorizes much lower royalty payments for airing music on terrestrial radio broadcasts and YouTube than on music streaming services, would make George Washington weep. Historical and legal circumstances have led to a different set of licenses and fees for the use of music over terrestrial radio, satellite radio, and interactive or non-interactive streaming services. In music circles, this is called the value gap.[29]

Radio Rip-off

Under long-standing copyright law, American radio stations do not pay for recorded music performance rights; they pay only for composition rights. As a result, Aretha Franklin was not paid when her iconic rendition of "Respect" was played on the radio, but the song's composer, Otis Redding, or his estate, was paid royalties. Iran and North Korea are the only other countries that do not require the payment of performance rights to artists when songs are played on the radio, a peculiar axis for the United States to be a party of.

---

* Alexander Hamilton assisted President Washington in writing his Farewell Address. This fact is commemorated in Lin-Manuel Miranda's song "One Last Time," which envisions Washington instructing Hamilton, "Pick up a pen, start writing / I wanna talk about what I've learned / The hard-won wisdom I've learned."

In the past, it was argued that performers benefited from having their songs played on the radio because it promoted their work and increased record sales. In other words, performance royalties were unnecessary in light of the in-kind benefits performers received. But whatever merit this argument may have had in the twentieth century is moot in the digital age. Streaming services, such as Spotify, Amazon, and Apple Music, provide promotional benefits for touring that rival those offered by radio stations, yet these services do pay substantial performance royalties. Moreover, economic consultant Barry Massarsky has noted that just over half of the music currently played on radio stations is from the back catalog (two years old or older), so it is inaccurate to argue that radio promotes new music. Massarsky argues that music promotes radio, rather than the other way around.

The differential treatment of radio and streaming services violates the neutrality principle, to the benefit of owners of radio stations. Figure 9.1 shows that music radio stations pay out a much smaller share of their revenues to music rights holders than do satellite music stations or streaming services.[30] This creates a profitable business model for radio stations: music radio stations pay out only 4.6 percent of their operating budget for music, although music makes up two-thirds of their on-air content. And radio station owners, who are located in nearly every congressional district, and their trade group, the National Association of Broadcasters, have successfully lobbied to avoid paying performance royalties for decades, in a successful exercise of rent-seeking.

Non-interactive streaming services, such as Sirius XM and Pandora, where users cannot select a specific song to play, qualify for a compulsory license with royalty rates set by the Copyright Royalty Board (CRB). But the neutrality principle is further muddied because the two services pay different royalty rates, as they are subject to different legal standards and different CRB rulings.

Figure 9.1: Music Licensing Fees as a Share of Revenue, by Format, 2017

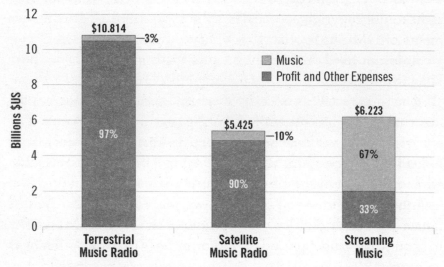

Source: Massarsky Consulting. Note that the revenue base is adjusted to exclude revenue that is not subject to royalties.

On-demand (or interactive) streaming services such as Spotify, Amazon Music, and Apple Music, where the user can select which song to play, must obtain a license from copyright holders for the use of sound recordings. And, as explained in Chapter 8, they negotiate royalty rates directly with the rights owners.

YouTube Rip-off

Perhaps the biggest violation of the neutrality principle belongs to YouTube, the giant online video-sharing platform. More music is listened to over YouTube than on Spotify and Pandora combined.[31] YouTube is covered by the 1998 Digital Millennium Copyright Act (DMCA). The DMCA creates a safe harbor from copyright infringement for user-uploaded content on Internet platforms, provided certain requirements are met. Most important is that the platform must remove content in a timely fashion when it receives a request to do so, known as a *takedown notice*, from a copyright holder. YouTube is not required to pay for the right to use copyrighted material so long as it meets the requirements of DMCA. Spotify, Pandora, and other ad-supported services do not have this luxury because their music catalog is not uploaded by users.

YouTube receives millions of takedown notices every week, but the system has become a losing game of whack-a-mole for copyright holders. Once popular content is removed, users often upload the same or similar copyrighted material again. This system is particularly problematic for less successful artists, who lack the wherewithal and the legal team to constantly search and police YouTube's billions of postings. An obvious fix would be to require YouTube and other platforms to permanently remove copyrighted material once they receive a notification that the copyright holder does not want that material made available on their service. But Internet service providers have resisted this solution, for obvious reasons. Instead, record labels have negotiated from a weak position for a relatively small share of the ad revenue that YouTube collects. This situation provides YouTube with a significant economic advantage over Spotify, for example, which many users consider a close substitute.

When President Clinton signed the DMCA, it was meant as a temporary measure, one that would allow the Internet to grow and evolve; the law was to serve as a stopgap until more thoughtful and appropriate regulation could be devised after the Internet had matured and it became more clear what shape platforms were taking. The Clinton administration did not anticipate that Google, which would later acquire YouTube, and other Internet service providers would become so large and powerful that it would be a Herculean task to unwind the temporary protection that DMCA afforded and legislate a more reasonable balance between content creators and Internet platforms. This is another example of the power of rent-seeking.

Modernizing Copyright for a Digital World

Early in this chapter I warned that music copyright rules can make your head spin. The lines that divide legitimate copyright protection from excessive copyright exploitation are blurred, the laws that dictate copyright fees and licensing requirements across different platforms are uneven, and the restrictions that govern the organizations that collect and distribute music royalties are antiquated. Marty Gottesman, who worked for the performing rights organization BMI for many years, aptly summed up this sad state of affairs when he told me, "Copyright rules don't need to split so many hairs over minutiae that don't matter anymore."[32]

After decades of infighting and failed efforts to reform the system, almost the entire music industry supported a set of proposals that were bundled together in the Music Modernization Act (MMA). This legislation, which was signed into law in 2018, establishes a new organization to collect and distribute royalties from digital streaming services; creates a public database that associates recordings with songwriters and publishers to streamline payments; creates a method for producers and engineers to receive royalties when their music is streamed; creates copyright protection for music recorded before 1972; changes the standard for setting rates used by the CRB to a free market standard; limits the liability of streaming platforms such as Spotify in copyright infringement lawsuits under certain circumstances; and introduces a variety of other technical changes.[33] Although the act was unanimously passed by the House of Representatives in April 2018—an exceedingly rare feat—some last-minute wrangling was necessary to carry it across the finish line in the Senate in September 2018. For example, at the last minute Sirius XM managed to add language that locked in its current royalty rate (15.5 percent as of 2018) for an extra five years, from 2022 to 2027.[34]

The MMA reforms, though significant, represent the lowest common denominator that all interest groups could support, and only scratch the surface of what is needed to modernize copyright laws for a digital era. The MMA does not address the distortionary value gap in radio and YouTube royalty payments, for example. And copyright royalty rates are still highly regulated, rather than determined by market forces.

A much more significant step would be to level the playing field by moving to a uniform, market-based system: allow music rights holders or their delegates (e.g., performing rights organizations and record labels) to negotiate directly with *all* streaming services, radio stations, video-sharing services, and anyone else seeking to gain access to their music. This system is currently used for sound recordings by interactive streaming services, movies, and videogames. Why not extend it to AM and FM radio, YouTube, and other platforms?

Legal researchers Peter DiCola and David Touve conducted more than thirty confidential interviews with individuals directly involved in negotiating access to rights for music for more than twenty interactive streaming services. They found that "licensing an Internet music service can take as little as nine months." The median streaming service took eighteen months to negotiate for the rights to stream enough songs to launch their service.[35] Although the time required to negotiate rights did not decline over the first decade of the 2000s, the volume of songs covered by the negotiations grew to the millions. It thus appears feasible for the market to work in an efficient fashion. Moving to a uniform system that requires all platforms to obtain the rights to use music, instead of imposing a compulsory license at an administratively determined fee for some platforms, would also enable artists to retain creative control over their works, which is a major objective for musicians.

Even Lines

A driver listening to music in her car can seamlessly switch from a terrestrial radio station to a satellite radio station to an Internet radio station to a streaming service without noticing the difference. Yet U.S. policy dictates differential royalty fees and licensing requirements for these platforms. The upshot is that government policy currently favors some formats over others, impeding progress. The uneven and blurry lines that policy makers have drawn for copyright laws have too often been etched to protect and expand the interests of rent-seekers, and not often enough to support the creative instincts of musicians, composers, and innovators.

CHAPTER 10

The Global Market for Music

Though the mountains divide
And the oceans are wide
It's a small world after all.

—Richard and Robert Sherman, 1964

*T*he first concert I attended outside the United States was performed by Air Supply in Hong Kong in 2001, four years after the city-state was returned to Chinese rule. The sold-out crowd never stood up, never danced, and never sang along. The audience seemed more like they were observing a chess match than attending a rock concert. The Australian-English duo of Russell Hitchcock and Graham Russell soldiered on, singing one love ballad after another: "Even the Nights Are Better," "Dance with Me," "Here I Am," "All Out of Love." The audience was respectful, but hardly anyone seemed familiar with their hits.

The music that people listen to and the ways they engage with live entertainment are different around the world. But they are rapidly converging. The Chinese authorities recently started allowing concertgoers to stand and dance during a show—but they have to stand on their chairs! Another change is the growth in the number of music festivals in China. International stars have participated in the Ultra festival in Beijing and Shanghai, for example. And more music is streamed in China than in any other country in the world.

Digital technology is transforming the global music market. For centuries, countries have used music to forge their national identity and establish a unique cultural heritage. Canada, France, Australia, New Zealand, and several other countries require radio stations to broadcast a minimum amount of domestic content to promote the nation's music. But streaming—which provides listeners with access to the entire world's catalog of music—is breaking down those barriers. A decade from now, the global music market will likely look more homogenous than it does today. In the future, you probably will be listening to more music produced by international stars from foreign countries.

In this chapter I use the lens of economics to highlight the differences and similarities in music markets around the world. I focus in particular on China, because China for decades lagged far behind the rest of the world in music production, dissemination, and access as a result of the Cultural Revolution, isolationist policies, and lack of copyright protection. But that is rapidly changing. Scale matters in a superstar market. With the world's largest population and second-largest economy, China is poised to be a world leader in music. China has also begun to enact and enforce copyright protection for music. According to the superstar model (see Chapter 4), China will likely soon begin to produce a growing number of Mandarin-music mega-stars.

If China is a sleeping giant in music, Sweden is the mouse that roars (or at least sings loudly). With a population of under ten million, Sweden punches well above its weight in the music market. The Scandinavian nation has produced such iconic groups as ABBA and Roxette, leading-edge music technology companies like Spotify, and chart-topping composers like Max Martin. Why? The answer probably lies in Sweden's widespread music education, its citizens' proficiency in English, and its embrace of the global economy. The Scandinavian country also benefited from what economists call *agglomeration economies*, meaning positive spillovers from having others in the same industry nearby who foster creativity and productivity. Agglomeration benefits sometimes start by chance, and of course chance or luck plays a big role in the success of music. But agglomeration economies can have lasting effects. Other countries, too, such as Japan and India, have their own idiosyncrasies that influence the development of their music markets.

The Global Music Market

Measured by consumer spending, the United States is the largest music market in the world. Japan is a distant second. The United Kingdom, Germany, and France round out the top five music markets. China recently broke into the top ten.[1]

Countries with larger populations and higher income tend to spend more money on music. The scatter graph in Figure 10.1 plots spending on recorded music (vertical axis) against GDP (horizontal axis) for forty-nine countries with available data. The axes use a logarithmic scale. The upward-sloping line shown on the graph indicates that spending rises in proportion with a country's GDP, on average. Most countries cluster near the line, but there is one notable outlier: China. Total spending on recorded music in China is about $2 billion *below* what one would predict based on the size of its economy.

Indonesia, India, Russia, and Singapore are the next-largest negative outliers. Inadequate copyright protection likely contributes to underspending in these countries. India's music market is also distinct in that it is dominated by Bollywood soundtracks. Charming Hindi songs and dance routines are integral to Bollywood movies, which in turn spur interest in Bollywood songs. As much as 80 percent of music revenue in India is derived from Bollywood songs.[2] The preference for Bollywood music likely crowds out demand for other genres of music, which might explain the lower-than-expected spending on music in India. Streaming services, such as Spotify, have found India a challenging market as well, and will have to cater to Indian tastes for Bollywood songs to succeed there.

Figure 10.1: Spending on Recorded Music and GDP Across 49 Countries, 2017

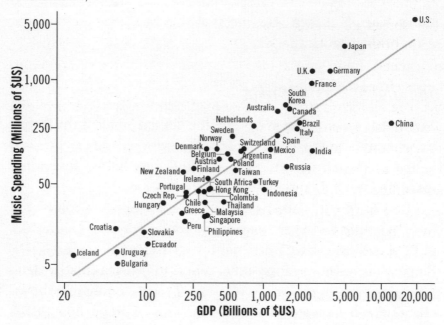

Source: Author's calculations based on data from IFPI Global Music Report and the World Bank. Music spending is wholesale figures converted to U.S. dollars using 2017 exchange rates. The indicated line is based on an ordinary least squares regression of the logarithm of spending on the logarithm of GDP.

Japan, the United Kingdom, and Sweden spend substantially more on recorded music than would be predicted from the size of their economies alone. The fact that Japan is the largest positive outlier is consistent with the country's long-running commitment to CDs and its slow adoption of Internet streaming platforms for music distribution.[3] In this respect, the Japanese music market resembles the U.S. market circa 2000, when revenue was at a peak. Music also plays a big role in the popular anime and video-game industry in Japan. The United Kingdom and Sweden have a long tradition of producing innovative music, which may boost spending in those countries.

It's a Smaller World

The spread of digital downloading and streaming platforms around the globe has greatly expanded the set of songs available to listeners. Long gone are the days when music lovers could only choose from the limited set of albums stocked by Sam Goody and other retail record stores. Sales of physical records (vinyl or CDs) were subject to various "trade frictions," because consumers could only choose from what was in stock, and because knowledge was limited to a small set of artists and songs. Streaming platforms and online stores enable users to discover and listen to music created by a nearly unlimited supply of musicians from all over the world, regardless of where they live.

Evidence suggests that the decline in trade frictions brought about by streaming and digital downloads is beginning to alter the pattern of music people listen to in various countries. The most frequently played and purchased music in a diverse set of countries appears to be converging toward a common tapestry of songs produced by musicians from around the world, rather than a dominant genre produced by musicians from a single country. Music is still a superstar affair, and probably even more so with streaming, but the national origins of the superstars are changing.

Economists who study international trade have discovered a strong "home bias" in trade patterns, meaning a tendency for people to purchase domestically produced goods and services of all kinds, as opposed to goods and services produced in other countries.[4] National borders matter for trade.

In a series of studies, the economist Joel Waldfogel and his co-authors have applied a similar set of tools to analyze the national origins of the music purchased by consumers in several countries.[5] This work requires some strong statistical assumptions to overcome data limitations (for example, sales are inferred from chart rankings using a power law assumption), but the results nonetheless provide important insights into the listening habits of people in different countries and the ways digitization is changing old habits and shifting demand for various types of music around the world.

For decades, the music that people listened to and purchased around the globe exhibited a strong home-country bias, as it does for other products. Swedish musicians, for example, are more likely to reach the top of the Swedish pop charts than are musicians from any other country, and Japanese musicians are most likely to reach the top of the charts in Japan. Some of this home bias is explained by language differences: there is a pronounced tendency to listen to music in one's native language. But language does not explain the whole phenomenon. In the United Kingdom, for example, English groups are more likely to make it to the top of the pop charts than are American groups, and in the United States the reverse holds.

Waldfogel's research reveals that this home bias, though still strong, started to erode after 2004, following the launch of the Apple iTunes store (April 2003) and the proliferation of streaming services. Approximately 40 percent of the home bias preference for domestic music has dissipated since 2004. And less of a tendency for home bias is exhibited on music streamed over Spotify than in chart rankings (which are based on radio airplay, sales, streaming spins, and other measures), suggesting that streaming will likely continue to break down barriers.

Another consequential finding of this line of research is that the mixes of music that people listen to in different countries are growing closer together. Waldfogel refers to this as a "leveling of the playing field," where the share of popular music attributable to past giants, including U.S. recording artists, is shrinking. As a result, people around the globe are listening to music created by musicians from a more diverse and far-flung set of countries. The music world has indeed grown smaller with streaming.

Sweden has had one of the largest trade surpluses in music in the world starting in the 1990s. Although the country has produced fewer stars since the early 2000s—and its most recent international star, Avicii, died at age twenty-eight in 2018—it nonetheless continues to be a hit maker in many respects. Max Martin and Denniz Pop formed a remarkably successful song-writing and producing team until Pop died of stomach cancer in 1998, and afterward Martin carried on the tradition. American stars such as Bon Jovi, Christina Aguilera, Ricky Martin, Kelly Clarkson, the Backstreet Boys, and Britney Spears have flocked to Sweden to produce music.[6]

Many hypotheses have been floated to explain Sweden's out-sized success in music, but a definitive test is lacking. Quincy Jones told me that Sweden was a popular destination for American jazz musicians, which spread knowledge and generated inter-est.[7] A night owl, he also noted the long Swedish winter nights. Max Martin attributed his own success to Swedish support for public school music education: all first-graders are taught to use a recorder, music education is required until age nine, and sub-sidized after-school music programs are widely available.[8] After the success of ABBA, a sophisticated infrastructure developed to produce music and support the music business, including pub-lishing, recording studios, and videography. Many of these con-ditions exist outside of Sweden (in Denmark, for example), so it may be that Sweden was just lucky—a few fortunate superstars helped to put Sweden on the music map, and the infrastructure to produce more stars followed. Abroad, Swedish musicians out-perform on Spotify compared with their rankings based on the charts, radio play, and album sales, suggesting that the expansion of Spotify and streaming will help Sweden continue to be an ex-port powerhouse in music.

If the music world continues to grow smaller, American musi-cians and record labels will face greater competition both at home and abroad. One response to this new environment is for record labels to seek to diversify their rosters and recruit recording art-ists from around the globe. It could also make sense for bands to become more geographically diverse by embracing members and music from other countries, instead of just one local area.

Among some recent collaborations by international stars on the vanguard of this trend are "Despacito" by Luis Fonsi and Daddy Yankee of Puerto Rico and Justin Bieber of Canada; "Lean On" by Major Lazer of the United States, DJ Snake of France, and MØ of Denmark; and "Waka Waka (This Time for Africa)" by Shakira of Colombia and Freshlyground of South Africa. The spread of streaming could lead to even more crossover artists, who cross over in new and different directions.

Music in the Middle Kingdom

Although some American music executives believe "China is the country of the future for music, and always will be," the future may arrive sooner than many expect. Music sales grew faster in China than in any other country except Argentina from 2012 to 2017, according to IFPI data. More people speak Mandarin than any other language. The superstar model predicts that the Chinese market is ripe for superstars. Sooner or later, China is likely to produce its own home-grown stars, who will dominate the music market in Asia and perhaps other continents.

Even if China remains a relative music backwater, the nation's music business illustrates several lessons in economics, and serves as a microcosm for the Chinese economy in general. All seven of the economics lessons I emphasize throughout this book (supply, demand, and all that jazz; preconditions for superstars; power of luck; complementarities; price discrimination; cost disease; and the magical property of music) can readily be seen in the Chinese music market.

To learn more about the Chinese music market firsthand, I visited China in March 2018 and interviewed a dozen executives from the live and recorded music industry, and a handful of musicians. If the music business in the United States is less than transparent, in China it is positively opaque. John Cappo, who was president and CEO of AEG China from 2008 to 2016, describes the Chinese music industry by pointing to a Chinese saying that translates as "Murky waters have all the fish."[9] Business matters are often cloaked in layers of secrecy and insider dealing, because this arrangement enables powerful parties to capture a larger slice of the pie.

There is an acute shortage of data on the music business in China, and business practices are often murky, monopolistic, and fraudulent. The government also keeps a watchful eye on the music business, censoring some music and strictly regulating concerts. The situation is changing, however, and becoming more commercial.

The Heavenly Queen: Wong Fei

Perhaps no story better illustrates the *mishegoss* of the Chinese music market than the saga of Wong Fei's New Year's concerts in Shanghai in 2016. The singer Wong Fei (called Faye Wong in the West) was born in Beijing and moved to British-ruled Hong Kong at age eighteen in 1987. She became famous in the early 1990s singing pop songs in Cantonese (the dialect of Hong Kong), although she has mostly recorded in her native Mandarin since the late 1990s. She has also been a movie star and TV actress.

Wong Fei may be the Madonna of China; her nickname is "the Heavenly Queen." After not performing publicly for six years, she agreed to hold two concerts at Shanghai's Mercedes-Benz Arena on December 29 and 30, 2016. Here is where the details become murky. She apparently committed to not performing another concert in China for at least five years, which elevated the already high demand for her show. Jack Ma, Alibaba's founder, reportedly paid Wong Fei $16 million for each show.[10] The first show was described as a private event for Ma's friends, and the second one was open to the public. Tickets for the December 30 show were listed for $260 to $1,100. But here's the rub: only a fraction of the arena's more than eight thousand seats were reportedly sold to the public. The majority of tickets were apparently sold through ticketing agencies and scalpers, for prices that often far exceeded the list price.

The sky-high ticket prices and minimal number available for public purchase became an embarrassment to the government, which launched an investigation into the incident and barred the arena from holding shows for a period of time. Individuals involved prefer not to talk about what happened. The fact that many devoted fans were willing and able to part with tens of thousands of dollars to watch the forty-seven-year-old diva perform is an indication of the high income inequality that now pervades China.*

Live Events

In China, as in the United States, musicians earn most of their income from performing live shows. Live events account for more than 60 percent of music spending in China, a higher share than in Taiwan, Japan, South Korea, and Australia.[11] The live event market in China can fairly be described by imagining Bill Graham Presents, the legendary San Francisco promoter's operation, on steroids.

The standard practice is that venues contract with promoters to put on concerts, and promoters distribute the tickets. This is where the waters become cloudy. Although Chinese people routinely use WeChat and Alipay apps on their smartphones instead of cash to pay for almost everything, the ticket market still relies on old-fashioned paper tickets. This antiquated technology is used so tickets can be duplicated, resold, distributed to friends and family—and not tracked. Ticket distribution does not go through traditional channels, like a box office or Ticketmaster.

---

* Jack Ma, China's wealthiest man, may be Wong Fei's number one fan: he recorded a duet with the diva for a movie he produced.

Instead, there is a highly structured and sophisticated scalping market that operates largely offline and uses cash.

John Cappo recalled that when he started promoting concerts in China in 2009, the scalper market was run by regional cartels that would fight, literally, over territory. They would budget money to take their victims to the hospital after disputes were settled, he said. Fortunately, the market has become less violent.

Another peculiarity is that the Public Security Bureau (i.e., the police) requires an allotment of tickets that can run from 10 to 20 percent of available seats. The police sometimes double- or triple-print the same ticket to sell or give to friends and family. This creates an obvious problem, as two or three people may arrive at a show holding tickets for the same seat. Promoters must hold extra seats open to accommodate the police and, in some cases, their guests and customers.

The government plays a heavy hand in screening concerts. Every aspect of the show—including the lyrics, videos, costumes, and dance routines—must be cleared with the authorities in advance. The practice stifles spontaneity and creates bureaucratic red tape.

Artists also can be banned from performing for taking politically sensitive positions or for offensive behavior.* Selena Gomez, Maroon 5, Jon Bon Jovi, and others have been banned because of their association with the Dalai Lama.[12] Björk was banned after chanting "free Tibet" at a concert in Shanghai. Katy Perry, who has performed in China, was barred from performing again because she inadvertently displayed a Taiwanese flag that she was handed by a fan. In 2017, Beijing's Ministry of Culture judged Justin Bieber too "badly behaved" to allow him to tour.

The Chinese authorities do not allow general admission tickets at concerts, and the number of people who can be seated on

---

* Artists who are banned from touring may nonetheless have their music available for streaming.

the floor is strictly limited. Concertgoers are prohibited from standing in the aisle or row and dancing. At a Dua Lipa show at the Convention Center in Shanghai on September 13, 2018, some fans were forcibly removed by security guards after dancing and waving a rainbow flag.[13]

Exact figures are unavailable, but several observers told me that the most popular performers in China are from Taiwan and Hong Kong. The band Mayday and Jay Cho are popular Taiwanese acts, and Jacky Cheung and Eason Chan are popular Hong Kongese singers. Korean boy bands were extremely popular until recently (even though they often lip-sync during live performances), and Chinese teenage girls memorized their lyrics in Korean. But K-pop was banned for political reasons in 2016. Electronic dance music is going through a boom-and-bust cycle.

John Cappo estimates that the share of concert acts originating from greater China (mainland plus Hong Kong and Taiwan) is currently up to around 90 percent. In the past, he said, 10 to 15 percent of concerts had consisted of Western acts, and 10 to 15 percent were Korean and Japanese acts.[14]

There is a void in the music that Chinese citizens are familiar with because of the country's isolation during the Cultural Revolution. Many have never heard of the Beatles. Mention David Bowie, Neil Diamond, or Billy Joel, and you are met with blank stares. Elton John is popular only because of the show *The Lion King*. Chinese students who have studied abroad, however, have helped to raise interest in and demand for Western music.

Eric de Fontenay moved to China from the United States in 2010 to manage Chinese rock bands such as Second Hand Rose and help bring Western indie bands to perform in China. De Fontenay is bullish on the Chinese music market. He estimates that ticket prices, which are tightly controlled by the government, have risen by 30 to 50 percent since he arrived. "There has been a marked increase in the number of venues that have opened, especially over the past two to three years in first-, second-, and even third- and fourth-tier cities."[15] And existing venues are operating at higher capacity, he added.

After the Wong Fei fiasco, venues increased their fees, as **demand** had long exceeded **supply**. In addition, the government eased constraints on how much venues could charge because promoters, many under investigation for tax compliance problems, were not in a strong position to resist. And ticketing has become more professional and traceable since Alibaba acquired the ticketing company Damai in May 2016.

More and more top Western acts perform in China as part of their Asian tours. Metallica and the Rolling Stones have toured in China twice. Taylor Swift brought her 1989 Tour to China in 2015.* Sam Smith, Mariah Carey, Pink Martini, and Charlie Puth have shows scheduled. Western acts increasingly view China as a profit center.

For bands like Metallica, ticket prices (to the extent that they can be measured) are at least as high in China as in the United States. Part of the reason for the high prices is that it is expensive to transport personnel and equipment to China, so artists must be compensated for their additional costs.

John Cappo pointed out another aspect of the superstar model that makes the Chinese market ripe for superstar performers. Concert conditions used to be chaotic; today they are more standardized and professional. In the past, it was costly and burdensome for artists to tour, even in major cities. And the fan experience was less than desirable. The temperature in the venue was often too hot or too cold; the bathroom facilities could be unusable or nonexistent; concession stands could be empty; and setting up a stage could take five or six days, given lax supervision

---

* Although the choice of 1989 had nothing to do with China (it is Swift's birth year), the government banned Swift's merchandise because the reference to 1989 conjured images of the 1989 Tiananmen Square protest. And it didn't help that Swift's initials, T.S., printed on some of her merch, happen to be the initials for Tiananmen Square. Nevertheless, pirated T.S. merchandise was widely available outside the arena.

and the lack of rigging capabilities or load-bearing roofs. Today, the venues are much better managed. "The infrastructure now exists in China for bigger shows and can deliver a better fan and artist experience," Cappo said. "The Mercedes-Benz Arena in Shanghai and the Wukesong Arena [now called the Cadillac Arena] in Beijing are world-class facilities, on par with the Staples Center in LA."

The market in China is also becoming more consolidated and commercialized. When Jacky Cheung toured mainland China in the past, he required dozens of promoters, one for each market. That is no longer the case. Multi-city tours organized by the same promoter are now common. Live Nation and AEG operate in China. CMC Live Entertainment, in a joint venture with Creative Artists Agency, is trying to build a nationwide music conglomerate, encompassing both a horizontal monopoly that promotes shows across China and throughout Asia and a vertical monopoly that develops and manages talent.[16] In 2018, CMC Live promoted Jacky Cheung and Mayday tours in cities both large and small, as well as hundreds of other shows.

John Cappo has turned his attention from working with American acts visiting China to producing and managing Chinese acts touring in China and elsewhere in Asia. He plans to bring his show to Las Vegas and Canada. Still, few mainland Chinese acts sell enough tickets to fill a large arena, even in a city with fifteen or twenty million people. And perhaps only Jacky Cheung and Wong Fei can fill an arena for more than two or three nights in a row.

Eric Zho: Creator of My Way, My Show *and the STORM Festival*

Eric Zho was born in Taiwan and raised in the United States. He attended Brown University and graduated in 1999 with a joint degree in economics and philosophy. I interviewed Zho in Shanghai on March 19, 2018.

Zho came to China in 2002, expecting to stay for just one year. His first project was a reality television singing competition show similar to *American Idol*, in a joint venture with the Shanghai Media Group and Universal Music. At the time China had few local stars. The music most Chinese people listened to was Mando-pop by pop singers from Taiwan or Hong Kong. The name of Zho's show translates to *My Way, My Show*, which connotes an edgy, independent streak. Contest winners were signed to a record contract and artist management deal by Universal to capitalize on the publicity.

The show quickly vaulted to the top spot on Chinese television. Thirty million viewers watched the first episode, and more than 100 million tuned in for the second. At its peak, Zho said that 150 million people watched each episode, on par with the viewership of the Super Bowl.

The success quickly spurred copycats. "China is great at copying," Zho said. Seemingly overnight, more than thirty networks produced competitors. As an indication of the format's popularity, the state regulatory agency thought the music competition shows were "polluting the airwaves," so it limited the number of series to two per network.

Zho's show was a launching pad for mainland Chinese pop stars such as singer Jason Zhang. Winners of Chinese TV music competition shows now tour in Singapore, Malaysia, and elsewhere in Asia, and occasionally in North America and Europe.

Zho said that success didn't just happen by accident. He carefully constructed artists' stories to attract interest in the contestants. He hired a hundred interns to post positive comments about the singers on the Baidu message board. This strategy created a critical mass, leading to more comments being posted, and soon some of the singers went viral—yet another example of network effects and compound advantage in the music business. He is proud of the "buzz creation methodology that we created."

The show ran for seven seasons, but Zho left after the third season to strike out on his own. His friends urged him to stay in China because of the opportunity to shape the nation's culture. As someone who was fluent in Chinese, yet raised and educated in the West, he felt uniquely positioned to bridge two cultures.

He soon moved to the live music business. With backing of investors and sponsors, he hit on the idea of creating the STORM Electronic Music Festival.

Launched in 2013, STORM leveraged the growing popularity of dance music in China. Zho told me that he looked for a product that could be branded. "If you promote an artist's concert, the artist owns the brand," and, with competitors, there is little the promoter can capitalize on. If you create a successful festival, however, you own the brand and can earn higher margins.

Using his marketing expertise, he first created a story for the festival. Why STORM? The backstory, he explained, "is about Arcturian aliens who were expelled from the Andromeda galaxy, and roamed around for two thousand years before discovering planet Earth and creating the STORM Festival." The story invokes futuristic images of aliens and high tech. In 2017 the STORM Festival was held in seven cities in China (Beijing, Shanghai, Chengdu, Guangzhou, Shenzhen, Nanjing, and Changsha) and drew a total of 190,000 fans.

Next Eric Zho aspires to create STORM Academies, to educate and develop the next generation of music talent in China.

Music Festivals

As music festivals gain popularity in China, they pose their own unique set of challenges. Festivals are typically held in a park, and parks in China are considered "the people's parks." Archie Hamilton, a tall Scot who has been organizing festivals in China since 2007, told me that he was shocked to discover a group of retirees practicing tai chi in the park on the day of his first festival. And it is not uncommon for the police to take down a rope cordon that prevents non-paying customers from entering a festival, or for security to open an unauthorized entrance. Festivals, however, do allow general admissions, standing, and dancing, and in those respects resemble festivals in the United States and elsewhere.

China's first annual rock festival was the Midi Music Festival, begun in Beijing in 1997.[17] Hamilton estimates that there are more than four hundred music festivals a year currently being held in China. Electronic dance music festivals, with international stars and world-class DJs, are growing particularly rapidly. Live Nation Asia, for example, announced a multi-year partnership with Budweiser to present the Creamfields dance music festival in China, Hong Kong, and Taiwan, so the explosive growth of festivals is likely to continue—as long as the government permits it.

Eric Zho, founder of the STORM Festival, said that there has been intense competition for festivals in recent years. The STORM Festival is one of the largest in China. The 2017 Shanghai edition drew 70,000 fans over two days, featuring three stages and eight acts a day per stage. There are three pricing tiers for admission: general admission tickets for $50 (380 RMB), VIP treatment for $140 (980 RMB), and VVIP tables with champagne service like a private club for $2,900 to $8,700 (20,000 RMB to 60,000 RMB). Zho said STORM offers an early-bird special for general admission tickets targeted by demographic group, an effort to price-discriminate and sell more tickets by charging less to those who are more price sensitive. It is critical to fill the general admission spots, he noted, because VIPs do not want to look out at a half-empty field.

Zho estimated that about 40 percent of festival revenue comes from ticket sales, 40 percent from sponsorships by companies like Budweiser and Adidas, and 20 percent from food and beverage sales. Sponsorship revenue is even greater in China than in the United States, as Chinese millennials have substantial disposable income. Approximately half the festival budget goes toward paying the performers.

The economics of festivals in China is becoming highly competitive. In addition to Live Nation and AEG, wealthy individuals are launching their own festivals, often at a loss. The competition has bid up artist fees and cut into profit margins. The Chainsmokers, I was told, were paid $1 million to perform at the 2017 Shanghai Ultra festival, substantially more than the nightly fee for their Las Vegas residency at the time. Festival organizers vie to lock performers into exclusive deals, preventing them from performing at other events in China for a period of time before and after the festival.

That said, shows and festivals can be cancelled at the last

minute without warning or explanation. The Ultra festivals were cancelled in Beijing and Shanghai in 2018, for example.[18] And Nicki Minaj flew to Shanghai to perform in November 2018, but declined to go onstage because the event was underattended and possibly fraudulent. This environment creates obvious risk for fans, promoters, venues, and artists.

Still, China has come a long way. "Ten years ago," Archie Hamilton said, "no one knew what live music was, concert or festival. Now it has become a *thing* among a certain generation."[19]

Copyright Protection: From Confucius to QQ

China does not have a historical tradition of respecting copyright. In fact, Confucius participated in copying others' folk songs in the classic book *Poetry* (also translated as the *Book of Songs*). According to professors David Herlihy and Yu Zhang, Confucius "believed that intellectual knowledge of these songs was the common heritage of all Chinese people and could not be owned by private individuals."[20]

China enacted regulations to restrict the transmission of copyrighted material over the Internet in 2006. The regulations were weak tea, however, and piracy and unauthorized uploading and downloading of music remained rampant. In 2010, copyright law was strengthened to remove plagiarized material and unauthorized modifications from the web. Non-profit management organizations representing copyright owners were formed and regulated by the National Copyright Administration of China. In July 2015, the National Copyright Administration issued a "Notice on Ordering Internet Music Service Providers to Stop Communicating Unauthorized Music Products," which threatened severe penalties for violators. Nearly two million songs were subsequently deleted from the web.

Sam Jiang, an investor and former executive at Tencent, told me that piracy, once a major problem in China, has been greatly reduced recently for two reasons: the government cracked down on the practice, and streaming companies began policing one another to ensure that no competitor has an unfair advantage by streaming unauthorized music.[21] Copyright protection in China is probably stronger for music today than it is for movies or other forms of intellectual property. Nonetheless, copyright royalties are lower in China than they are in the West, especially for publishing rights.

Bill Zang: The Man Who Brought Michael Jackson's Music to China

Now in his late sixties, Bill Zang lists five affiliations on his business card, including vice president of the China Audio-Video and Digital Publishing Association. I interviewed him in Shanghai on March 20, 2018.

Why did he devote his career to the music business? Through a translator, he explained: "For a very personal reason. In the Cultural Revolution period people could access very little culture, but I was touched by a recording of *Swan Lake*, the Russian classic. It was magical. I decided right then that I would spend my career working in music if I could, because it was so beautiful."

Zang witnessed the evolution of music in post–Cultural Revolution China. From 1980 through 1995, China opened the door to music from Hong Kong and Taiwan, he said. Schools mostly taught classical music. But most people had a strong preference for pop. In the 1990s, students educated abroad brought Western music back to China. In the early 2000s, Korean and Japanese music influenced the development of Chinese music, and the government supported the spread of South Korean pop music and dance. Since 2007, China has been touched by a growing number of European and American artists. He is especially proud of having played a part in bringing Michael Jackson's music to China, and he regrets that he could not arrange for Jackson to visit in person.

Mr. Zang's prediction for the next decade: "Western countries will influence Chinese music more because young people are exposed to it and open to it. Pop, jazz, R&B, rock, EDM are all growing fast. Music from Hong Kong and Taiwan is now growing more slowly."

He envisions a future where there will be international cooperation between artists in international companies, and music will combine traditional Chinese music with Western influences. "American music combines
African, jazz, and hip-hop," he noted. "Chinese music can combine with
Western music to make a world song."

Music Production and Dissemination

Partly because of the legacy of weak copyright protection, the
recording business is in an embryonic stage in China. Entertainment lawyers who understand music copyright and licensing
agreements barely exist. Music is produced by four main groups:
the major labels (Universal, Sony, and Warner); Taiwan's Rock
Records; small independent mainland music companies, such as
Vibe 9; and independent artists. There is no Chinese equivalent
of the major labels, but Tencent Music Entertainment (TME)
has been acquiring labels to produce its own music and may well
become a force in music production in China. Because China
tolerates large, multi-industry monopolies, Tencent could leverage its position to provide live entertainment as well.

Music companies in China are often broader in scope than
American record labels. A music company can manage an artist's
entire career and extract most of his or her income. Eric Zho said
that the main difference in the music business between China
and the United States is that the United States has a separation
of responsibilities, "from managers to agents to promoters to
the whole ecosystem. In China, you can be a promoter, and a
manager, and an agent—and a relative—all at once." It is an arrangement that breeds conflicts of interest, a problem that was
common in the United States in the 1960s. And music companies do relatively little to develop artists or promote their music.
Instead, they look to capitalize on singers who are already going
viral. Some lucky Chinese singers become Internet phenoms,
streaming their music directly through their smartphones.

Chinese artists often look for **complementary activities** to leverage their celebrity status in order to earn a living. A common strategy is to sell merchandise and work as a brand sponsor. The band Mayday, for example, reinvests most of its earnings from touring and recording back into its music production, and earns substantial income from merch sales. The band wears its merchandise onstage to advertise its product.

New companies are also sprouting up to disseminate music, enforce copyright protection, promote music, and collect royalties for individual artists and labels. An example is HiFive, a two-year-old company with ninety employees, headquartered in Chengdu. The company publishes music, places songs on streaming platforms, collects royalties, promotes artists, monitors "audio fingerprints" across the web to police unauthorized copies of songs, and acts as an agent for booking shows. It represents a catalog of ten million tracks. HiFive also invests in music promotion, which could involve paying streaming services to post banners and push music. In exchange for its services, HiFive receives a 30 percent share of artist royalties.

Another innovative startup is Kanjian Music, which works both with foreign labels to place their music on Chinese streaming services (QQ, Netease, etc.) and collect royalties, and with foreign streaming services (Spotify, Apple, etc.) to export Chinese music.[22] The four-year-old company has approximately four million tracks under a licensing agreement. Kanjian shared with me its top one hundred imports for the twelve months ending in April 2018. They mainly include indie Western artists, such as Tobu (Lithuanian), Alex Krindo (Danish and Norwegian), and Nightwish (Finnish), as well as the American production company Two Steps from Hell, which produced songs for hit movies such as *X-Men*, *Interstellar*, and the Harry Potter films. Streaming is highly skewed toward the top songs in China, as elsewhere. Kanjian's top ten songs accounted for as much streaming and downloading activity as the next ninety songs.

Chinese music companies are responsible for screening songs, artwork, and music videos for domestic consumption to ensure that they do not include offensive lyrics or images. Companies like HiFive and Kanjian are required to administer the first line of censorship.

In a widely publicized incident in early 2018, the rapper GAI was abruptly dropped from a popular reality television show called *Singer*, just as his fans were anticipating his second appearance on the program. The State Administration of Press, Publication, Radio, Film and Television (SAPRFT), China's top media regulator, issued an edict banning performers belonging to the hip-hop culture or other subcultures, including anyone with tattoos, from appearing on televised shows. In earlier years, several rap songs were blacklisted.[23]

The pressure to conform embodied in Chinese culture and enforced by government policy could inhibit the development of a world-class music industry. Even apart from government censorship, Chinese education typically emphasizes rote learning, rather than creativity and independence. Top Western musicians often come from a counterculture environment and use music to express extreme feelings of love, anger, sadness, pain, and joy. It remains to be seen whether Chinese musicians can make the leap to expand the musical frontiers along the lines of earlier iconoclastic visionaries such as Beethoven, Miles Davis, Chuck Berry, Bob Dylan, the Beatles, Aretha Franklin, Carole King, Freddie Mercury, James Hetfield, and Dr. Dre.

Streaming Is Surging in China

Following the crackdown on piracy, streaming of recorded music is flourishing in China. Live-streaming and reality music television shows are also immensely popular. Nearly one billion Chinese people, making up 72 percent of the population, listen to music every week, according to a 2016 Nielsen survey.[24] The average listener spends sixteen hours per week listening to music, and two-thirds of listeners report using a streaming service. Some seven billion songs are streamed a day.

Tencent Music Entertainment, or TME, is the largest music streaming conglomerate in China. TME operates QQ, Kugou, and Kuwo, three distinct streaming platforms. The platforms attract different groups of users. QQ, for example, is more popular in tier-one cities, such as Beijing and Shanghai, than is Kugou and Kuwo. Combined, the three streaming services had six hundred million monthly users in 2017, and two hundred million daily users.[25]

NetEase Cloud Music is the second-most-popular streaming company. The company claims to have four hundred million monthly users.[26] Despite its efforts, Alibaba has made a relatively unsuccessful foray into streaming so far. Spotify, Google, and Amazon Music are not available in China, and Apple Music has a small presence. Spotify and TME are strategic partners, however, and have swapped roughly 10 percent of each other's stock.[27]

As in the United States, in China streaming platforms offer a "freemium" (ad-supported) service and a paid subscription service. The Chinese streaming business is overwhelmingly supported by ad revenue, not subscription payments. Only 4 percent of users of QQ Music, for example, are paid subscribers, and Kuwo and Kugou have an even lower percentage of paid subscribers, just 2 percent. In an example of **price discrimination**, TME offers some exclusive content that only paid subscribers can download, and enables paid subscribers to download higher-quality music (what it calls "Super Quality Music").[28]

Tencent Music Entertainment pays out more than 50 percent of its revenue net of costs in royalties. In 2016, $400 million in royalties were paid out, and in 2018 that figure was estimated to have doubled to $800 million. Revenue was $1.3 billion in the first half of 2018, up 92 percent from a year earlier. About half of the revenue generated by TME is from live-streaming, an indication of the popularity of home-grown Internet phenoms.

In May 2017, TME and Universal Music Group signed a multi-year licensing agreement that enables QQ, Kugou, and Kuwo to stream music from Universal's catalog.[29] TME has similar arrangements with several other labels.

Tencent Music Entertainment's library of songs increased from between fifteen million and seventeen million in 2017 to twenty million in 2018. According to Andy Ng, vice president of TME, English-language songs make up over 60 percent of the tracks in TME's catalog, while Chinese songs make up just 4 percent. But over 80 percent of users listen only to the Chinese catalog.

Tencent Holdings Limited, the largest company in Asia and the world's largest Internet company, is the parent company of TME. It is unclear whether TME is earning an operating profit from streaming music. Unlike Spotify, however, TME can afford to lose money on streaming if it raises demand for WeChat, videogames, and other apps that its parent produces. Thus, TME yields **complementary** benefits to Tencent's other activities, just as Amazon's Alexa provides a complementary portal to drive demand for Amazon's core retail business, and Apple Music is complementary to the manufacturer's core device business.

With hundreds of millions of users, China's streaming platforms collect enormous volumes of Big Data on users' preferences and listening habits, which can be used to tailor recommendations to users, target concert tours, and guide music production. Because the services are new, however, the use of Big Data is still in its infancy.

Although China is one of the largest and fastest-growing music markets in the world, TME investor Sam Jiang noted that the total amount of money spent on online music in China "is about the same size as one real estate project in a tier-one city." Still, with hundreds of millions of people streaming music every day, the business is a powerful force shaping Chinese culture, leisure activities, and consumption. In China, as elsewhere, music punches well above its weight.

Risk and Opportunity in China

China provides endless potential for entertainers—both new and old, Western and Asian—to reach a vast audience. The signs bode well for China to launch international music superstars. Massive audiences partake in streaming and live shows, and the infrastructure for nationwide touring is improving and becoming more standardized. Music impresario John Cappo is optimistic about the prospects for the Chinese music market. He points out that "hundreds of millions of Chinese listen to music on their smartphones," and he expects rapid growth over the next decade.

Eric Zho expects a "Yao Ming of music" to come along and become an internationally famous Chinese superstar, much like the original Yao Ming became a basketball phenomenon in the United States. "I go around the world to conferences and preach on this," he said. "The pie in China is so big now. A couple of international Chinese superstars will make the pie much bigger."

China could indeed create a new "world song," as Bill Zang idealistically envisions. And the world may be ready: countries' musical preferences are moving in the direction of a tapestry of world songs in an era of frictionless global streaming catalogs.

Still, there are enormous risks. The Chinese government could step in and shut down the entire enterprise. Music streamed on the Internet could be more tightly controlled. Concerts and festivals, with mass gatherings of energized young people, could pose a special threat to orderly government rule.

Archie Hamilton has highlighted critical paradoxes at the heart of modern China, which could determine not just the future of its music market but also the nation's role in the world economy.[30] According to what he calls the "paradox of scale," "in China, as long as you're marginal, as long as you're not reaching more than 100, 200, 300 people," the authorities give a lot of latitude. "You can do whatever you want on the margin and get away with it." But if you grow too big, you are at risk. "The hip-hop thing was very much that paradox of scale. It was small and emerging and underground, and suddenly it is huge and it's influential and it's crazy. And they discouraged it. They say that doesn't exist anymore."

Sounding like an economist, Hamilton observed, "China seems to pursue an export-driven expansionist policy on trade, and an import-substitution policy on culture." He calls this the "paradox of engagement," and it involves the contrast between "China's outward expansion and inward containment." As a practical matter, this tension requires a bureaucratic approval process for music, which places the state's moral concerns and values above economic and business considerations.

So far the government has haltingly allowed the Chinese music business to develop and grow. Even the hip-hop ban is far from complete. Hip-hop is still allowed as long as it is devoid of offensive language, misogynistic references, and tattoos. But it remains to be seen if China can influence the world's music without allowing the world's music to influence China too abruptly, and possibly cause the government to push the stop button.

CHAPTER 11

Music and Well-Being

I have been rich, and I have been poor. Believe me, baby, rich is better!

—Ella Fitzgerald

Al Stenner began his career as a Presbyterian minister and later earned a Ph.D. in philosophy at Michigan State University. He moved to St. Louis in the 1960s to teach at Washington University and raise his family. Al was also a talented pianist. When Ella Fitzgerald brought her jazz band to town to play the Kiel Auditorium, her longtime pianist Paul Smith came down with the flu, so she asked around for the best piano player in St. Louis. Someone recommended Al Stenner, and he eagerly filled in. Feeling that he had risen to the occasion, after the show the philosophy professor asked the First Lady of Song to grade his performance. Al was only slightly deflated when she replied that he had done "a good job but missed a few notes."

Unfortunately, Alzheimer's disease robbed Al of his memory later in life. By the time I met him, he could not remember most of the milestones of his life, including accompanying Ella Fitzgerald, or his scholarly publications in philosophy. His son Jack told me the story about Al and Ella Fitzgerald. Although Al's memory had faded, he could still play the piano—quite well. He seemed transported in time when I saw him energetically play "Mack the Knife," "Moon River," "Summertime," and other tunes from memory, without missing a note.

Al Stenner's experience is not atypical. Music therapy has

been shown to stir memories and emotions in people afflicted by neurological disorders. The documentary film *Awake Inside* provides vivid examples of how patients suffering from dementia and other memory disorders can come alive when they hear music of their youth. As the late physician Oliver Sacks has written, "Musical perception, musical sensibility, musical emotion and musical memory can survive long after other forms of memory have disappeared."[1] Part of the reason for the durable power of music appears to be that listening to music engages many parts of the brain, triggering connections and creating associations, according to neuroscience research.[2]

Listening to music can profoundly affect people's emotional experiences during their daily activities as well. It is impossible for me to watch James Corden's "Carpool Karaoke" with Paul McCartney (and other guests) and not smile, or to listen to Billy Joel and not feel nostalgic. Beyond anecdotes, there is a voluminous literature on the psychological and physiological impacts of music on our lives. From an economic standpoint, this research documents that music contributes to our "utility," the satisfaction we derive from the goods and services we consume. Simply put, music makes us happier. Music can also help people to regulate their emotions, and it can provide an enjoyable distraction from everyday mundane tasks. And because music is more widely available today, the contribution of music to human welfare is greater than ever.

If You're Happy and You Know It

Many approaches have been used to measure the psychological effects of music on our well-being, and they point to a wide range of benefits resulting from listening to music.

Because listening occurs in real time, the most direct approach is to examine how music affects people's emotional states while they are listening. Studies find that time spent listening to music ranks among the most enjoyable activities that people undertake in their daily lives. My research with the psychologist Danny Kahneman and others, for example, found that music is in the same class as participating in sports, religious worship, and attending a party in terms of the presence of positive emotions (such as feeling happy) and absence of negative ones (such as feeling stress and anger).[3] And, of course, music is often combined with these other activities.

Listening to music is most often a secondary activity—a welcome distraction while driving to work, doing chores, or exercising. It is often playing in the background during parties, conversations, and meals. Maybe you're even listening to music while you read this chapter!

Recent research finds that listening to music as a secondary activity, while focusing attention on some other activity, tends to make the other activity more enjoyable. This finding emerges, for example, from an in-depth study of 810 women in Columbus, Ohio, and 820 women in Rennes, France, that I conducted with Kahneman and others.[4] Specifically, we asked the women to list the activities they engaged in during the previous day, and how happy, stressed, or sad they felt during each episode. Our survey approach, known as the day reconstruction method (DRM), included many innovations. We asked respondents to divide their days into episodes and identify all of the activities that they engaged in during each episode. If multiple activities were reported, they indicated the one that seemed most important at the time. Although we published many results using the data, we did not previously focus on music.

Of the 22,715 episodes reported, a total of 1,572 involved listening to music.[5] In only 7 percent of these incidents, however, was music considered the main activity. Listening to music was more common in the United States than in France, and more likely to be a secondary activity in the United States than in France.

What were the subjects focused on while listening to music? The most frequent non-music-related activities indicated as most important while listening to music were commuting or traveling, working, talking or conversation, and doing housework or cooking. For each of these four focal activities, Figure 11.1 shows the average rating of happiness (on a 0 to 6 scale) that respondents reported, depending on whether or not they were also listening to music at the time. The figure also reports results for all activities, divided by whether or not music was listened to as a secondary activity during the episode.

Commuting, for example, is one of the most unpleasant activities that people report in their daily routines.[6] The average happiness rating reported for occurrences of commuting or travel that did not involve music was 3.7, and the average rating during commuting or travel time that also included listening to music was 4.0. Turning on music while commuting improves the experience to close to the overall average happiness rating.

In each of the four activities shown in Figure 11.1, listening to music while doing the activity is associated with greater reported happiness. Listening to music appears especially beneficial while working and having conversations.

Across all activities of daily life in which music is not the main focus, the average happiness rating is 4.0, and across all activities in which listening to music is a secondary activity, the average happiness rating is 4.3. The difference amounts to almost one-fifth of a standard deviation of reported happiness ratings across all daily episodes.

Not only is reported happiness higher, but negative emotions, such as feeling stressed or impatient, are less intense when music is playing in the background. Music can make you feel happier and chase the blues away.

Two important statistical concerns must be addressed before reaching the conclusion that listening to music *itself* causes people to have better emotional experiences. First, it is possible that music is combined with activities that are generally highly enjoyable, such as parties or recreation. Although this is not an

Figure 11.1: Average Happiness Rating (0–6 scale) During Activities with and Without Music

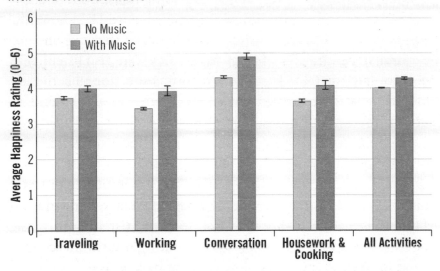

Source: Author's calculations from French-American survey conducted with the day reconstruction method. Whiskers indicate width of a 95 percent confidence interval.

issue when looking at occurrences of, say, commuting, it could be a confounding factor when looking across all episodes. If one statistically controls for the main activity that took place during the episode, however, the results are hardly changed.[7]

Second, and more important, it is possible that the subset of people who listen to music while engaging in other activities are just happier souls. For example, those who choose to listen to music while commuting may be happier, regardless of whether or not they are listening to music, than those who do not listen to music while commuting. Fortunately, with the data we collected, it is possible to compare the *same* person over separate episodes of the same activity that occurred during a day, some when she combined music with commuting and some when she did not, for example. Such a comparison indicates that personal differences account for less than half of the benefit that seems to accrue when music is listened to while other activities are taking place.[8] Thus, listening to music during an activity seems to improve a person's perception of her experience compared with her perception of other episodes of the same activity that occurred during the day without music.

Similar results were found in a DRM study of 207 men and women conducted in Sweden by Daniel Västfjäll and co-authors.[9] Positive emotions, such as feeling happy or joyful, were more common and more intense during musical episodes than during non-musical episodes. Subjects were also more likely to express higher degrees of arousal (e.g., feeling inspired or energized) during musical episodes. The Swedish researchers added a new wrinkle to the DRM: they asked participants to indicate their motives for listening to music. "The most common motives for listening to music among the participants were to *get energized, to relax, to affect one's emotions, to get some company* and *to pass the time*," they found. These findings suggest that people use music to help regulate their emotional states.

Economists have long been skeptical that researchers can take at face value what people say about what makes them happy or sad. My profession prefers to infer people's preferences from the choices they make, rather than rely on what they tell us about what they like or dislike. Although this predilection for "revealed preference" is slowly fading with the emergence of behavioral economics, there are good reasons to focus on objective data over subjective reports, when possible. In this regard, the fact that many people choose to devote a large amount of leisure and work time to listening to music is a strong indication that they find the experience satisfying, consistent with what psychological studies tell us.

There is another reason to trust what people report about their emotions when listening to music: physiological studies establish that listening to music produces positive biological and neurological reactions, similar to those generated during other positive experiences. And, as I explain next, those physiological functions are also related to positive health outcomes.

Good Vibrations

An entire academic journal is dedicated to the psychology of music, and stacks of books have been written on music and health and well-being. Even a cursory survey of this literature reveals the many benefits of music for markers of health and well-being, such as on the level of stress hormones, and for health itself, including for patients suffering from neurological disorders.

Marie Helsing, a researcher at the Karolinska Institute in Stockholm, and co-authors, for example, designed a field experiment to test the effect of listening to music on subjects' levels of cortisol, a stress hormone.[10] Participants were randomly assigned to either a treatment group (twenty-one women) or a control group (twenty women). The treatment group selected music that they liked to listen to, which was loaded on an MP3 player. In the first week of the experiment, both groups were instructed to relax for thirty minutes at home after work without listening to music. After a week, the treatment group was instructed to listen to music during their relaxation time each workday over the next two weeks, while the control group continued their protocol of relaxing for thirty minutes without music. The results indicated that salivary cortisol levels significantly declined after subjects listened to thirty minutes of music, compared with the control group. Self-reported stress also declined, further suggesting that responses to survey questions regarding emotional experiences related to music provide meaningful results. The authors concluded, "Together these results suggest that listening to preferred music may be a more effective way of reducing feelings of stress and cortisol levels and increasing positive emotions than relaxing without music."

A bevy of other research supports similar conclusions. Researchers Saoirse Finn and Daisy Fancourt conducted a thorough review of forty-four studies of the biological impact of listening to music, twenty-seven of which were based in clinical settings.[11] Biomarkers included cortisol, immune function, and blood glucose as outcome measures. "Thirteen of 33 biomarkers tested were reported to change in response to listening to music," they noted, and concluded that "the primary way by which music listening affects us biologically is via modulations of stress response. Effects were shown irrespective of genre, self-selection of the music, or duration of listening, although a majority did use classical music."

Music is increasingly being used in therapy for patients suffering from a range of disorders, as highlighted in the film *Alive Inside*. Although the underlying mechanisms by which music helps memory are still uncertain, accumulating evidence from case studies, clinical work, and a handful of experiments suggests that familiar music is salient and memorable for Alzheimer's patients in ways that many other stimuli are not.[12] A survey of the research literature by music therapy professors Blythe LaGasse and Michael Thaut concludes, "The vast amount of evidence from rehabilitation science has demonstrated that rhythmic stimuli can help to recover function in persons who have decreased functioning due to stroke, traumatic brain injury, spinal cord injury, Parkinson's disease, and multiple sclerosis."[13]

Neuroimaging studies find that the medial prefrontal cortex, a region of the brain that supports retrieval of autobiographical information, is particularly active while people listen to music that was popular during their adolescent years. And there is further evidence that music heard during childhood and adolescence creates more salient or durable memories than music heard at other ages.[14]

Interestingly, research on the listening choices of Spotify users by Seth Stephens-Davidowitz finds that people of all ages most frequently listen to music that was popular in their adolescent years.[15] Consider the Radiohead song "Creep," for example, which was released in 1993. In 2018, "Creep" was the 164th-most-streamed song among thirty-eight-year-old men, who were fourteen years old when the song was released; it was not even in the top three hundred songs for men born ten years earlier or ten years later. Looking across all songs that topped the *Billboard* charts from 1960 to 2000, Stephens-Davidowitz finds that the "most important period for men in forming their adult tastes were the ages 13 to 16" and "for women . . . the ages 11 to 14." Adolescence appears to be a particularly important time for forging our musical tastes and memories.

The writer Harlan Coben reflected on the role of music in forging his identity while growing up in suburban New Jersey. "Inside, I was panicked about being directionless. My rebellion, mild as it seems, consisted of listening to bands like Steely Dan."[*] He was particularly struck by "Deacon Blues." "I heard it as a song about someone trapped in the suburbs trying to break free." Later he became interested in writing, "and found my own way to break free."

I once asked Q Prime founders Cliff Burnstein and Peter Mensch why they regularly attend spring training for Major League Baseball. Peter answered, "We are trying to extend our adolescence." Cliff added with a smile, "We are sort of in the business of extending adolescence."[16]

A Great Bargain

Music is arguably one of the best bargains ever created. For listeners, music is a kind of elixir with seemingly magical properties: it improves unpleasant experiences and makes pleasant activities more enjoyable. Music can also help individuals regulate their moods. For society, music has the capability to unite people of disparate backgrounds, tear down walls, and rally people to support causes. Music is present at almost every major milestone in our lives: high school proms, weddings, funerals, birthdays, parades, sporting events, college reunions, and presidential inaugurations.

For all of these benefits, Americans spend less money on

---

[*] Harlen Coben, "Novelist Harlan Coben on Steely Dan," *Wall Street Journal*, November 15, 2016.

recorded music in a typical year than they do on potato chips. The average consumer spends less than a dime a day on recorded music. Yet the average person spends three to four hours a day listening to music. Few activities absorb as much time as music yet provide as much pleasure. What's more, the time we spend listening to music is up, while spending on music is down by 80 percent in real terms since 1999. A great deal has gotten even better!

Live entertainment also offers fans a great bargain. Although the cost of attending live events by top performers has increased much faster than overall price inflation in recent decades, more people are attending concerts than ever, indicating that consumers still consider live entertainment a good bargain. And more stars than ever are touring.

Seven Keys to Economics of Music

The music industry is certain to change as new apps and business models are developed, fans' tastes change, and entirely new genres and performers rise and fall. But the seven key economic lessons for understanding the music business are likely to endure and continue to be helpful for understanding developments in the industry.

Supply, demand, and all that jazz of human desire for fair treatment and government policy relating to copyright and scalping, for example, will always play a central role in determining the direction of the music business. Although technology will enable further disintermediation, and provide new avenues for artists to create, market, and distribute their music, the music industry will likely continue to be dominated by a relatively small number of superstars given the scale of the market, the uniqueness of performers, and the role of networks in determining popularity. And luck, along with talent, will likely continue to play an outsized role in determining which superstars seize the momentum and break through in an ever more crowded market with many performers vying for an audience.

Successful artists and businesses will continue to take advantage of complementary activities, such as live performances and selling merchandise, find ways to price-discriminate without offending fans in order to maximize revenue, and avoid incurring unnecessary costs. Music will always affect listeners' moods, and scientists may find new and better ways of treating patients with musical therapy.

A journalist in China recently asked me, "What does your book have to say about the latest hit app, TikTok?" To be honest, I had never heard of TikTok, a fast-growing social media platform for creating and sharing short videos, with five hundred million users. But I explained that a lesson of this book is that consumers demand quick and convenient service, which is why streaming platforms such as Apple, Amazon, and Spotify have been able to attract users from sites offering free pirated music, and that music is a social activity that spreads through networks. As the music industry evolves and new apps emerge, the lessons of rockonomics will help us to understand these exciting yet disruptive developments and place them in a broader context.

Closing Time

In his 1930 essay "Economic Possibilities for Our Grandchildren," John Maynard Keynes posited that a hundred years hence, the main economic problem confronting people will be what to do with our leisure time:

> Thus for the first time since his creation man will be faced with his real, his permanent problem—how to use his freedom from pressing economic cares, how to occupy the leisure, which science and compound interest will have won for him, to live wisely and agreeably and well.[17]

Most people are not nearly as free of pressing economic concerns as Keynes had envisioned, partly because of the rise in inequality in our increasingly winner-take-all economy, and that situation is unlikely to change in the next decade when we reach Keynes's one-hundred-year marker. Still, Keynes's forecast has merit. As Daniel Hamermesh has observed, "Our ability to purchase and enjoy goods and services has risen much more rapidly than the amount of time available for us to enjoy them."[18] Keynes anticipated that "it will be those peoples, who can keep alive, and cultivate into a fuller perfection, the art of life itself and do not sell themselves for the means of life, who will be able to enjoy the abundance when it comes."

Indeed, economic activity and consumer spending are increasingly dependent on experiences, entertainment, and culture. Research by the Nobel Prize winners Angus Deaton and Danny Kahneman finds that Ella Fitzgerald's famous quote about being "rich is better" is only partly correct: higher income is associated with greater life satisfaction, but beyond a certain level—$75,000 of income a year in their estimation—additional income is unrelated to day-to-day emotional well-being. In their words, "High income buys life satisfaction but not happiness." A wealth of psychological research finds that experiences, family and friendships, health, and personal values are what matter most for our well-being, not the amount of material goods that we purchase.[19] For this reason, advice books commonly recommend that to improve our lives, we should spend money on memorable, enjoyable experiences, not on tangible goods.

Music is a quintessential component of the experience economy. And while we can hope that we will someday soon face Keynes's dilemma of figuring out what to do with excessive leisure time, listening to music will continue to be a significant element of how we improve our experiences both during leisure time and during work time. That is an essential element of rockonomics: music is almost uniquely situated to enhance experiences, reinforce memories, help people find purpose and meaning in their lives, and build sustainable communities. And enabling people to reach these goals is the ultimate purpose of the economy.

Keynes closed his essay on the future by observing:

> The pace at which we can reach our destination of economic bliss will be governed by four things—our power to control population, our determination to avoid wars and civil dissensions, our willingness to entrust to science the direction of those matters which are properly the concern of science, and the rate of accumulation as fixed by the margin between our production and our consumption; of which the last will easily look after itself, given the first three.
>
> Meanwhile there will be no harm in making mild preparations for our destiny, in encouraging, and experimenting, in the arts of life as well as the activities of purpose.
>
> But, chiefly, do not let us overestimate the importance of the economic problem, or sacrifice to its supposed necessities other matters of greater and more permanent significance. It should be a matter for specialists—like dentistry. If economists could manage to get themselves thought of as humble, competent people, on a level with dentists, that would be splendid!

My dentist actually helps manage her son's electronic music band, Space Jesus, in her spare time. There is even more to learn from dentists than Keynes anticipated! Rockonomics provides a splendid model for learning about the economy and life on the journey to economic bliss.

Evaluation of the Pollstar Boxoffice Database

*T*he Pollstar Boxoffice Database is used in Chapters 4 and 6 to describe trends in concert prices and revenue. The Pollstar data have a variety of commercial applications: they are used by the media (e.g., the *Wall Street Journal* and *Forbes*) to determine the size of the concert industry and celebrity earnings; by Pollstar to select bands for touring honors; by promoters to determine the likely number of tickets that could be sold for tours; and by merch sellers to determine a band's potential for merchandise sales. Pollstar is considered the gold standard for data on concert attendance, revenue, and prices, but a number of music business insiders mentioned to me that Pollstar data are incomplete. Data quality should always be a concern, especially in the music industry, where there is a lack of transparency and where managers, promoters, and venues may have incentives to misreport data or fail to report altogether. (As a public company, however, Live Nation has a legal duty to report accurately.) This appendix assesses the coverage, accuracy, and reliability of the Pollstar data.*

The underlying concert data are reported to *Pollstar* magazine by venues, promoters, and managers. The reported information

---

* These terms have a specific statistical meaning. *Coverage* refers to the share of concerts contained in the Pollstar data; *accuracy* refers to whether statistics computed from the data tend to be correct, on average; and *reliability* refers to the strength of correlation between the data reported to Pollstar and the actual box office records.

consists of the date of the event, the headline act and opening acts, the promoters, the name and location of the venue, box office revenue, number of tickets sold, and high and low prices. In this Appendix, I compare the Pollstar data for a subset of concerts to more accurate and comprehensive data from other sources. The main conclusion of my analysis is that although there are some lapses in the coverage of the Pollstar data, the Pollstar Boxoffice Database provides reasonably comprehensive, accurate, and reliable data on concert revenue for top artists, especially since the 1990s and in the United States.

A comparison of the Pollstar data to other sources is possible because (1) the website Setlist.fm crowdsources information on concerts for major performers and (2) a large state university that operates two sizable arenas shared its confidential box office data with me on the condition that the name of the university remain anonymous.[1] These two arenas do not directly report information to Pollstar, but managers and promoters of shows performed at the venues often do report the data.

Both of these alternative sources have their own strengths and weaknesses: Setlist.fm lacks information on prices, attendance, and revenue, but it is quite comprehensive for top artists. The large state university represents only two venues that do not report data directly to Pollstar, but it provided me with unassailable box office records on all of its shows. Taken together, the two sources help paint a picture of the coverage, accuracy, and reliability of the Pollstar data. I first considered the coverage of the Pollstar data by comparing it to Setlist.fm, and then I turned to the accuracy and reliability of the price and revenue data.

Evidence on Coverage

This analysis focuses on twenty-six major acts who headlined more than 23,000 shows reported to Setlist.fm since the early 1980s. Specifically, the artists are Beyoncé, Billy Joel, Bon Jovi,

Britney Spears, Bruce Springsteen, Bruno Mars, Cher, Cold-play, Céline Dion, Dave Matthews Band, Jay-Z, John Mayer, Justin Bieber, Kenny Chesney, Lady Gaga, Madonna, Mariah Carey, Maroon 5, Metallica, Pink, Rihanna, Shania Twain, Taylor Swift, U2, Usher, and Whitney Houston. I scraped data on the date, location, and headline act for each of their shows from Setlist.fm. Once the data were collected, an effort was made to exclude award shows, TV appearances, MTV, and other non-concerts from the Setlist.fm data. Nevertheless, it is possible that some non-concerts remain in the Setlist.fm list, which would make the Pollstar data appear less comprehensive than is actually the case. The Pollstar sample of concerts is almost a proper subset of shows reported to Setlist.fm, which suggests that Setlist.fm covers close to the entire universe of concerts.

Table A.1 reports the number of concerts contained in the Pollstar database as a proportion of the number of concerts in Setlist.fm for those twenty-six major headliners. The results are presented separately for events in the United States (column 3) and for all countries in which Pollstar and Setlist have data (column 6). If the Setlist.fm compilation of concerts is taken as the universe of all concerts, then the Pollstar data captured more than 80 percent of concerts performed by top acts in the United States in the 2000s. The proportion of concerts covered by Pollstar slipped for a period when Live Nation ceased reporting to Pollstar, though it has since resumed reporting. Pollstar's coverage outside the United States has improved each decade and currently approaches the coverage rate of concerts in the United States.

Table A.1: Number of Concerts in Setlist.fm and Pollstar for 26 Headliners

Decade	US ONLY			ALL		
	Setlist	Pollstar	Pollstar/ Setlist	Setlist	Pollstar	Pollstar/ Setlist
	(1)	(2)	(3)	(4)	(5)	(6)
1980s	1,876	1,121	60%	2,906	1,173	40%
1990s	2,553	1,794	70%	4,343	2,174	50%
2000s	5,585	4,884	87%	8,569	6,340	74%
2010s	4,337	3,529	81%	7,342	5,786	79%

Notes: Author's analysis of Pollstar Boxoffice Database and Setlist.fm. See text for list of artists. An effort was made to remove non-concerts from the Setlist.fm list of events.

Evidence on Accuracy and Reliability

Even though the operator of the two venues at the large state university that shared data with me does not report data directly to Pollstar, artist managers and promoters of shows performed at the venues can report the data to Pollstar. The university shared data with me on live events held at its venues from mid-2010 to the end of 2017. In this period, there were 135 concerts that appeared in the Pollstar Boxoffice Database. This represents 57 percent of the total number of concerts that were performed in the two venues, which not surprisingly is less comprehensive than the Pollstar data overall, given that this venue operator does not report directly to Pollstar.

It is reassuring that the data for these 135 concerts reported to Pollstar were quite similar, on average, to the data for those same shows that the large state university provided. Revenue per show was $801,086 according to Pollstar and $776,170 according to the university data, a discrepancy of just 3 percent for the 135 shows in both data sets. The average number of tickets sold was 11,324 according to Pollstar and 11,191 according to the university records, yielding a discrepancy of just 1 percent. And the

Figure A.1: Revenue According to University vs. Revenue According to Pollstar (Millions of Dollars)

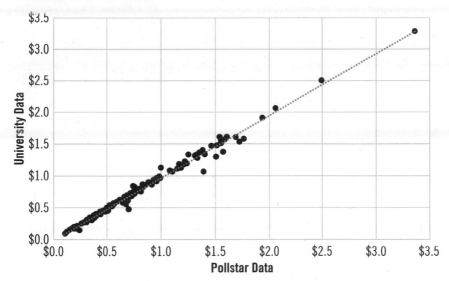

average price (derived as revenue per number of tickets sold for each show) was $70.74, according to Pollstar, and $69.36, according to the university records. Surprisingly, there was a tendency for shows with more tickets sold to be underreported to Pollstar. Nonetheless, this comparison suggests that the data reported to Pollstar are quite accurate.

The Pollstar data are also remarkably highly correlated with the actual box office data. Figure A.1 provides a scatter diagram of revenue per show as provided by the university (vertical axis) and as reported to Pollstar (horizontal axis). The correlation between the two measures is 0.99, and a fitted line is close to a 45-degree line, which implies that in most cases the revenue figures reported to Pollstar were almost identical to the revenue data recorded by the university. Interestingly, in the handful of outlying data points, the deviations from the fitted line tend to be below the line, which suggests that the revenue figures reported to Pollstar were occasionally exaggerated by managers or promoters.

Figure A.2: Tickets Sold According to University vs Tickets Sold According to Pollstar

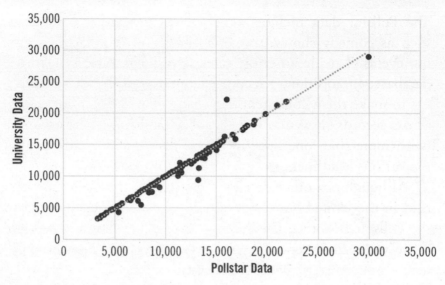

Figure A.2 shows there is also a tight correspondence between the number of tickets sold per show as reported by the university and as reported in the Pollstar data. (Note that the one show with 30,000 tickets sold represented two performances by the same performer on adjacent days combined.) And the average price per show is similar in both the Pollstar and university data. The correlation between the two sources is 0.99 for both tickets sold and average price, suggesting that the data available in the Pollstar Boxoffice Database are highly reliable.

Lastly, the university-reported data and Pollstar data also display similar trends over time. From 2011 to 2017, for example, the average ticket price rose by 27 percent for shows held at the two venues according to the Pollstar data, while the average ticket price for the complete universe of shows held at the two venues increased by 24 percent according to the university data. The correlation between the annual average ticket price calculated with the Pollstar data and the university data from 2010 to 2017 is 0.93.

Cleaning the Pollstar Data

The Pollstar data include some events that are not concerts, such as comedy shows, traveling Broadway shows, and sporting events. I made an effort to remove non-concerts from the database. In addition, I recoded names reported for some artists to make them consistent (e.g., consistent use of ampersands) across records. Revenue from festivals and joint performances (with more than one headliner) was distributed evenly among the various headliners.

Although box office data on a majority of the major concerts held in the United States and around the world are reported to the Pollstar Boxoffice Database, in early years shows were more likely to be underreported, and even in recent years the database is not complete. Missing data on concerts is a concern when it comes to examining multi-decade trends in total revenue for individual artists. Consequently, to derive the figures on artists' cumulative revenue in Figures 4.3a and 4.3b in Chapter 4, the Pollstar data were scaled up according to the inverse of the share of each artist's concerts that were not reported to Pollstar, using the artist-specific ratio based on the Setlist.fm and Pollstar data in the relevant decade. If ticket revenue earned in the excluded shows, on average, equals the revenue earned in the included shows, this approach would correct for incomplete reporting of concerts.

Conclusion

The Pollstar sample does not contain the universe of concerts, but it represents the lion's share of concerts performed by top headliners in recent years. Incomplete coverage is not necessarily problematic for determining trends in average prices or the distribution of revenue because shows may be missing at random and because the available data appear to be accurate and reliable. But relying on Pollstar figures alone to determine the size of the concert industry as a whole or individual artists' total income results in underestimates, because approximately 20 percent of shows over the past two decades were not reported to Pollstar.

ACKNOWLEDGMENTS

I have a confession to make: I am only an average music fan. That means that I listen to music about a couple of hours a day. True, I have gone to more than my share of concerts—starting with Billy Joel, Judy Collins, Steve Miller, George Benson, and Henry Mancini in the late 1970s—and I played the drums (very poorly) in the orchestra until eighth grade. But I am not a fanatic. I like to sing along and tap my feet to the rhythm, but I am hardly a music encyclopedia.

Throughout my career, I have followed U3 (the official unemployment rate) much more closely than U2 (the Irish rock band). But having some remove from a subject can help to understand it better, or at least to see the big picture, which I hope to have conveyed in this book. And the fact that music has played such an integral role in my life, the life of an average fan, suggests that it is at least as important in the lives of millions of readers.

As I reflect on it, music has had a profound impact on my life. I listened to music in my bedroom while trying to figure out what I wanted to be when I grew up, and how to fit in. I listened to music when I exercised, and when I took the bus home from sporting events. I danced to music at my prom and at my wedding. Like many others in my generation, I quoted song lyrics in my high school yearbook that were particularly meaningful to me. I chose the prologue to one of ABBA's least popular songs, "Move On":

> *If I explore the heavens, or if I search inside*
> *Well, it really doesn't matter as long as I can tell myself I've always tried*

That sentiment has been something of an inspiration and beacon for me. This book is a product of that journey.

I get by with more than a little help from my family, friends, research assistants, and students. I could not have written this book without the assistance, encouragement, and advice of many others. My wife, Lisa, read every chapter and encouraged the project from the start. Rafe Sagalyn, my book agent and friend, enthusiastically encouraged me to write about rockonomics. My editor, Roger Scholl, instantly saw what I was trying to achieve and guided me through the process of writing a trade book. Erin Little at Penguin Random House skillfully assisted with the production of this book.

Several research assistants helped with data analysis and other research tasks. While training for the U.S. Olympic rowing team, Max Meyer-Bosse assisted with the analysis of the Pollstar Box-office Database. Amy Wickett and James Reeves expertly provided assistance analyzing streaming data, tabulated ACS and *Billboard* data, and performed countless other tasks, from making graphs to running down footnotes. Grace Kwon, Brendan Wang, and Jun Ho Choi spent a summer tracking down the backgrounds of top musicians.

Princeton University has been a supportive employer and environment for my research for three decades. Ed Freeland of the Princeton University Research Center helped design and carry out the MIRA Musician Survey.

My brother, Richard Krueger, and childhood friend Jeff Kolton provided feedback on several chapters and tutored me on the intricacies of music, musicians, and bands from their extensive experience.

My children, Ben and Sydney, read several chapters of the manuscript and provided valuable advice. They are also responsible for reinvigorating my interest in live music, when they lobbied to see *NSYNC perform many years ago. Sydney's Columbia classmate Paul Bloom provided an informative summary of research on the neuroscience of music.

Several people in the music industry provided me with data. Gary Smith and Gary Bongiovanni, the founders of *Pollstar*, were particularly generous in giving me access to the Pollstar Boxoffice Database, and the new owners of *Pollstar* honored their arrangement. Tinko Georgiev of Kanjian provided streaming data and tutored me on the Chinese music market. David Price of IFPI provided me with the latest international data on recorded music revenue. Marco Rinaldo, Karolina Bressan, and Andrea Barattini generously provided streaming data from Rehegoo.

Too many people in the music business to mention individually tutored me on the inner workings of the business, but I want to especially acknowledge Adam Fell, Quincy Jones, John Eastman, Eric Berman, Don Passman, Marty Gottesman, and Rob Levine for their advice and help. John Cappo, Eric de Fontenay, Qingman Liu, and J. P. Mei helped me to understand the Chinese music market. And I am particularly grateful to Cliff Burnstein and Peter Mensch for sharing their stories and insights, arranging for me to see Metallica from the mixing station, and encouraging my research. I hope to join them at spring training next year.

I learned a tremendous amount that is reflected here from my partners in the Music Industry Research Association, including Joel Waldfogel, Alan Sorensen, Marie Connolly, Dan Ryan, Julie Holland Mortimer, and Jeannie Wilkinson. And Per Krusell tutored me on the Swedish music scene. Dan Pink helped me organize my thoughts. My colleague Orley Ashenfelter provided encouragement and advice, and paved the way for my work in this field with his research on wine economics. Amy Brundage and Sam Michel provided valuable feedback at various steps along the way of this project.

The incredibly talented and dedicated musicians Max Weinberg, Steve Ferrone, Dan Wilson, Jacob Collier, and Gloria Estefan generously and patiently gave me a window into their lives and craft. They inspire me and their fans. I have tried my best to represent their stories and the economics of their industry as faithfully as possible.

Chapter 1: PRELUDE

1. See Mikal Gilmore, "Why the Beatles Broke Up," *Rolling Stone*, Sep. 3, 2009.

2. Jon Pareles, "David Bowie: 21st Century Entrepreneur," *New York Times*, Jun. 9, 2002.

3. Mark Mulligan, "Why Profit Doesn't Come into It for Apple Music," *Music Industry Blog*, Aug. 28, 2015.

4. Barbara Charone, "Ladies and Gentlemen . . . Emerson, Lake & Palmer," *Gig Magazine*, Sep. 1977, http://ladiesofthelake.com/cabinet/77 Tour.html.

5. This quote comes from an interview with John Eastman on Mar. 2, 2018, in New York City.

6. Neil Young, "My My, Hey Hey (Into the Black)," *Rust Never Sleeps*, Reprise Records, 1979.

7. Chris Moukarbel, dir., *Gaga: Five Foot Two*, Netflix, 2017.

8. David J. Hargreaves, "The Effects of Repetition on Liking for Music," *Journal of Research in Music Education* 32, no. 1 (1984): 35–47; Robert B. Zajonc, "Attitudinal Effects of Mere Exposure," *Journal of Personality and Social Psychology* 9, no. 2, pt. 2 (1968): 1–27.

9. Tasneem Chipty, "FCC Media Ownership Study #5: Station Ownership and Programming in Radio," Federal Communications Commission, Jun. 24, 2007, https://docs.fcc.gov/public/attachments/DA-07-3470A6.pdf.

10. Gary Trust, "Ask Billboard: Max Martin Notches Another No. 1," *Billboard*, Nov. 25, 2014; Ed Christman, "Billboard's 2018 Money Makers: 50 Highest-Paid Musicians," *Billboard*, Jul. 20, 2018.

11. Marc Myers, "Steely Dan's Donald Fagen Tours with Young 'Nightflyers,'" *Wall Street Journal*, Jul. 26, 2017.

12. Alfred Marshall, *Principles of Economics* (New York: Macmillan, 1947).

13. Chris Anderson, *The Long Tail: Why the Future of Business Is Selling Less of More* (New York: Hyperion, 2006).

14. Author's calculations using information from Pollstar Boxoffice Database.

15. Facundo Alvaredo, Lucas Chancel, Thomas Piketty, Emmanuel Saez, and Gabriel Zucman, "World Inequality Report," World Inequality Lab, 2018.

16. Gerry Mullany, "World's 8 Richest Have as Much Wealth as Bottom Half, Oxfam Says," *New York Times*, Jan. 16, 2017.

17. Michael Wheeler, "The Luck Factor in Great Decisions," *Harvard Business Review*, Nov. 18, 2013.

18. See Chapter 6.

19. "Concert Tickets' Expensive Rocknomics: Our View," *USA Today*, Aug. 8, 2013.

20. Richard E. Caves, *Creative Industries: Contracts Between Art and Commerce* (Cambridge, MA: Harvard University Press, 2002). See also Peter Tschmuck, *The Economics of Music* (New Castle upon Tyne: Agenda Publishing, 2017).

21. IFPI, "Global Music Report 2018: Annual State of the Industry," 2018.

22. Jason Huang, David H. Reiley, and Nickolai M. Riabov, "Measuring Consumer Sensitivity to Audio Advertising: A Field Experiment on Pandora Internet Radio," working paper, 2018, https://davidreiley.com/papers/PandoraListenerDemandCurve.pdf.

23. See Alan B. Krueger, Daniel Kahneman, David Schkade, Norbert Schwarz, and Arthur A. Stone, "National Time Accounting: The Currency of Life," in *Measuring the Subjective Well-Being of Nations: National Accounts of Time Use and Well-Being*, ed. Alan B. Krueger (Chicago: University of Chicago Press, 2009).

24. From presentations by Dave Bakula, Nielsen, and Russ Crupnick at the 2017 MIRA Conference at UCLA, Los Angeles, CA. See https://themira.org/program-1.

25. Author's calculations using data from Statista (https://www.statista.com/outlook/40110200/109/potato-chips/united-states) and IFPI, "Global Music Report 2018."

26. Maria L. Bringas et al., "Effectiveness of Music Therapy as an Aid to Neurorestoration of Children with Severe Neurological Disorders," *Frontiers in Neuroscience* 9 (2015): 427.

Chapter 2: FOLLOW THE MONEY

1. Simon was originally quoted in Jon Landau, "Paul Simon: The Rolling Stone Interview," *Rolling Stone*, Jul. 20, 1972.

2. The statistics in this paragraph on the size of the music industry and in the next section are derived from Statista, "Music Dossier," 2017 (https://www.statista.com/study/10499/music-industry-in-the-united-states-statista-dossier), 10, 11, and 17, and the Bureau of Economic Analysis.

3. Mikal Gilmore, "The Rolling Stone 20th Anniversary Interview: Bruce Springsteen," *Rolling Stone*, Nov. 5, 1987.

4. Spotify's chief economist, Will Page, has argued with some justification that measures of recording industry revenue undercount copyright payments. But even taking such undercounting into account, global music spending is still well below 0.1 percent of worldwide GDP. See Tim Ingham, "The Global Music Copyright Business Is Worth More Than You Think—and Grew by Nearly $1bn Last Year," *Music Business Worldwide*, Dec. 13, 2016.

5. Quoted from an interview with Russ Crupnick on May 17, 2017, in Nashville, TN.

6. See Darren Heitner, "Sports Industry to Reach $73.5 Billion by 2019," *Forbes*, Oct. 19, 2015.

7. Daniel Kaplan, "NFL Revenue Reaches $14B, Fueled by Media," *Sports Business Journal*, Mar. 6, 2017, and author's calculation using data from the U.S. Department of Education (https://ope.ed.gov/athletics/#).

8. See Jennifer Maloney and Saabira Chaudhuri, "Against All Odds, the U.S. Tobacco Industry Is Rolling in Money," *Wall Street Journal*, Apr. 23, 2017. Advertising expenditures were $8.9 billion in 2015, according to the CDC; see "Smoking & Tobacco Use: Fast Facts," Centers for Disease Control and Prevention, https://www.cdc.gov/tobacco/data_statistics/fact_sheets/fast_facts/index.htm.

9. See IHRSA, "U.S. Fitness Center/Health Club Industry Revenue from 2000 to 2016 (in Billion U.S. Dollars)," Statista, www.statista.com/statistics/236120/us-fitness-center-revenue, and Ana Swanson, "What Your Gym Doesn't Want You to Know," *Washington Post*, Jan. 5, 2016.

10. These and other quotes in this chapter are from a telephone interview with Cliff Burnstein on Jul. 5, 2017.

11. Alan B. Krueger and Ying Zhen, "Inaugural Music Industry Research Association (MIRA) Survey of Musicians," *MIRA Conference Report 2018*.

12. Quote from meeting with Avery Lipman, New York, NY, Nov. 10, 2017.

13. "Vinyl (Still) Rocks \m/," *RIAA Music Note Blog*, Mar. 23, 2016; Elizabeth King, "Why Are CDs Still a Thing?," *Motherboard*, Apr. 8, 2016.

14. Allison Stewart, "What Genres Have Benefited Most from the Streaming Era of Music," *Chicago Tribune*, Apr. 4, 2018.

15. Hugh McIntyre, "What Do the Major Streaming Services Pay per Stream," *Forbes*, Jul. 27, 2017.

16. Jem Aswad and Janko Roettgers, "With 70 Million Subscribers and a Risky IPO Strategy, Is Spotify Too Big to Fail?," *Variety*, Jan. 24, 2018.

17. Donald S. Passman, *All You Need to Know About the Music Business* (New York: Free Press, 2012).

18. AudienceNet, "2017 Music Consumption: The Overall Landscape." These data are based on a nationally representative online survey of 3,006 U.S. residents age sixteen and older.

19. Goldman Sachs Equity Research, "Music in the Air," Aug. 28, 2017, 25.

20. "A Billion Reasons to Celebrate Music on YouTube," *YouTube Official Blog*, Dec. 6, 2016; Rob LeFebvre, "YouTube Music Head Says Company Pays Higher Royalties Than Spotify in US," Engadget, Aug. 7, 2017.

21. These statistics are from "David Byrne and Thom Yorke on the Real Value of Music," *Wired*, Dec. 18, 2007.

22. "BuzzAngle Music 2017 U.S. Report," BuzzAngle, 2017.

23. This information is drawn from Amanda Palmer's Patreon page, https://www.patreon.com/amandapalmer.

24. Passman, *All You Need to Know About the Music Business.*

25. The statistics in this subsection are drawn from *Billboard*'s top moneymakers in 2016 and 2017 and author's calculations using these data. See Ed Christman, "Billboard's 2018 Money Makers: 50 Highest-Paid Musicians," *Billboard*, Jul. 20, 2018.

26. Gary Trust and Keith Caulfield, "Eminem Marks Sales, Hot 100 Milestones," *Billboard*, Mar. 21, 2014.

27. Fleetwood Mac, "Dreams," *Rumors*, Warner Bros., 1977.

28. Dan Kopf, "Amid Controversy, the NFL Is Still Thriving Financially," *Quartz*, Sep. 9, 2018.

29. Presentation by David Bakula, VP of Global Product Leadership and Industry Insights for Music at Nielsen, at the 2017 MIRA Conference at UCLA, Los Angeles, CA (https://themira.org/program-1); AudienceNet, "2018 Music Consumption: The Overall Landscape," 2018.

30. AudienceNet, "2017 Music Consumption: The Overall Landscape."

31. "Time with Tunes: How Technology Is Driving Music Consumption," *Nielsen Insights*, Nov. 2, 2017.

32. Robert B. Zajonc, "Attitudinal Effects of Mere Exposure," *Journal of Personality and Social Psychology* 9, no. 2, pt. 2 (1968): 1–27.

33. See Erik Kirschbaum, *Rocking the Wall: Bruce Springsteen; The Berlin Concert That Changed the World* (New York: Berlinica, 2015).

34. Eric Alper (@ThatEricAlper), "What album or song or musician has changed your life?," Twitter, Dec. 26, 2017, 10:30 a.m., https://twitter.com /ThatEricAlper/status/945723501746454528.

35. See Ben Cosgrove, "Concert for Bangladesh: Photos from the First-Ever Rock 'n' Roll Benefit Show," *Time*, Jul. 30, 2013.

36. See Amy Robinson, "Michael Jackson 'We Are the World,'" The Borgen Project, Jan. 27, 2014, https://borgenproject.org/michael-jackson-world.

37. See Catherine McHugh, "Live Aid 30th Anniversary: The Day Rock and Roll Changed the World," Biography.com, Jul. 12, 2015.

38. Milton Friedman and Rose D. Friedman, *Capitalism and Freedom* (Chicago: University of Chicago Press, 1962).

39. Larry Fink, BlackRock, "A Sense of Purpose," annual letter to CEOs, 2017.

40. Author's calculation using BuzzAngle Total Streaming data.

41. Michael Agresta, "The Redemption of Sinead O'Connor," *Atlantic*, Oct. 3, 2012.

42. Brian Hiatt, "Natalie Maines: A Dixie Chick Declares War on Nashville," *Rolling Stone*, May 20, 2013.

43. Trigger (Kyle Coroneos), "Destroying the Dixie Chicks—Ten Years After," *Saving Country Music* (blog), Mar. 10, 2013.

44. Gayle Thompson, "15 Years Ago, Natalie Maines Makes Controversial Comments About President George W. Bush," The Boot, Mar. 10, 2018, http://theboot.com/natalie-maines-dixie-chicks-controversy.

45. "North American Concerts Gross $61M for Dixie Chicks," *Austin Business Journal*, Aug. 18, 2003.

46. "Banging the Drum for Music," BBC Arts, http://www.bbc.co.uk /programmes/articles/5lgpCss83SfgN1FJks8gJkB/banging-the-drum-for -music. Accessed Oct. 16, 2018.

Chapter 3: THE SUPPLY OF MUSICIANS

1. Andy Greene, "Max Weinberg Talks 43 Years with Bruce Springsteen, Health Scares," *Rolling Stone*, Mar. 7, 2017.

2. Bruce Springsteen, "Ain't Got You," *Tunnel of Love*, Columbia Records, 1987.

3. The figures in this section are based on my tabulations of the American Community Survey (ACS) for the years 2000–2016 and the 1970, 1980, and 1990 censuses. Salaries are for the preceding twelve months. Workers' occupations are classified based on their current or most recent job duties. The count of workers is based on those who worked for pay in the previous week. The 2016 ACS sample consisted of interviews conducted with 2.2 million households. Sample weights were used to attempt to make the weighted responses representative of the U.S. population.

4. Randall Filer in "The 'Starving Artist'—Myth or Reality? Earnings of Artists in the United States," *Journal of Political Economy* 94, no. 1 (1986): 56–75, finds that in 1980 artists as a whole, including musicians, earned less money, on average, than other workers primarily because they were younger. He concludes that the starving artist is a myth. The myth, however, is more of a reality in the 2000s, as musicians grew older and better educated than the rest of the workforce, yet continued to earn considerably less than other workers, on average.

5. Statistics in this paragraph are based on Alan B. Krueger and Ying Zhen, "Inaugural Music Industry Research Association (MIRA) Survey of Musicians," *MIRA Conference Report 2018*.

6. Lawrence F. Katz and Alan B. Krueger, "Understanding Trends in Alternative Work Arrangements in the United States," NBER Working Paper No. 25425, 2019.

7. Andrea Domanick, "The Dollars and Desperation Silencing #MeToo in Music," Noisey.com, Mar. 15, 2018.

8. "Artists and Health Insurance Survey," *Future of Music*, Oct. 15, 2013.

9. Krueger and Zhen, "Inaugural Music Industry Research Association (MIRA) Survey of Musicians."

10. "Freelancing in America: 2017," Freelancers Union & Upwork, 2017.

11. Focus group with New Jersey musicians on Feb. 21, 2018.

12. See Alan B. Krueger, "The Impact of Non-Traditional Jobs and the Role of Public Policy," Moynihan Lecture, 2017, http://www.aapss.org/news /alan-krueger-delivers-2017-moynihan-lecture.

13. Eric Alper, "Billy Joel on His Advice to Younger Musicians," *That Eric Alper* (blog), Jan. 14, 2018.

14. Dan Wilson (@DanWilsonMusic), "Even to be a moderately successful musician . . . ," Twitter, May 10, 2018, 8:48 a.m., https://twitter.com/DanWilsonMusic/status/994604978625900550.

15. Kurt Cobain, *Kurt Cobain Journals* (London: Viking Books, 2002).

16. Shawn Rending, "Music Legend Nile Rodgers to SXSW Crowd: 'Don't Be a Snob,'" KVUE, Mar. 15, 2017.

17. Patti Smith, *Just Kids* (New York: Ecco, 2010).

18. Bob Dylan, *Chronicles: Volume One* (New York: Pocket Books, 2005).

19. lEIGh5, "Jason Pierce (Spiritualized) Interview: 2011," *Digging a Hole* (blog), May 11, 2011, http://guestlisted.blogspot.com/2011/05/jason-pierce-spiritualized-interview.html.

20. Interview with Jacob Collier on Feb. 16, 2018, in Miami Beach.

21. Krueger and Zhen, "Inaugural Music Industry Research Association (MIRA) Survey of Musicians."

22. These data come from author's calculations of data on CEO compensation of publicly traded companies, athletes, and musician earnings. See "Equilar | New York Times 200 Highest-Paid CEOs," Equilar, May 25, 2018; "The World's Highest-Paid Athletes," *Forbes*, June 13, 2018; and Ed Christman, "Billboard's 2018 Money Makers: 50 Highest-Paid Musicians," *Billboard*, Jul. 20, 2018.

23. Adam Smith, *An Inquiry into the Nature and Causes of the Wealth of Nations* (London: W. Strahan and T. Cadell, 1776).

24. Grateful Dead, "Playing in the Band," *Ace*, Warner Bros., 1972.

25. Frank Sinatra, *Sinatra at the Sands*, Reprise Records, 1966.

26. Author's calculations using data from *Billboard* Top 100 Songs.

27. Skype interview with Dan Wilson on Jun. 29, 2018.

28. Gary Trust, "Happy Birthday, Billboard Charts! On July 27, 1940, the First Song Sales Chart Debuted," *Billboard*, Jul. 27, 2017.

29. Robert Daniels, "The Hip Hop Economy Goes Free Trade," *Fortune*, Apr. 25, 2012.

30. Jacob Slichter, *So You Wanna Be a Rock & Roll Star: How I Machine-Gunned a Roomful of Record Executives and Other True Tales from a Drummer's Life* (New York: Broadway Books, 2004).

31. Telephone interview with Cliff Burnstein, Jul. 5, 2017.

32. James Brown and Bruce Tucker, *James Brown: The Godfather of Soul* (London: Head of Zeus, 1987).

33. Dan Epstein, "Metallica's Black Album: 10 Things You Didn't Know," *Rolling Stone*, Aug. 12, 2016.

34. Fred Bronson, "Metallica, Afghanistan National Institute of Music Named 2018 Polar Music Prize Laureates," *Billboard*, Feb. 14, 2018.

35. Interview with Quincy Jones on Aug. 11, 2017, in Los Angeles, CA, and Quincy Jones remarks at Inside ETF conference, Hollywood, FL, Jan. 23, 2017.

36. Interview with Adam Fell on Aug. 11, 2017, in Los Angeles, CA.

37. Quoted from an interview with Steve Ferrone on Mar. 14, 2018, in Los Angeles, CA.

38. Statistics in this section are based on the 2018 MIRA musician survey, 2016 National Survey on Drug Use and Health, and 2015–16 National Health and Nutrition Examination Survey (NHANES). See Krueger and Zhen, "Inaugural Music Industry Research Association (MIRA) Survey of Musicians."

39. See Martin Wolkewitz, Arthur Allignol, Nicholas Graves, and Adrian G. Barnett, "Is 27 Really a Dangerous Age for Famous Musicians? Retrospective Cohort Study," *BMJ* 343, no. 7837 (2011); Mark A. Bellis, Tom Hennell, Clare Lushey, Karen Hughes, Karen Tocque, and John R. Ashton, "Elvis to Eminem: Quantifying the Price of Fame Through Early Mortality of European and North American Rock and Pop Stars," *Journal of Epidemiology and Community Health* 61, no. 1 (2007): 896–901.

40. Socioeconomic indicators and geography of musicians were compiled using a variety of sources, including interviews, articles, biographies, etc. Socioeconomic status was determined using several factors, including family structure, housing type (i.e., public housing), and parental occupation. Parental occupations were classified into income categories using data from the 2010 American Community Survey.

41. Raj Chetty, Nathaniel Hendren, Patrick Kline, and Emmanuel Saez, "Where Is the Land of Opportunity? The Geography of Intergenerational Mobility in the United States," *Quarterly Journal of Economics* 129, no. 4 (2014): 1553–623.

42. "Melanie C Talks Spice Girls and Sexism at AIM's Women in Music," *Music Week*, Jan. 18, 2018.

43. Krueger and Zhen, "Inaugural Music Industry Research Association (MIRA) Survey of Musicians."

44. Trigger (Kyle Coroneos), "In 2017, Women Only Made Up 7.5% of Country Radio's Top 40," *Saving Country Music* (blog), Dec. 27, 2017.

45. Judy Klemesrud, "Is Women's Lib Coming to the Philharmonic?," *New York Times*, Apr. 11, 1971.

46. Melinda Newman, "Where Are All the Female Music Producers," *Billboard*, Jan. 19, 2018.

47. Claudia Goldin and Cecilia Rouse, "Orchestrating Impartiality: The Impact of 'Blind' Auditions on Female Musicians," *American Economic Review* 90, no. 4 (2000): 715–41.

48. Katharine Zaleski, "Job Interviews Without Gender," *New York Times*, Jan. 6, 2018.

49. Patrick Doyle, "The Last Word: Billy Joel on Self-Doubt, Trump and Finally Becoming Cool," *Rolling Stone*, Jun. 14, 2017.

Chapter 4: THE ECONOMICS OF SUPERSTARS

1. Thomas Piketty and Emmanuel Saez, "The Evolution of Top Incomes: A Historical and International Perspective," *American Economic Review* 96, no. 2 (2006): 200–205.

2. Lucas Chancel Facundo, Thomas Piketty, Emmanuel Saez, and Gabriel Zucman, "2018 World Inequality Report," World Inequality Lab, 2018.

3. This and other quotes are from Alfred Marshall, *Principles of Economics*, 8th ed. (London: Macmillan, 1930).

4. This and other quotes are from Sherwin Rosen, "The Economics of Superstars," *American Economic Review* 71, no. 5 (1981): 845–58.

5. William Barclay Squire, "Billington, Elizabeth," in *Dictionary of National Biography*, ed. Leslie Stephen (London: Smith, Elder, 1886).

6. This is based on the Bank of England's inflation calculator and a pound-dollar exchange rate of 1.40. See Zack O'Malley Greenburg, "The World's Highest-Paid Women in Music 2017," *Forbes*, Nov. 20, 2017.

7. Author's calculation using information from the Pollstar Boxoffice Database.

8. Author's calculation using BuzzAngle data. Estimates are based on the assumption that there are three million artists currently on streaming platforms. Artists are ranked by number of albums sold in 2017.

9. Jon Pareles, "David Bowie: 21st Century Entrepreneur," *New York Times*, Jun. 9, 2002.

10. Quoted from a telephone interview with Cliff Burnstein on Jul. 5, 2017.

11. Donald S. Passman, *All You Need to Know About the Music Business* (New York: Free Press, 2012).

12. Lucy Williamson, "The Dark Side of South Korean Pop Music," BBC News, Jun. 15, 2011.

13. "BuzzAngle Music 2017 U.S. Report," BuzzAngle, 2018.

14. I made this calculation assuming an eighty-year life span, sixteen hours of listening time a day, and five minutes per song.

15. David J. Hargreaves, "The Effects of Repetition on Liking for Music," *Journal of Research in Music Education* 32, no. 1 (1984): 35–47; Robert B. Zajonc, "Attitudinal Effects of Mere Exposure," *Journal of Personality and Social Psychology* 9, no. 2, pt. 2 (1968): 1–27.

16. For a technical discussion of this process, see David Easley and Jon Kleinberg, *Networks, Crowds, and Markets: Reasoning About a Highly Connected World* (Cambridge, MA: Cambridge University Press, 2010), ch. 18.

17. Matthew J. Salganik, Peter Sheridan Dodds, and Duncan J. Watts, "Experimental Study of Inequality and Unpredictability in an Artificial Cultural Market," *Science* 311 (2006): 854–56.

18. This is from an interview with Jacob Collier on Feb. 16, 2018, in Miami Beach.

19. See Mark E. J. Newman, "Power Laws, Pareto Distributions and Zipf's Law," *Contemporary Physics* 46, no. 5 (2005): 323–51; Dimitrios Rafailidis and Yannis Manolopoulos, "The Power of Music: Searching for Power-Laws in Symbolic Musical Data," working paper, Department of Informatics, Aristotle University, Thessaloniki, Greece, 2008.

20. Stephen Gandel, "Beware, Bitcoin Buffs, Bubbles Often Bite," *Bloomberg*, Sep. 29, 2017.

21. Chris Anderson, *The Long Tail: Why the Future of Business Is Selling Less of More* (New York: Hyperion, 2006).

22. Paul Krugman, "Is This (Still) the Age of the Superstar?," *New York Times*, Jun. 13, 2013.

23. Author's calculation using information from the Pollstar Boxoffice Database.

24. Anita Elberse, *Blockbusters: Hit-Making, Risk-Taking, and the Big Business of Entertainment* (London: Macmillan, 2013).

25. Smith and Telang make a related argument: "Long-tail processes can and will be used to produce not only long-tail products but also blockbuster products." Michael D. Smith and Rahul Telang, *Streaming, Sharing, Stealing: Big Data and the Future of Entertainment* (Cambridge, MA: MIT Press, 2016), 76.

26. Questlove interviewed by Tom Healy at the Bass Museum, Apr. 15, 2018, Miami Beach, FL.

27. Author's calculations using information from the Pollstar Boxoffice Database.

28. Lawrence Mishel, Elise Gould, and Josh Bivens, "Wage Stagnation in Nine Charts," Economic Policy Institute, Jan. 6, 2015.

29. Steven Kaplan and Joshua Rauh, "It's the Market: The Broad-Based Rise in the Return to Top Talent," *Journal of Economic Perspectives* 27, no. 3 (2013).

30. David Autor, David Dorn, Lawrence F. Katz, Christina Patterson, and John Van Reenen, "The Fall of the Labor Share and the Rise of Superstar Firms," NBER Working Paper No. 23396, 2017; David Wessel, "Is Lack of Competition Strangling the U.S. Economy," *Harvard Business Review*, Mar. 2018.

31. Wessel, "Is Lack of Competition Strangling the U.S. Economy."

32. Paul Resnikoff, "Two-Thirds of All Music Sold Comes from Just 4 Companies," *Digital Music News*, Aug. 3, 2016.

33. "Tech Firms Shell Out to Hire and Hoard Talent," *The Economist*, Nov. 5, 2016.

34. "Knorr, Wabtec Settle with U.S. over Agreements to Not Poach Workers," Reuters, Apr. 3, 2018.

35. Adam Smith, *An Inquiry into the Nature and Causes of the Wealth of Nations* (London: W. Strahan and T. Cadell, 1776).

36. Federal Trade Commission, "Antitrust Guidance for Human Resource Professionals," Department of Justice, Antitrust Division, Oct. 2016.

37. David Clark, "Antitrust Action Against No-Poaching Agreements: Obama Policy to Be Continued by the Trump Administration," *National Law Review*, Jan. 26, 2018.

Chapter 5: THE POWER OF LUCK

1. Transcribed from Elton John's appearance on *The Late Show with Stephen Colbert*, Nov. 13, 2017.

2. Peter Carlin, *Homeward Bound: The Life of Paul Simon* (New York: Henry Holt, 2016).

3. Frank H. Robert, *Success and Luck: Good Fortune and the Myth of Meritocracy* (Princeton, NJ: Princeton University Press, 2016).

4. Superstars would emerge even if all contenders were equally talented and equally hardworking. See Moshe Adler, "Stardom and Talent," *American Economic Review* 75, no. 1 (1985): 208–12, for an extension of Sherwin Rosen's superstar model where everyone is equally talented.

5. Chris Hastings and Susan Bisset, "Literary Agent Made £15m Because JK Rowling Liked His Name," *Telegraph*, Jun. 15, 2003.

6. Shaun Considine, "The Hit We Almost Missed," *New York Times*, Dec. 3, 2004.

7. Mike Sigman, "John Hammond Looks Back (II)," *Record World*, Oct. 7, 1972.

8. See Robert Burnett, "Dressed for Success: Sweden from Abba to Roxette," *Popular Music* 11, no. 2 (1992): 141–50.

9. Interview with John Eastman on Apr. 12, 2018, in New York City.

10. Larry Rohter, "A Real-Life Fairy Tale, Long in the Making and Set to Old Tunes," *New York Times*, Jul. 20, 2012.

11. Jennifer Ordoez, "Pop Singer Fails to Strike a Chord Despite the Millions Spent by MCA," *Wall Street Journal*, Feb. 26, 2002.

12. Statistics in this section are based on author's calculations using *Billboard* Year-End Top 100, 1960–2017.

13. Fran Strine, *Hired Gun*, Vision Films, 2016.

14. See Matthew J. Salganik and Duncan Watts, "Leading the Herd Astray: An Experimental Study of Self-Fulfilling Prophecies in an Artificial Cultural Market," *Social Psychology Quarterly* 71, no. 4 (2008): 338–55. My description of their work combines two of their alternative universes to provide a simplified overview of their experiment, but it is faithful to their main findings.

15. Duncan Watts, "Is Justin Timberlake a Product of Cumulative Advantage?," *New York Times*, Apr. 15, 2007.

16. Bruce Springsteen, *Born to Run* (New York: Simon & Schuster, 2017), 324–25.

17. Andy Greene, "Max Weinberg Talks 43 Years with Bruce Springsteen, Health Scares," *Rolling Stone*, Mar. 7, 2017.

18. Alex Arbuckle, "A Young Frank Sinatra, Dapper and Rebellious from Birth," *Mashable*, Oct. 19, 2015.

19. Geoff Boucher, "Allen Klein Dies at 77; Powerful Figure in Music World," *Los Angeles Times*, Jul. 5, 2009.

20. "Princeton University's 2012 Baccalaureate Remarks," Princeton University, Jun. 3, 2012, www.princeton.edu/news/2012/06/03/princeton-universitys-2012-baccalaureate-remarks.

21. Orley Ashenfelter and Alan B. Krueger, "Estimates of the Economic Return to Schooling from a New Sample of Twins," *American Economic Review* 84, no. 5 (1994): 1157–83.

22. See Philip Oreopoulos, Till Von Wachter, and Andrew Heisz, "The Short- and Long-Term Career Effects of Graduating in a Recession," *American Economic Journal: Applied Economics* 4, no. 1 (2012): 1–29; Lisa B. Kahn, "The Long-Term Labor Market Consequences of Graduating from College in a Bad Economy," *Labour Economics* 17, no. 2 (2010): 303–16.

23. Paul Oyer, "The Making of an Investment Banker: Stock Market Shocks, Career Choice and Lifetime Income," *Journal of Finance* 63, no. 6 (2008): 2601–28.

24. Lawrence Mishel and Jessica Schieder, "CEO Pay Remains High Relative to the Pay of Typical Workers and High-Wage Earners," Economic Policy Institute, Jul. 20, 2017.

25. Marianne Bertrand and Sendhil Mullainathan, "Are CEOs Rewarded for Luck? The Ones Without Principals Are," *Quarterly Journal of Economics* 116, no. 3 (2001): 901–32.

26. David Cho and Alan B. Krueger, "Rent Sharing Within Firms," draft working paper, 2018.

27. This draws from an interview with Cliff Burnstein on Jul. 27, 2018, in New York City.

28. Burton Malkiel, *A Random Walk down Wall Street: Including a Life-Cycle Guide to Personal Investing* (New York: W. W. Norton, 1999).

29. Burton Malkiel, "Index Funds Still Beat 'Active' Portfolio Management," *Wall Street Journal*, Jun. 5, 2017.

30. Chana Schoenberger, "Peter Lynch, 25 Years Later: It's Not Just 'Invest in What You Know,'" *MarketWatch*, Dec. 28, 2015.

31. Joan Goodman, "*Playboy* Interview with Paul and Linda McCartney," *Playboy*, Dec. 1984.

32. Brad M. Barber and Terrance Odean, "The Courage of Misguided Convictions: The Trading Behavior of Individual Investors," *Financial Analyst Journal* 55, no. 6 (1999): 41–55; Brad M. Barber and Terrance Odean, "Boys Will Be Boys: Gender, Overconfidence, and Common Stock Investment," *Quarterly Journal of Economics* 116, no. 1 (2001): 261–92.

33. Interview with Gloria Estefan, Oct. 4, 2018.

34. Frank Bruni, "Am I Going Blind?," *New York Times*, Feb. 23, 2018.

35. George Palathingal, "Life Not So Sweet for 'Sugar Man' Sixto Rodriguez," *Sydney Morning Herald*, May 29, 2014.

36. Larry Rohter, "A Real-Life Fairy Tale, Long in the Making and Set to Old Tunes," *New York Times*. Jul. 20, 2012.

Chapter 6: THE SHOW MUST GO ON

1. Figures on U2's tours are from Bob Grossweiner and Jane Cohen, "Madonna Tour Wraps with $280 Million-Plus Gross," *TicketNews*, Dec. 23, 2008, and Brian Boyd, "Bono's Injury and U2's Shrinking Tour," *Irish Times*, May 8, 2015.

2. Quoted from the 2018 Pollstar Live! convention in Los Angeles, CA.

3. This and other quotes in this chapter are from a phone interview with Cliff Burnstein on Jul. 5, 2017.

4. Author's calculation based on information from the Pollstar Boxoffice Database.

5. Thor Christensen, "Gouge-a-Palooza? Rock Artists' Soaring Ticket Prices Amplify Cries of 'Sellout,'" *Dallas Morning News*, Jun. 2, 2002.

6. Donald S. Passman, *All You Need to Know About the Music Business* (New York: Free Press, 2012).

7. Ron Howard, dir., *The Beatles: Eight Days a Week*, Polygram Entertainment, 2016.

8. Ethan Smith, "Ticketmaster, Live Nation Near Merger," *Wall Street Journal*, Feb. 4, 2009.

9. Deborah Speer, "Pollstar Live! Q&A: Michael Rapino," *Pollstar*, Feb. 2, 2018.

10. Ben Sisario and Graham Bowley, "Live National Rules Music Ticketing, Some Say with Threats," *New York Times*, Apr. 1, 2018.

11. Dave Brooks, "AEG Says It Will Continue to Block-Book the O2 and Staples Center," *Billboard*, Sep. 1, 2017.

12. Jem Aswad, "AEG-MSG Turf Battle Heats Up: Acts That Play L.A. Forum Cannot Play London's O2 Arena," *Variety*, Jun. 30, 2017.

13. Jem Aswad, "Sharon Osbourne Slams AEG over Staples-O2 Booking Policy, Jay Marciano and Irving Azoff Respond," *Variety*, Feb. 7, 2018.

14. Associated Press, "In Move to Discourage Scalping, Rock Band Won't Honor Tickets," *New York Times*, Jul. 2, 1996.

15. MTV News Staff, "Box Office Employee Convicted in N.Y. Ticket Scam," *MTV News*, June 18, 1998.

16. Sarah Pittman, "Listen to Michael Rapino's Pollstar Live! Keynote Q&A: Promoter 101 Podcast," *Pollstar*, Feb. 19, 2018.

17. Neil Irwin, "Why Surge Prices Make Us So Mad: What Springsteen, Home Depot and a Nobel Winner Know," *New York Times*, Oct. 14, 2017.

18. See, for example, Julie Holland Mortimer, Chris Nosko, and Alan Sorensen, "Supply Responses to Digital Distribution: Recorded Music and Live Performances," *Information Economics and Policy* 24, no. 1 (2012): 3–14; Alan B. Krueger, "The Economics of Real Superstars: The Market for Rock Concerts in the Material World," *Journal of Labor Economics* 23, no. 1 (2005): 1–30.

19. Quoted from email correspondence with John Eastman on Mar. 5, 2018.

20. In 2009, Ticketmaster's then CEO, Irving Azoff, testified before a Senate Judiciary Subcommittee on the Ticketmaster–Live Nation merger, "You know, Ticketmaster was set up as a system where they took the heat for everybody else. Ticketmaster gets a minority percentage of that service charge. In that service charge are credit card fees, the rebates to the buildings, rebates sometimes to artists, and sometimes rebates to promoters." Stephen Dubner, "Why Is the Live-Event Ticket Market So Screwed Up?," *Freakonomics Radio*, WNYC, Dec. 6, 2017.

21. Irwin, "Why Surge Prices Make Us So Mad."

22. Author's calculations using information from the Pollstar Boxoffice Database.

23. "What Other Bands Can Learn from Ed Sheeran," *Stage Right Secrets*, Jan. 10, 2015.

24. David Wild, "10 Things That Piss Off Tom Petty," *Rolling Stone*, Nov. 14, 2002.

25. This material is from Garth Brooks's panel at the Pollstar Live! conference, Los Angeles, CA, Feb. 2, 2018.

26. Ben Popper, "8 Business Secrets of the Grateful Dead," *Business Insider*, Aug. 5, 2010.

27. Pittman, "Listen to Michael Rapino's Pollstar Live! Keynote Q&A."

28. Gregory Mankiw, "I Paid $2,500 for a 'Hamilton' Ticket. I'm Happy About It," *New York Times*, Oct. 21, 2016.

29. Phillip Leslie and Alan Sorensen, "Resale and Rent-Seeking: An Application to Ticket Markets," *Review of Economic Studies* 81, no. 1 (2014): 266–300.

30. Aditya Bhave and Eric Budish, "Primary-Market Auctions for Event Tickets: Eliminating the Rents of 'Bob the Broker'?," NBER Working Paper No. 23770, 2017.

31. "What Is Ticketmaster Verified Fan?," Ticketmaster, https://help.ticketmaster.com/s/article/What-is-Ticketmaster-Verified-Fan. Accessed Oct. 22, 2018.

32. Kaitlyn Tiffany, "How Ticketmaster's Verified Fan Program Toys with the Passions of Fandom," *The Verge*, Feb. 7, 2018.

33. Dave Brooks, "Taylor Swift Has Concert Industry Embracing 'Slow Ticketing' Model," *Billboard*, Dec. 14, 2017.

34. Dave Brooks, "Slow Ticketing Helps Jay-Z Net $48.7M on 2017 Tour," *Billboard*, Jan. 11, 2018.

35. See William J. Baumol and William G. Bowen, *Performing Arts, the Economic Dilemma: A Study of Problems Common to Theater, Opera, Music, and Dance* (New York: Twentieth Century Fund, 1966).

36. Quoted from an interview with Rob Levine on Aug. 3, 2017.

37. Quoted from an interview with Michael Lorick on Apr. 5, 2018.

38. Material in this section comes from an interview with Peter Lubin on Dec. 5, 2017.

39. This comes from a lecture Dan Ryan presented at Princeton University on Oct. 11, 2017.

40. Ethan Smith and Sara Silver, "To Protect Its Box-Office Turf, Ticketmaster Plays Rivals' Tune," *Wall Street Journal*, Sep. 12, 2006.

41. Barry Ritholtz, "Markets, Music and a Defense on Wall Street: Barry Ritholtz," *Washington Post*, Dec. 22, 2017.

Chapter 7: SCAMS, SWINDLES, AND THE MUSIC BUSINESS

1. I interviewed John Eastman on Mar. 2 and Apr. 12, 2018.

2. Richard E. Caves, *Creative Industries: Contracts Between Art and Commerce* (Cambridge, MA: Harvard University Press, 2000), 65.

3. Justin M. Jacobsen, "The Artist & Record Label Relationship— A Look at the Standard 'Record Deal' [Part 1]," *TuneCore*, May 11, 2017.

4. Ray Waddell, "Update: Madonna Confirms Deal with Live Nation," *Billboard*, Oct. 16, 2007.

5. Peter C. DiCola, "Money from Music: Survey Evidence on Musicians' Revenue and Lessons About Copyright Incentives," *Arizona Law Review* 55, no. 2 (2013): 301–70.

6. Donald S. Passman, *All You Need to Know About the Music Business* (New York: Free Press, 2012).

7. Richard Smirke, "Indie Labels Raked in $6 Billion Last Year, Accounting for 38 Percent of Global Market: New Study," *Billboard*, Oct. 23, 2017.

8. Nate Rau, "Lumineers' Success Hasn't Changed Label's Formula," *Tennessean*, Apr. 4, 2014.

9. Dylan Owens, "Four Years Later, the Lumineers Stage a Surprising Second Act," *Denver Post*, Mar. 31, 2016.

10. Bruce Springsteen, *Born to Run* (New York: Simon & Schuster, 2016), 251.

11. Colin Stutz, "Lil Pump Signs New Contract with Warner Bros. for Roughly $8M: Sources," *Billboard*, Mar. 12, 2018.

12. Jem Aswad, "It's Official: 'Gucci Gang' Rapper Lil Pump Re-Signs with Warner Bros. Records," *Variety*, Mar. 13, 2018.

13. Rafa Alvarez, "A Hip-Hop Signing Frenzy Sends New Record Deal Prices Soaring," *Billboard*, Mar. 29, 2018.

14. This is from a conversation and the Q&A session with Tom Corson at the Jun. 26, 2018, MIRA Conference at the Village Studio in Los Angeles.

15. Fred Goodman, *Allen Klein: The Man Who Bailed Out the Beatles, Made the Stones, and Transformed Rock and Roll* (New York: Houghton Mifflin Harcourt, 2015), 195.

16. "Jay Van Dyke, formerly of the Lumineers: Music Biz 101 & More Podcast," *Music Biz 101*, Dec. 7, 2017.

17. This comes from a lecture Dan Ryan presented at Princeton University on Oct. 11, 2017.

18. Passman, *All You Need to Know About the Music Business*.

19. Peter Bogdanovich, dir., *Tom Petty and the Heartbreakers: Runnin' Down a Dream*, Warner Bros., 2007.

20. Fred Goodman, "How Tom Petty Beat the Labels," *Billboard*, Oct. 6, 2017.

21. Richard Harrington, "Billy Joel's Midlife Confessions," *Washington Post*, Oct. 17, 1993.

22. Nick Paumgarten, "Thirty-Three-Hit Wonder," *New Yorker*, Oct. 27, 2014.

23. Mary Braid, "Sting's Adviser Jailed for £6m Theft from Star," *Independent*, Oct. 18, 1995.

24. Guy Lynn and George Greenwood, "Musicians Hit by 'Management Scam,'" BBC, Mar. 29, 2018.

25. John Robinson, "Get Back and Other Setbacks," *Guardian*, Nov. 21, 2003.

26. "Colonel Tom Parker Biography," Biography.com, Apr. 16, 2018.

27. Jerry Osborne, *Elvis: Word for Word* (New York: Harmony Books, 2000).

28. Dave Brooks, "Kanye West Splits with Longtime Manager Izzy Zivkovic: Exclusive," *Billboard*, Mar. 28, 2018.

29. "How I Became the Fresh Prince of Bel-Air | Storytime," YouTube, posted by Will Smith, May 10, 2018, https://www.youtube.com/watch?v=y_WoOYybCro.

30. "Singer Shakira Under Investigation in Spain for Possible Tax Evasion," *USA Today*, Jan. 24, 2018.

31. Carlson Kyle, Joshua Kim, Annamaria Lusardi, and Colin F. Camerer, "Bankruptcy Rates Among NFL Players with Short-Lived Income Spikes," *American Economic Review: Papers and Proceedings* 105, no. 5 (2015): 381–84.

32. Astrid Baumgardner, "How to Take Charge of Your Finances as a Musician," *I Care If You Listen* (blog), Nov. 11, 2014.

Chapter 8: STREAMING IS CHANGING EVERYTHING

1. Source: RIAA, U.S. Sales Database, https://www.riaa.com/u-s-sales-database. Note that these are retail figures. See Michael D. Smith and Rahul

Telang, *Streaming, Sharing, Stealing* (Cambridge, MA: MIT Press, 2016), ch. 6, for a comprehensive summary of the literature on the effects of piracy on music sales.

2. Source: Josh Friedlander of RIAA, presentation at MIRA, Jun. 26, 2018, Los Angeles, CA. According to Friedlander, subscription-supported audio streaming accounted for 31 percent of all music streams in 2017, Internet radio accounted for 35 percent, ad-supported video accounted for 26 percent, and ad-supported audio accounted for 8 percent.

3. Tim Arango, "Digital Sales Surpass CDs at Atlantic," *New York Times*, Nov. 25, 2008.

4. "Vinyl Still Rocks \m/," *RIAA Music Note Blog*, Mar. 23, 2016; Elizabeth King, "Why Are CDs Still a Thing?," *Motherboard*, Apr. 8, 2016.

5. Steve Knoppwer, "The End of Owning Music: How CDs and Downloads Died," *Rolling Stone*, Jun. 14, 2018.

6. Friedlander, presentation at MIRA, Jun. 26, 2018.

7. Figures in this paragraph come from Ben Sisario, "After Driving Streaming Music's Rise, Spotify Aims to Cash In," *New York Times*, Mar. 13, 2018; Paul Resnikoff, "Apple Music Just Surpassed Spotify's U.S. Subscriber Count," *Digital Music News*, Jul. 5, 2018; "2017 Letter to Shareholders," Amazon, Apr. 18, 2018; Erin Griffith, "Pandora Learns the Cost of Ads, and of Subscriptions," *Wired*, Apr. 30, 2018; "Tencent Platforms Overview in Q1 2018; WeChat MAU Exceeded 1bn," *China Internet Watch*, May 17, 2018.

8. From Marc Geiger's presentation at MIRA in Los Angeles, CA, 2017.

9. Jem Aswad and Janko Roettgers, "With 70 Million Subscribers and a Risky IPO Strategy, Is Spotify Too Big to Fail?," *Variety*, Jan. 24, 2018.

10. Some further complications are that the mechanical rate component of royalties for interactive streaming services is set by the Copyright Board, and labels could negotiate for minimum payments. Also, as explained later in this chapter, the labels and streaming services can negotiate for promotion and other benefits in addition to streaming royalties. Some contracts also base royalties on a complicated formula involving the greater of a share of revenue, a per stream basis, and a per customer basis.

11. See Colin Stutz, "Spotify Subscribers Demand Refunds over Too Much Drake Promotion," *Billboard*, Jul. 2, 2018; Micah Singleton, "Drake's Scorpion Pulls In over 1 Billion Streams in Its First Week," *The Verge*, Jul. 8, 2018.

12. Josh Constine, "Spotify 'Sponsored Songs' Lets Labels Pay for Plays," *TechCrunch*, Jun. 19, 2017.

13. See Nicholas Deleon, "Best Music Streaming Services," *Consumer Reports*, May 18, 2018; "Amazon Music," Amazon, https://www.amazon.com/gp/dmusic/promotions/AmazonMusicUnlimitedFamily. Accessed Oct. 16, 2018.

14. "U.S. Music Mid-Year Report 2018," Nielsen, Jul. 6, 2018.

15. This is based on author's calculations using BuzzAngle Music data for Jan. 5, 2018, through Jun. 28, 2018. This calculation understates the effect on other artists of removing Drake because the total number of streams was calculated just for the top four thousand artists.

16. See, for example, Ben Sisario, "As Music Streaming Grows, Royalties Slow to a Trickle," *New York Times*, Jan. 28, 2013.

17. "Billboard Finalizes Changes to How Streams Are Weighted for Billboard Hot 100 & 200," *Billboard*, May 1, 2018.

18. These and other figures about Spotify come from Spotify Technology, "Spotify Technology S.A. Releases Financial Outlook for First Quarter and Fiscal Year 2018," Mar. 26, 2018, https://www.sec.gov/Archives/edgar/data/1639920/000119312518095067/d560151dex991.htm; and Spotify Technology S.A., "Form F-1 Registration Statement Under the Securities Act of 1933," Feb. 28, 2018.

19. Brian Braiker, "Pandora Wants to 'Evolve out of' Autoplay Video Ads," *Digiday*, Mar. 15, 2016.

20. See Jason Huang, David H. Reiley, and Nickolai M. Riabov, "Measuring Consumer Sensitivity to Audio Advertising: A Field Experiment on Pandora Internet Radio," working paper, 2018, https://davidreiley.com/papers/PandoraListenerDemandCurve.pdf.

21. Shelly Banjo, "Yes, You're Hearing More Ads on Pandora These Days," *Quartz*, Jul. 24, 2015.

22. Luis Aguiar and Joel Waldfogel, "Platforms, Promotion, and Product Discovery: Evidence from Spotify Playlists," NBER Working Paper No. 24713, 2018.

23. See Joel Waldfogel, "How Digitization Has Created a Golden Age of Music, Movies, Books, and Television," *Journal of Economic Perspectives* 31, no. 3 (2017): 195–214, for an analysis of the growth in music production in response to technological change.

24. "Database Statistics," MusicBrainz, 2018.

25. "Music Production," Rehegoo Music, 2018, https://rehegoo.com/music-production.html.

26. Marc Hogan, "Uncovering How Streaming Is Changing the Sound of Pop," *Pitchfork*, Sep. 25, 2017.

27. My research assistant Amy Wickett listened to all of the songs that involved collaborations to determine the singers that appeared in the first thirty seconds or later in the song. This paragraph reports on her findings.

28. For an early analysis of how digital downloading unbundled albums and reduced sales, see Anita Elberse, "Bye-Bye Bundles: The Unbundling of Music in Digital Channels," *Journal of Marketing* 74, no. 3 (2010): 107–23.

29. George Garner, " 'You Can't Capture Lightning in the Bottle Again': Rihanna Producer JR Rotem on the Key to Writing Hit Songs," *MusicWeek*, Feb. 28, 2018.

30. Abigail Tracy, "Jay-Z's Tidal Music Streaming Service Says Goodbye to Another CEO," *Forbes*, Jun. 23, 2015.

31. Keith Caulfield, "Taylor Swift's 'Reputation' Becomes Only Album Released in Last Two Years to Sell 2 Million Copies in U.S.," *Billboard*, Mar. 21, 2018.

32. Taylor Swift, "For Taylor Swift, the Future of Music Is a Love Story," *Wall Street Journal*, Jul. 7, 2014.

33. This paragraph is based on "Apple Music Changes Policy After Taylor Swift Stand," BBC News, Jun. 22, 2015.

34. Ian Courtncy, "The Bob Lefsetz Podcast: Steve Boom," *Celebrity Access Encore*, Jun. 27, 2018.

35. Stephen Witt, "Billboard Power 100 Cover: Amazon's Jeff Bezos & Steve Boom on Starting a New 'Golden Age' for Music," *Billboard*, Feb. 9, 2017.

36. This is based on Marc Geiger's interview with Hannah Karp at the 2017 MIRA Conference.

37. Quoted from Alan B. Krueger and David A. Anderson, *Explorations in Economics* (New York: Worth, 2013).

Chapter 9: BLURRED LINES

1. *Williams v. Gaye*, 885 F.3d 1150 (2018).

2. Philip Caulfield, "Sam Smith Gives Tom Petty Songwriting Credit on 'Stay with Me,' " New York *Daily News*, Jan. 26, 2015.

3. Michelle Fabio, "Bruno Mars and Mark Ronson's 'Uptown Funk' Faces (Yet Another) Copyright Infringement Suit," *Forbes*, Dec. 30, 2017.

4. Kory Grow, "Led Zeppelin Face Retrial in 'Stairway to Heaven' Suit," *Rolling Stone*, Sep. 28, 2018.

5. From an interview with Quincy Jones on Jan. 22, 2018, in Hollywood, FL.

6. Kurt Dahl, "The 2 Copyrights in a Song (or the Most Important Concept in the Music Business)," *Lawyer Drummer*, Oct. 2, 2013.

7. Paul Goldstein, *Copyright's Highway: The Law and Lore of Copyright from Gutenberg to the Celestial Jukebox* (New York: Hill and Wang, 1995), 4.

8. For an excellent overview of the economics of copyright, see Stan Liebowitz and Richard Watt, "How to Best Ensure Remuneration for Creators in the Market for Music? Copyright and Its Alternatives," *Journal of Economic Surveys* 20, no. 4 (2006): 513–45.

9. Alan Greenspan, "Statement re S. 31 Before the Subcommittee on Patents, Copyrights and Trademarks, Senate Committee on the Judiciary," Oct. 25, 1983.

10. Nilay Patel, "Metallica Sued Napster 15 Years Ago Today," *The Verge*, Apr. 13, 2015.

11. Todd Bishop, "Rhapsody Will Rebrand as Napster, Creating 'One Global Brand' for Longtime Music Service," *GeekWire*, Jun. 14, 2016.

12. See, for example, Joseph Plambeck, "Court Rules That File-Sharing Service Infringed Copyrights," *New York Times*, May 12, 2010.

13. Joel Waldfogel, "Copyright Protection, Technological Change, and the Quality of New Products: Evidence from Recorded Music Since Napster," *Journal of Law and Economics* 55, no. 4 (2012): 715–40.

14. Michela Giorcelli and Petra Moser, "Copyrights and Creativity: Evidence from Italian Operas," SSRN Working Paper No. 2505776, 2016.

15. Frederic M. Scherer, *Quarter Notes and Bank Notes: The Economics of Music Composition in the Eighteenth and Nineteenth Centuries* (Princeton, NJ: Princeton University Press, 2012).

16. Questlove, *Creative Quest* (New York: Ecco, 2018).

17. Quoted from email correspondence with John Eastman on May 30, 2018.

18. Petra Moser, "Patents and Innovation in Economic History," NBER Working Paper No. 21964, 2016.

19. This point has been emphasized by the Nobel Prize–winning economist Paul Romer, who wrote, "When more people start prospecting for gold

or experimenting with bacteria, more valuable discoveries will be made." See Paul M. Romer, "The Origins of Endogenous Growth," *Journal of Economic Perspectives* 8, no. 1 (1994): 3–22.

20. See Lorie Hollabaugh, "Florida Georgia Line, Bebe Rexha Hit One Billion Streaming Mark," *MusicRow*, May 30, 2018; Jim Asker, "Bebe Rexha & Florida Georgia Line's 'Meant to Be' Breaks Record for Longest Rule in Hot Country Songs Chart's History," *Billboard*, Jul. 30, 2018.

21. Quoted from Raney Schockne's discussion at 2018 MIRA meeting in the Village Studio in Los Angeles, CA.

22. Ben Kaye, "David Bowie, King of Turning People Down, Turned Down the Trainspotting Soundtrack," *Consequence of Sound*, Feb. 26, 2016.

23. Kelsey McKinney, "Songwriter Aloe Blacc Has a Plan to Save the Music Industry," *Vox*, Jan. 22, 2015.

24. Avery Avapol, "Steven Tyler Demands Trump Stop Playing Aerosmith at Rallies," *The Hill*, Aug. 22, 2018.

25. Steven Tyler (@IamStevenT), "This is not about Dems vs. Repub," Twitter, Aug. 22, 2018, 2:20 p.m., https://twitter.com/iamstevent/status/103 2376949358788608?lang=en.

26. Kory Grow, "The Last Word: Lars Ulrich on Metallica's Darkest Times, Making His Own Rules," *Rolling Stone*, Nov. 7, 2016.

27. George A. Akerlof et al., "The Copyright Term Extension Act of 1998: An Economic Analysis," AEI-Brookings Joint Center for Regulatory Studies, Brief 02-1, 2002.

28. Megan MacGarvie, John McKeon, and Jeremy Watson, "It Was Fifty Years Ago Today: Recording Copyright Term and the Supply of Music," working paper, 2017.

29. International Federation of the Phonographic Industry, "Fixing the Value Gap," *IFPI Global Music Report 2018*.

30. These figures were generously provided by Barry Massarsky. The percentages of revenue reported in the charts differ from other estimates that are commonly reported because the revenue base is broadly defined for satellite music stations.

31. AudienceNet, "2017 Music Consumption: The Overall Landscape."

32. Quoted from an interview with Marty Gottesman on Jul. 24, 2018.

33. For more details, see "The Music Modernization Act," SoundExchange, https://www.soundexchange.com/advocacy/music-modernization-act. Accessed Oct. 16, 2018.

34. Ed Christman, "Music Modernization Act Passes Senate: Should End Confusion on Sirius XM Pre-1972 Settlement," *Billboard*, Sep. 19, 2018.

35. Peter DiCola and David Touve, "Licensing in the Shadow of Copyright," *Stanford Technology Law Review* 17 (2014): 397.

Chapter 10: THE GLOBAL MARKET FOR MUSIC

1. Statistics in this section are based on author's calculations using 2018 IFPI Global Music Market Data.

2. Cherie Hu, "How India, the Global Music Industry's Sleeping Giant, Is Finally Waking Up," *Forbes*, Sep. 23, 2017.

3. Mun Keat Looi, "Why Japan Has More Old-Fashioned Music Stores Than Anywhere Else in the World," *Quartz*, Aug. 19, 2016.

4. Helliwell, for example, finds that trade of goods between Canadian provinces was about twelve times greater than goods trade between Canadian provinces and American states of comparable size and distance apart. Interprovincial trade in services was twenty-five to thirty times as dense as Canada-U.S. trade in services. He also finds that national borders have a substantial, though smaller, effect on trade between EU countries: internal trade densities are about six times greater than international trade densities, and lower for countries that share a common language. See John Helliwel, *How Much Do National Borders Matter?* (Washington, DC: Brookings Institution Press, 1998).

5. See Fernando Ferreira and Joel Waldfogel, "Pop Internationalism: Has Half a Century of World Music Trade Displaced Local Culture?," *Economic Journal* 123, no. 569 (2013): 634–64; Luis Aguiar, Joel Waldfogel, and Estrella Gomez-Herrera, "Does Digitization Threaten Local Culture? Music in the Transition from iTunes to Spotify," mimeo, 2018.

6. Josh O'Kane, "The Other Stockholm Syndrome," *Globe and Mail*, Jan. 12, 2018.

7. From an interview with Quincy Jones on Aug. 11, 2017.

8. John Seabrook, "Blank Space: What Kind of Genius Is Max Martin?," *New Yorker*, Sep. 30, 2015.

9. This draws from an interview with John Cappo on Mar. 19 and 20, 2018.

10. This pieces together reporting from Wang Han, "Faye Wong's Shanghai Concert: The Return, or Fall, of a Legend?," *Global Times*, Jan. 4, 2017; Viola Zhou, "The Rise and Fall of Scalped Faye Wong Concert Tickets," *South China Morning Post*, Dec. 26, 2016; and "Jack Ma Pays $32.5 Million for Faye Wong Concert in Shanghai: Report," *Asia One*, Jun. 23, 2016. I assume a 6.9 yuan per dollar exchange rate, which was the rate at the time.

11. This is based on Nielsen's "Asia-Pacific Dance Music Study," commissioned by A2LiVE, Oct. 2017.

12. This paragraph is based on Fred Hwang, "Touring in China Remains Unpredictable as Gov't Keeps a Watchful Eye on Music Industry," *Billboard*, Sep. 18, 2018, and Jiayang Fan, "Why Justin Bieber Got Banned from Performing in China," *New Yorker*, Jul. 26, 2017.

13. See Hwang, "Touring in China Remains Unpredictable"; Laura Snapes, "Dua Lipa 'Proud' of Fans Ejected from Concert for Waving LGBT Flags," *Guardian*, Sep. 13, 2018.

14. Doug Strub, "John Cappo: Bringing Music to the Mainland," *Amcham Shanghai*, Jul. 20, 2017.

15. This and other quotes are from an interview with Eric de Fontenay on Mar. 18, 2018, in Beijing and email correspondence.

16. "Headlines from China: China Media Capital Launches CMC Live," *China Film Insider*, Jan. 10, 2018.

17. "Midi Modern Music Festival to Leave Beijing," China.org, Mar. 18, 2009.

18. "Ultra Shanghai Forced to Cancel Only a Week Before Taking Place, Ultra Beijing Dates Reconfirmed," *EDM Sauce*, Sep. 3, 2017.

19. This and other quotes are from an interview with Archie Hamilton on Mar. 20, 2018, in Shanghai.

20. David Herlihy and Yu Zhang, "Music Industry and Copyright Protection in the United States and China," *Global Media and China* 1, no. 4 (2016): 394. Other details in the next two paragraphs also draw on their article.

21. From an interview with Sam Jiang in Beijing, Mar. 18, 2018.

22. This draws on an interview I conducted with Tinko Georgiev, global business director at Kanjian Music in Shanghai, on Mar. 20, 2018.

23. Lorraine Schmucker, "China's Ban on Hip-Hop from Television Causes Many to Speak Their Minds," *IR Insider*, Feb. 9, 2018.

24. Mark Savage, "China's Music Listening Habits Revealed," BBC News, Feb. 2, 2016.

25. This is based on data presented by Andy Ng, group vice president of TME, at the 2017 Midem Conference in Cannes, France. Source: "Keynote: Andy Ng, Tencent—Midem 2017," YouTube, posted by Midem, Jun. 6, 2017, https://www.youtube.com/watch?v=eCDPOkfpIYw.

26. NetEase Cloud Music, "NetEase Cloud Music Hits 400 Million User Mark," PR Newswire, Nov. 21, 2017.

27. Marsha Silva, "Spotify Is Poised to Make Another $3 Billion—Thanks to Tencent Music's Upcoming IPO," *Digital Music News*, Jul. 8, 2018.

28. Unless otherwise noted, information on TME in the rest of this section is based on my interview with Sam Jiang in Beijing, Mar. 18, 2018, and a subsequent email correspondence, or on TME's prospectus filed with the Securities and Exchange Commission in October 2018.

29. "Universal Music Group and Tencent Music Entertainment Group Enter into Strategic Agreement Significantly Expanding Chinese Music Market," Universal Music Group, May 16, 2017.

30. For an elaboration of Hamilton's paradoxes, see Archie Hamilton, "Weathering Storms: The Paradox of China's Music Industry in 2018," LinkedIn, Feb. 26, 2018.

Chapter 11: MUSIC AND WELL-BEING

1. Oliver Sacks, *Musicophylia* (New York: Knopf, 2007), 373.

2. See Daniel Levitin, *This Is Your Brain on Music* (New York: Plume/Penguin, 2007), 186–88.

3. See Alan B. Krueger, Daniel Kahneman, David Schkade, Norbert Schwarz, and Arthur A. Stone, "National Time Accounting: The Currency of Life," in *Measuring the Subjective Well-Being of Nations: National Accounts of Time Use and Well-Being*, ed. Alan B. Krueger (Chicago: University of Chicago Press, 2009), 9–86. Analysis of the more recent 2010, 2012, and 2013 American Time Use Well-Being module data yields broadly similar results.

4. The sample was recruited by random-digit dialing in 2005. Each subject was paid $75 for participation, and filled out four packets containing questions and a time diary in a central location. This type of survey yields many more instances of multitasking than traditional time-use surveys, such as the American Time Use Survey, which is conducted by phone.

The questionnaire and data are available here: https://rady.ucsd.edu/faculty/directory/schkade/pub/fa-study.

5. Weighted by the duration of episodes, music was reported during 7.5 percent of people's awake time.

6. See Daniel Kahneman, Alan B. Krueger, David A. Schkade, Norbert Schwarz, and Arthur A. Stone, "A Survey Method for Characterizing Daily Life Experience: The Day Reconstruction Method," *Science* 306, no. 5702 (2004): 1776–80.

7. If the happiness rating for each episode is regressed on an indicator for whether music was present during the episode and indicator variables for the main activity, episodes that involve music have a 0.281 higher happiness rating, with a standard error of 0.043.

8. Specifically, if the happiness rating for each episode is regressed on an indicator for whether music was present during the episode, indicator variables for the main activity, and unrestricted indicators for each person, episodes that involve music have a 0.157 higher happiness rating, with a standard error of 0.038. If there are random recall errors in individuals' reports of whether music was listened to during each episode, as is likely, then controlling for person effects will attenuate the estimated effect of listening to music.

9. See Daniel Västfjäll, Patrik N. Juslin, and Terry Hartig, "Music, Subjective Well-Being, and Health: The Role of Everyday Emotions," in *Music, Health, and Well-Being*, ed. Raymond A. R. MacDonald, Gunter Kreutz, and Laura Mitchell (Oxford: Oxford University Press, 2012), 405–23. The authors also report on an Experience Sampling Method study of theirs that quizzed thirty-two Swedish college students about their emotions and activities in real time at seven randomly chosen times a day over a two-week period. The authors found that self-reported stress was significantly lower during musical episodes than non-musical episodes.

10. See Marie Helsing, Daniel Västfjäll, Pär Bjälkebring, Patrik Juslin, and Terry Hartig, "An Experimental Field Study of the Effects of Listening to Self-Selected Music on Emotions, Stress, and Cortisol Levels," *Music and Medicine* 8, no. 4 (2016): 187–98.

11. See Saoirse Finn and Daisy Fancourt, "The Biological Impact of Listening to Music in Clinical and Nonclinical Settings: A Systematic Review," *Progress in Brain Research* 237 (2018): 173–200.

12. See Katlyn J. Peck, Todd A. Girard, Frank A. Russo, and Alexandra J. Fiocco, "Music and Memory in Alzheimer's Disease and the Potential

Underlying Mechanisms," *Journal of Alzheimer's Disease* 51, no. 4 (2016): 949–59.

13. A. Blythe LaGasse and Michael H. Thaut, "Music and Rehabilitation: Neurological Approaches," in *Music, Health, and Well-Being*, ed. Raymond A. R. MacDonald, Gunter Kreutz, and Laura Mitchell (Oxford: Oxford University Press, 2012), 159–60.

14. See Laurel J. Gabard-Durnam, Takao Hensch, and Nim Tottenham, "Music Reveals Medial Prefrontal Cortex Sensitive Period in Childhood," bioRxiv (2018), https://doi.org/10.1101/ 412007; Steve M. Janssen, Antonio G. Chessa, and Jaap M. Murre, "Temporal Distribution of Favourite Books, Movies, and Records: Differential Encoding and Re-Sampling," *Memory* 15, no. 7 (2007): 755–67.

15. Seth Stephen-Davidowitz, "The Songs That Bind," *New York Times*, Feb. 10, 2018.

16. From an interview with Cliff Burnstein and Peter Mensch on Mar. 1, 2018, in New York City.

17. See John Maynard Keynes, *Essays in Persuasion* (New York: W. W. Norton, 1963), 358–73.

18. Daniel Hamermesh, *Spending Time: The Most Valuable Resource* (London: Oxford University Press, 2018), 4.

19. Daniel Kahneman and Angus Deaton, "High Income Improves Evaluation of Life but Not Emotional Well-Being," *Proceedings of the National Academy of Sciences* 107, no. 38 (2010): 16489–93. Also see, for example, Richard Layard, *Happiness: Lessons from a New Science*, 2nd ed. (London: Penguin Books, 2011).

Appendix: EVALUATION OF THE POLLSTAR BOXOFFICE DATABASE

1. To obtain the data from the public university, in Feb. 2018 I officially became a contractor providing analytical services to the university for a fee of $100. The terms of the agreement required that the identity of the university and the individual venues involved in this analysis remain confidential.

Pandora (streaming service), 22, 31–33, 41, 93, 179, 180, 190–92, 192*f*, 225, 227
Parker, Colonel Tom, 172
Parker Theory (band), 26, 113
Passman, Donald, 169, 171
Patents, 209, 214
Paterno, Peter, 67
Patreon.com, 35, 39
Payola, 10, 183
Perry, Katy, 197, 241
Personalization, 39, 183, 191, 202
Petty, Tom, 15, 18, 44, 70–71, 140, 169–70, 206
Pierce, Jason, 58
Piracy, 30, 39, 55, 177, 178, 189, 200, 210, 211, 248–49
Pirate Bay, 189
Poetry (Confucius), 248
Political events, 217
Pollstar Boxoffice Database, 4, 84, 271–78
Pollstar data, 84, 271–78, 274*t*, 275*f*, 276*f*
Pollstar magazine, 4, 271
Popularity, 13, 79, 83, 86–90, 112–14, 193, 199, 214, 266
Pop-up stores, 156
Portfolio theory, 124
Positive externalities, 28
Post Break Tragedy (band), 113, 116
Post Malone, 116, 197
Power law, 13, 88–91, 93, 112
Power law distribution, 87, 88
Practice, 56–57
Presley, Elvis, 172
Price discrimination, 8, 36, 140, 148, 153, 184, 187, 197, 199, 213, 253, 267
Productivity, 148, 232

Promotion and promoters, 130–33, 134, 162–64, 193, 243, 251, 301n.10
Property rights, 23, 209
Publicity, 49
Publishing, 32, 37, 79, 170, 185, 202, 205
Puerto Rico, 46
Pyrotechnics, 150

Q Prime Management, 69, 120, 121, 124
QQ Music, 22, 190, 253
Questlove, 94, 213

R&B music, 185
Radio, 216–18, 224–26, 230, 232
Radiohead (band), 34, 35
Rapino, Michael, 132, 134
Rauh, Joshua, 102
Recognition, 216
Record companies, 33, 36, 40, 54, 159–63, 211, 250–52
Recorded music
    in China, 252
    compartmentalized, 65
    illegal copying of, 210–11
    income from, 11, 29, 30, 31, 31*f*, 37–40
    listeners reached by, 12
    and live performances, 39
    for popularity, 83
    and radio, 224
    replication and distribution, 18
    in restaurants and bars, 83
    revenue from, 30, 177, 178–79, 285n.4
    spending on, 233
    and streaming services, 22, 32, 185, 189–90

time spent listening to, 10

Recording Industry Association of America, 210

Record label(s), 301n.10
  complaints against, 163–64
  improved financial situation, 167
  music production in China, 250
  payola, 183
  and Petty, 169
  playlists, 193
  renegotiating unfavorable contracts, 166
  revenue from subscription services, 179
  risks of, 36
  and Spotify, 200, 201
  and streaming, 181, 182, 185, 198, 202
  underreporting sales, 161
  See also Record companies

Record stores, 22

Redding, Otis, 224

Rehegoo Music Group, 23, 194–96, 196f

Reiley, David, 191

Rent-seeking, 219, 225, 227

Repetition, 56

Reputation (album), 34, 36, 199

"Respect" (song), 224

Rexha, Bebe, 214–15

Richie, Lionel, 45

Rihanna, 88, 98, 112

Rinaldo, Marco, 194

Risk, 36, 255

Ritholtz, Barry, 157

Rock and Roll Hall of Fame (Cleveland), 1, 2, 25

"Rockanomics" (song), 21

Rockonomics
  definition of, 1, 21
  earliest use of term, 20
  keys to, 6–10
  for music and economy, 268–69

Rockonomics (Eliot), 20–21

Rodgers, Nile, 57

Rodriguez, Sixto, 26, 110, 116, 125–26

Roelofsen, Jasper, 171

Rolling Stones, 6, 57, 162, 243

Ronson, Mark, 206

Rosen, Sherwin, 80, 81, 82

Rossini, Gioachino, 213

Rotem, J.R., 197

Rouse, Cecilia, 76

Rowland, Steve, 110

Roxette (band), 109, 232

Royalties, 79, 130, 198
  in China, 249, 251
  contract, 36, 301n.10
  copyright, 249
  cut in, 18, 19
  fees, 230
  Ferrone on, 17
  from YouTube, 33
  Kobalt company, 34–35
  Lumineers,' 165
  musicians,' 211
  performance, 185, 225
  publishing, 37, 79, 185, 205
  rates, 162, 163, 208, 226
  Rehegoo, 195
  Spotify, 32, 181
  streaming, 5, 179, 181, 182, 199, 301n.10
  underreporting, 161

Rush (band), 120

Russell, Graham, 231

Ryan, Dan, 154, 168

From Byron, Austen and Darwin

to some of the most acclaimed and original contemporary writing, John Murray takes pride in bringing you powerful, prizewinning, absorbing and provocative books that will entertain you today and become the classics of tomorrow.

We put a lot of time and passion into what we publish and how we publish it, and we'd like to hear what you think.

Be part of John Murray – share your views with us at:

www.johnmurray.co.uk

 johnmurraybooks

 @johnmurrays

 johnmurraybooks